FAMILY FICTIONS

Family Fictions

Representations of the Family in 1980s Hollywood Cinema

Sarah Harwood

Foreword by
Janet Thumim

Consultant Editor: Jo Campling

First published 1997 by
MACMILLAN PRESS LTD
Houndmills, Basingstoke, Hampshire RG21 6XS
and London
Companies and representatives
throughout the world

ISBN 0–333–64843–9 hardcover
ISBN 0–333–64844–7 paperback

A catalogue record for this book is available
from the British Library.

This book is printed on paper suitable for recycling and made from fully managed and sustained forest sources.

10 9   8   7   6   5   4   3   2   1
06 05 04 03 02 01 00 99 98 97

Printed and bound in Great Britain by
Antony Rowe Ltd, Chippenham, Wiltshire

For my mother

Contents

Foreword
Janet Thumim

Popular cinema is marketed and received as entertainment, a commodity participating in the capitalist marketplace's drive to profit. As a direct consequence of this imperative it also contributes to the construction and maintenance of cultural specificities – a point not lost on the early financiers who invested in Hollywood production with a view to recouping their investments at least partly through the increased sale of US goods in overseas markets. US success in dominating the world stage throughout the twentieth century owes something, therefore, to the movies. But it is not only world trade that has proved susceptible to the examples purveyed in mass-marketed popular fictions. As well as urging the benefits of Coca-Cola or McDonalds, movies have offered models of being-in-the-world that have informed generations of cinemagoers. Consequently these models are of interest to those concerned with relations between society and its cultural artefacts, particularly where change or controversy are at issue.

The cinema industry has developed steadily through its 100-year history, displaying rather more sophistication in its industrial techniques of production and marketing than is generally evident in the social models offered in its fictions. The bottom line, as they say, is the maximisation of profit. This means low overheads in relation to potential sales: when overheads are to be high, large sales must, accordingly, be predictable. Nowadays the marketing budget of a film can be as high as its production budget. In order to ensure the necessarily huge exposure of the product its invitation to audiences must be as broadly-based as possible. One consequence of this is that though fantasy, spectacle, star and production values may be lavish, the narrative closures of mainstream Hollywood cinema continue to be deeply conservative.

The problem exercising historians interested in the relation between cinema and society concerns the ways in which this relation may be accounted for without resort to a simple (and now, I trust, wholly discredited), idea of film somehow 'reflecting' things as they are. Recent scholarship suggests a much more pro-active role for audiences than the notion of reflection allows, yet still we must account for the pleasures audiences derive from fictions in which the underlying narrative rationale is regressive, not to say repressive. A further difficulty, of course, is the sheer scale of the scholarly exercise entailed: it is a daunting matter to go beyond the relatively straightforward study of an actor, director or genre to consider the widely purveyed filmic propositions delivered through the combination of all these.

In order to proceed with any coherent description, analysis or speculation the film scholar – like any scholar – is obliged to select both appropriate questions and the body of material to which these questions may be put. Accordingly, this book sets out to consider filmic representations of the family, in a decade when this term was both widely contested and idealised in contemporary discourses of the social. Since it is precisely the articulation of these often contradictory discourses that is in question, the study takes as its representative films those which achieved a significant degree of success at the box-office in Britain. Either they were very well-liked by British audiences, or their marketing budgets ensured wide exposure, or both: in any case these were the 'box-office hits' with which the decade has subsequently been identified, films such as *E.T.*, *Out of Africa*, *Fatal Attraction*, *Raiders of the Lost Ark*. This is still, of course, a huge number of films displaying little or no generic consistency. It is greatly to Sarah Harwood's credit that she has managed the difficult task of balancing the general with the particular, of outlining a sufficiently large number of films to persuade readers of her arguments, while still delivering adequately detailed discussion of the texts which she has demonstrated to be exemplary.

On its own this would be an admirably useful contribution to film studies. However, this book goes further. Not only are filmic constructions of the family subjected to meticulous examination, but also the social and political discourses of the family, the discourses within which filmic constructions are circulated, are themselves accorded a characteristically careful and detailed attention. Consequently this work is an invaluable contribution to the social history of the eighties, a history which, as the book conclusively demonstrates, may be deduced from a study of the films but cannot be limited to them: 'our interest in analysing film representations in this context is to understand better how these representations work to expose, displace or anneal the gap between lived experience and cultural forms'. Turning this assertion the other way round, we can say that the experience of audiences outside the cinema, informed as it is by the social and political imperatives of the day, must have a bearing on their readings of popular fictions inside the cinema – even if these are 'just entertainment'. As the author reminds us 'we should take these films seriously precisely because they ask not to be'.

This is a fascinating study, breathtaking in its ambition, stimulating and provocative in its detail and thoroughly rewarding to all those of us concerned to unpick the apparently seamless productions of the Hollywood machine.

Acknowledgements

I have to be held entirely responsible for the words that appear between these covers but for the work that it represents I am indebted to others. Most obviously I owe a tremendous debt to those referenced in the text but equal thanks are due to those whose contributions are invisible. Firstly, to Phillip Drummond without whom I would never have contemplated publication and whose wise and incisive judgements have guided my doctoral research. Much love and gratitude also belong to Dorothy Leng who inspired me, wrestled with me over some of my most intractable dilemmas, listened to my problems and gave me the impetus to keep going.

Jo Campling provided a steady hand and reassurance throughout this process and the book certainly would not have been published without her. Janet Thumin's own writing and, later her advice, have been a great source of encouragement. Thanks are also due to the staff and students at the Institute of Education who saw rough drafts and were kind enough to offer their comments and insights.

Throughout the writing and research for this book, I have been wearing two hats and I am deeply obliged to my business partner, Chris Dyson, for his generosity over the time this has taken to complete.

My friends deserve much praise, particularly Peter Taylor, Sheila Tait and Janet Carrick, who have been unstintingly patient and generous in their friendship and have always been there to remind me of reality.

A book about the family must also acknowledge its debt to the author's own who, like all others, are (generally) wonderful.

Last, but most important, I owe an incalculable debt to Nigel Hathway who put up with both me and this book throughout its darkest hours. This book is also dedicated, with love, to him.

Introduction

Family n. A body of individuals living in one household, consisting of male, female, young, servants, dog, cat, dicky-bird, cockroaches, bedbugs and fleas – the 'unit' of modern civilised society.

Ambrose Bierce, *Devil's Dictionary*

In the final shot of *Fatal Attraction*, the camera zooms into the family photograph and holds it in the centre of the frame. It depicts the gilt framed image of Dan (the errant father), his wife, Beth (the perfect mother and his mistress's killer) and their daughter Ellen, in pride of place among a jumble of domestic items on the hall sideboard. Prominent among these items are a key rack and a set of keys, conventional symbols of domestic possession and residence. In the photograph itself, Beth holds Ellen close and both are smiling. Dan, his arm round his wife, looks enigmatically into the camera, his expression uncommitted while his posture is possessive; he leans towards his wife and child. This final shot is held for several seconds before the end-title comes up and the credits roll across it. The Gallaghers are a torn family, not completely restored at the end, yet are here represented back to themselves – and to us – as whole. The father is flawed (it was his indiscretion which caused the ensuing mayhem, and his actions which were inadequate to contain or resolve it) and yet he is represented as familial guardian, possessing and self-possessed. The mother, too, is a paradox, perfect but neglectful, caring but not careful enough, passive but active, the good mother who is also a murderer. Despite their encircling embrace, they have failed to protect the child, object of both desire and abuse throughout the film. This image also draws attention to fractures in the film's realist aesthetic and its status as chronicle. We are left with an image of a whole, restored family. Yet the photo is an old one, taken before the traumas of the film. To 'fix' this family, the narrative has to rely on invoking an earlier moment, fixing time as well as damage. To believe in the restoration of the family, we have to believe that the clock can go back, that time can be stopped, even reversed. Thus this resolution is fundamentally unreliable, neither the film nor the family can go back, the family has changed, the narrative unwound, the spectator has a memory of the transformational events. Closure is thrown into question precisely by the image selected to close it just as 'family values' were inadequate to heal the social fractures of the eighties.

This film attracted a huge amount of attention for its depiction of the nuclear family 'winning through' against the uncontrolled, predatory single woman. In a decade which based its reactionary political agenda on 'family values', the film was both celebrated for endorsing, but also denigrated for even threatening, the family. These debates were, of course, further complicated by the very intense relationships which audiences formed with the film. Audience exhortations to 'Kill the Bitch' made press headlines and raised complex issues of subjectivity and identification, especially for female spectators who, despite a predisposition to more mobile and paradoxical identifications, particularly in relation to gender, were still confronted with the destruction of an assertive woman.[1] These intense relationships were mirrored in the film's pre-release handling. At preview screenings, the ending was preferred to, and therefore determined against, an alternative closure depicting Alex's suicide, a marketing *volteface* which raises the thorny question of the relations of the industry to its product, the film to its spectators and text to contexts; issues which are central to disentangling the whole business of familial representation.

This shot encapsulates – or, rather, spills out – many of the questions and issues I have set out to address in this book, a book which is intent on teasing out the meanings and functions of the family in contemporary culture. Why was this film, one of the top grossers of the 1980s, constructed to close on this shot and why was the image of the family such a pivotal signifier of narrative resolution?[2] What (un)pleasures and meanings were there in the familial representation for audiences in the hugely popular movies dealt with in this book? And what relationship did these representations bear to other cultural and social formations? *Fatal Attraction* epitomises many of the key issues of contemporary familial representation. The family serves as moral touchstone, guarantor of resolution in the film while also being invoked in a bid to fix time and secure stasis in a period of great flux. Yet it cannot guarantee resolution, relying instead on a mythical earlier period to signify closure. Representations of individual family members also highlighted contemporary trends; the child is represented as innocent victim, the mother as neglected possession and the father-figure as highly problematic. This book explores why these family representations were so prevalent at this time and what functions each family term served within major film narratives.

But why choose to look at the *family* within film – specifically within popular Hollywood film? *Fatal Attraction* hit British screens towards the latter end of a decade in which the family was foregrounded and the gains made by feminists in the sixties and seventies were steadily diminishing. A New Right agenda had revolutionised both Britain and America. It was a time of massive change at all levels, and moral questions, following the challenges to moral and social certainties in the sixties and seventies, were becoming increasingly complex – and increasingly personalised. Post-Reformation secularism had heralded the first wave of 'moral privatisation', and the gradual substitution of State and legislature for religious guidance continued into the twentieth century. By the eighties, however, the frontiers of the state were being 'rolled back' and individuals increasingly searched for a moral framework within the forms of popular culture. The family was at the heart of this quest and became the moral centre for political and cultural rhetoric; a family which was held as metonymic, explicable and responsible for the social formation *in toto*. The family, like gender, is a social construction. It has its roots in ideology as firmly as in material reality. Indeed, in the 1980s, it became a primary way of organising and understanding that reality across all cultural forms, including film, a medium enjoying a renaissance in the eighties. Of course, film does not simply reflect its social and cultural context, but it does engage and contend with it, providing a rich resource for private and public reworkings, imaginings and desires. This book examines the social and cultural impulses which prompted the foregrounding of the family by examining how the most popular Hollywood films took up the family, recirculating and representing it in a continuing battle between social transformation and social conservation.

The first part of this book examines how the family became a primary – and controversial – site of political, social and cultural struggle during the 1980s and explores how that reverberated specifically within its representations.

Throughout this period, both Britain and America were experiencing crises in their national and international identities, in their economies and in their social structures. In times of turmoil, societies search for absolute values, unassailable moral positions which are apparently outside ideology, outside history and outside culture, in which it is possible to take refuge. In the eighties, the family was explicitly constructed as a moral domain. However, Althusser has observed, there is no 'outside' to ideology, and familial morality was as ideologically suffused as any other sociocultural formation.[3] Chapter 1 investigates the political and social paradoxes in the eighties which contributed to the construction of contemporary familism. Of course history is not mapped in strong, progressive, continuous strands. It is a conflictual, contradictory matrix of overlapping events, discourses and power formations, a reality which will always exceed any attempts to describe or explain it and to which no single account can ever be adequate. A history is, therefore, always a partial affair, elegantly defined by E.H. Carr as 'a continuous process of interaction between the historian and his facts, an unending dialogue between the past and the present'.[4] The role of the historian is to distinguish the underlying structures, what Ray Bhaskar has called the 'generative mechanisms', from the historical phenomena that litter the way and to assign some kind of priority to different levels of evidence.[5] In the eighties, powerful myths emerged to resolve and contain crises in national, economic and social arenas on both sides of the Atlantic. While the nature of these crises were specifically distinct in each country, there is sufficiently broad commonality to look primarily at Britain as the country of reception, while also looking to America as the country of origin, of our popular Hollywood movies.

Hollywood is both an industry and a geographic location, metonymically represented by a grand tradition of film texts. It is also an ideal – a classic metonymy in which both industry and location have been supplanted by their product. The process of that production is also effaced, as is the eventual destination of the revenue which is generated by it. Perhaps most importantly, 'Hollywood' has become a term which metonymically articulates the totality of American cinema and to whose industrial and stylistic tune almost all international film-making now marches. The dominance of US-produced cinema (in both its industrial and textual forms) has been well documented.[6] Indeed the benchmark for what constitutes a film – its conventions of length, dominant mode (narrative fiction), style and technical articulation – evolved from the Hollywood cinematic institution in its very earliest, entrepreneurial incarnations to the establishment of the Hollywood system and has been almost universally represented as an inevitable, linear development in the teleology of film history and production. The prevalence of the model owes as much to the economics and industrialisation of film production as it does to the films themselves.[7] Cultural and social theorists from the Frankfurt School onwards have concerned themselves with the damaging 'cultural imperialism' they see exemplified in the widespread export of American, particularly Hollywood, cinema. While I dispute the assumptions of simple semiotic instrumentality, audience passivity and 'false consciousness' implicit in these accusations, it is incontestable that the hegemony of Hollywood cinema has limited the range of cinematic resource available to spectators across the world. This argues for a far closer understanding of how the representations in circulation appealed to a spectatorship far broader than the immediate domestic audience and what uses and pleasures they drew from them.

In some respects the eighties were a reprise of trends which surfaced in the fifties. As Jackie Byars has identified, this period was also a time of massive upheaval and ideological change which 'threw the family into question'.[8] One vehicle for renegotiating a new moral order in the face of social crisis was melodrama, a cultural mode which, as Christine Gledhill has suggested, 'demarcates the desirable from the taboo'.[9] While Byars explicitly recognised the family's role in achieving such demarcations, her focus remained at the level of melodrama. Chapter 2 demonstrates how textual modes are but one piece in the cultural puzzle of representation. Hollywood itself was in a period of transformation and this intersected with broader cultural myths and contemporary anxieties over the role and representations of the family. Hollywood's own industrial structures and practices were affected by socioeconomic shifts which fed into social, economic and nationalist paranoia which, in turn, referenced the family. In Chapter 2, I look at how Hollywood's industrial and narrational structures dovetailed with broader cultural paradigms to privilege private and domestic spaces, continuing the Enlightenment project of interiorising and privatising value structures which served to establish and maintain the bourgeoisie. In concert with the emphasis on the home, leisure activity continued the domesticating, individuated trend seen since the Second World War. Home-based hobbies dominated non-work time, replacing outings to the pub. Technologies supporting domestic leisure proliferated in the form of computer games, VHS and CDs. Cinemas themselves developed into multiplexes, drawing on myths of choice and individualism. That this strategy of diversification chimed with a popular shift in leisure patterns is attested to by the resurgence in cinema audiences in the latter part of the decade. Britons were returning to the cinema in droves. As one newspaper attested: 'The British were eating films, they couldn't get enough.'[10] Like historical events, film texts cannot be isolated from the contexts of their production, from the industrial practices which shaped them and the audiences they were constructed for.

The family is a central problematic in the field of representation – a social phenomenon we have all had some experience of and around which a vast array of naturalised assumptions and prejudices circulate. It is, in addition, represented as the founding vehicle of maturation – sexual, social and psychic – and the mechanism by which we achieve our gender, our sense of self and our social status. However, the family is also a site of contradiction, revealing its uneasy ideological positioning. It is simultaneously represented as a 'natural', universal and inevitable form while also being constructed as a fragile, threatened entity requiring support for its survival. It is both the sanctioned forum for sexual reproduction and development and a realm in which sexuality is hidden and suppressed. It is constructed as private space, a haven from the public sphere, while also being a field for public enquiry and investigation and a site of violence and tension. It is a place of protection but also of abuse. It provides a space for individual self-expression and self-realisation but is also a strictly hierarchical group with clear divisions of labour, power and freedom. The family is both place of relaxation and place of work; a site of reproduction and a site of consumption. It is represented as requiring the constant presence of the mother but also needing the mother's income. It is a form which reinforces and recreates social development while being a form which damages that development. Finally it is a form which fosters 'natural' formation of sexualised subjects while also being represented as the sphere which constructs 'unnatural', coercive, gendered subjective identities. Neither paradigm, of course, is either comprehensive or adequate to some ideological authenticity. They do, however, represent the continuum along which family ideology and family representations oscillate and along which the 'family narrative' is driven.

While it is impossible to ascribe a universal form to household or family composition at any one period since this imposes an essential similarity on highly diverse institutions and practices, a refusal to begin this very specific analysis of the diversity of family forms is precisely to overlook them and to risk their appropriation by an ideological universalism. My own analysis engages with specific representations of the family and relates them to the variety and versatility of the social family while avoiding any simplistic reduction of one to the other. What underpins this is the recognition that material and ideological family forms are reciprocally developed and developing; that both ideological and material families change over time and that these changes can be traced to broader economic, cultural and historical frameworks. It is therefore not possible to speak of the social family but only of families. However, in speaking of familism, the ideology of the nuclear family, we must recognise that ideology is not a monolithic entity, but a site of struggle. Within any single ideological formation, such as 'family' or 'nation', there are competing ideologies, any grouping of which may assume precedence at a particular moment in history. What I elide to the singular term, 'ideology' is thus the dominant tendency of a configuration of ideologies contesting a common discursive content. Familism is therefore the hegemonising moment in a process of struggle over what the ideal family could, or should, look like. Its content is defined by psychic and cultural imperatives as much as by its material referent.

By looking at paradoxes inherent in family theory, Chapter 3 scrutinises both the social and ideological formations which characterised the eighties family. This chapter examines familial definitions, distinguishing demographics from familial ideology and assesses the social investment made in the ideological family form. Social institutions were increasingly formulated around assumptions implicit in familial ideology, and significant sociocultural effects resulted from a simple equation of ideological family type to the diversity of social and reproductive organisation. Finally, I look at representations of individual family members to explore how historically specific forms were developing across cultural forms.

If 'family values' was the rallying cry of dominant political, social and cultural discourse in the decade, then how successful were Hollywood films at representing the ideal family? Reproducing the ideological form of the nuclear family always has been the underpinning goal of classical Hollywood cinema and in Chapter 4 I assess the success of these texts in achieving it. Crudely summarised, Hollywood cinema has historically represented three family types. Firstly a stable, consensual entity, flawed only if one or more terms are missing or its boundaries and rules are broken. The second type has been the psychotic, perverse or 'other' family representation, usually inverted, such as vampire or cannibal families or families of other races. These usually carried out the same function as 'normal' families in that they were opposed to the private sphere, and were vehicles for socialisation and reproduction. Such representations did not challenge the familial representation itself but, inversely, endorsed it. The third type, which began to emerge in the eighties, was a family that was in itself flawed and unhealthy. Such representations are not inextricably tied to a specific period but appear more frequently at one time rather than others; they do not form a strict continuum but rather a spiral of change on which they intersect and reiterate each other. During the eighties, the second type of family only appeared in less popular films and genres, usually horror or science-fiction films. Although the dominant narrative driver was the first type, it was unachievable and it was generally the flawed family which was ultimately represented in the most popular films, questioning the very role and representation of the family itself.

Yet this crude summary does not tell us much about where and why such breakdowns occurred. I distinguished three dimensions which constructed specific, structuring familial paradigms in the eighties. Appendix 1 shows how the films are distributed across these paradigms while Appendix 2 gives a detailed synopsis for each film, along with an explanation of its assignation. What emerges is a complex picture of familial representation in which there is no simplistic reading of a dominant familial type, but a rich resource of familial possibilities where the nuclear family is certainly not represented as ideal.

The advantage of selecting the big Hollywood movies to analyse is to examine those with the financial and industrial muscle to ensure their widespread distribution and, reciprocally, the biggest financial investment tied up in their success. This level of risk compelled the major studios to keep a finger on the pulse of market demands and therefore indicates a more active relationship between audience and producer and, perhaps, between dominant ideologies and cultural representations. I have therefore deliberately chosen to look at the most popular films rather than select those films which are most obviously 'about' the family. While this limitation excludes certain texts which appear particularly susceptible to this form of analysis (*Parenthood, Parents, Baby Boom* or *The Good Mother*, for example), I wanted to examine family representations in those films which the greatest number of people paid to see rather than pick films to justify a particular polemic. The selection of films (the top ten box office hits in each year) is sufficiently broad to permit generalisation but sufficiently focused to permit close analysis.

Chapter 5 focuses in on the father. In common with many contemporary theorists, Yvonne Tasker has noted that 'sets of anxieties to do with gender identity were being inscribed almost exclusively over the tortured figure of the white male body'.[11] In analysing the family, it is clear that the father was the primary cause of familial breakdown in the most successful Hollywood movies. By analysing a broad range of films and combining structural analysis with cine-psychoanalysis, we can identify specific types of paternal failure which stimulate intriguing narrational forms and resolutions for the family. These failures engage with two structuring problematics for the patriarch: succession and individuation, and centre on contemporary anxieties over the separation, and respective roles, of private and public realms.

In Chapter 6, I have taken a smaller sample of films, concentrating on three in particular, *Out of Africa, Terms of Endearment* and *Fatal Attraction*. Narrowing the focus allows a closer attention to contextual as well as textual material. This is particularly important in analysing the maternal role as it was so frequently absent in the films themselves. All three films are concerned with the family and the role of the mother in particular. *Out of Africa* is constructed around the absence of the mother, while the other two films examine competing representations of the maternal role, one as a problematic of succession, the latter as a problematic of competition. The disturbances set up by the maternal representation intersect across the text and construct contradictory and unsettling spectatorial positions, providing a rich and diverse resource for engaging with social realities. The repercussions from these disturbances can be found in the films' reception in the press which suggests how the films engaged with, and became a vehicle for circulating, wider sociocultural anxieties. The maternal representation is far less susceptible to the narrative analysis deployed in Chapter 5. Using the tools of psychoanalysis, therefore, I attempt to show how the Oedipal scene is inadequate to position women, particularly mothers, in patriarchy, but can provide insights into the ways in which conventional theoretical approaches can be used to expose their own contradictions and inadequacies. All three films explore the problematic relationship between mother and daughter, suggesting that recent work in object relations theory is more productive than a straightforward application of a Freudian–Lacanian tradition of cine-pyschoanalysis.

The familial term which occupied the most privileged position in eighties films was that of the child. However, this was not by virtue of driving the narrative forward but because of the particular significations and narrational capital vested in the child in the decade. Children necessarily signify a future and this conflicted with the contemporary patriarchal drive to fix the present. Chapter 7 examines the different types of child represented within the text to identify the child's role in proposing different social orders and how these challenges were contained by narratives which were largely driven by the father and ruptured by his failure.

The final chapter in this section is a more detailed case study of one particular text, *E.T.*, the film which generated the highest box-office receipts of the decade and which exhibits many of the most common textual anxieties, thereby rendering it doubly deserving of sustained attention. *E.T.* is constructed around two families: one human, one alien. It thus begs the obvious questions, not only over relations between family and society so problematic in all the other films, but also over family and not-family, human and not-human. This chapter draws together the analytical approaches and cultural preoccupations and findings of previous chapters in a close analysis of the film's familial representations.

The concluding chapter summarises the key representational issues of the eighties and looks forward into the 1990s to show how some of these textual operations are being carried forward. This preliminary work is a powerful argument for a broader historical and social study which would explore how these contemporary paradigms resonate with those of previous decades and begin to fill in a representational map of the relations between culture and society.

ENDPIECE : SOME ASSUMPTIONS

The assumptions behind this book are fivefold. Firstly, that the family is an overused and underdefined term which conveniently collapses a

complex tapestry of individual and social activities, desires and power
relations into a single normative entity. The familial ideology which
achieved that collapse performed a specific function in the eighties, securing myths which attempted to resolve deep social fractures. My second
premise is that Hollywood cinema has always deployed romance and the
family to structure its narratives and to signify utopian endings; any deviation from a normative familial resolution will therefore indicate where
social and political projects might be causing or refracting dislocations at
a cultural level.[12] Hollywood cinema is thus a prime site for investigating
these. Thirdly, I propose that popularity itself provides a sufficient reason
for selecting the films to be studied. As Robert Ray insists in his study of
Hollywood cinema, '"popular" is a more verifiable term than "great" –
after all, we have box-office statistics'.[13] Yet the films' popularity is frequently proposed as the very reason for dismissing them as objects for
serious study. We should take these films seriously precisely because they
ask not to be. In doing so, however, we lay ourselves open to commonsense
ridicule that analysis of such films is spurious as they are 'just entertainment', a charge this book fundamentally refutes. The fourth assumption is
that a film text can only privilege meaning and propose a spectatorial
position, not guarantee it. The contexts of textual production and reception
will always produce a surplus of meaning and therefore film texts and their
spectators may confirm, contest or negotiate such hegemony. Nor do these
spectatorial positions follow a closed system model, inevitably linked to
biological determinants such as sex or race, but are culturally, cognitively
and psychically negotiated by each individual to produce a broad, and
often contradictory, range of readings. The fifth and final premise is that
ideology and materiality are separate but constantly articulating and transforming each other. Neither precedes the other or absolutely determines it.
The nuclear family was a dominant ideological form in the eighties, but
its material and ideological forms can, and should, be distinguished. While
the nuclear family may be neither achievable or even desirable in reality,
its production and reproduction were the hegemonic cultural goal for both
British and American societies in the eighties. Analysis of the family in
Hollywood cinema will therefore shed light on how social categories such
as the family, gender and class are constructed and contested through
popular forms.

   The position from which I have researched and written this book, therefore, is one that I can best describe as Feminist-Realist. That is, criticism
engaged with a specific political project within the philosophical and epistemological framework of Realism.[14] This book therefore assumes that
there is a 'real' upon which subjects can have impact and which is distinct

from, and independent of, our own subjectivity. A reality which, however, can only ever be partly known as it will always be mediated by language (a vehicle which is never transparent and therefore never objective), by culture and by our own sociohistorically specific relationship to it. My own Realism is, moreover, inflected by a preoccupation with the highly gendered nature of theoretical and discursive constructions in relation to the social reality they purport to reflect; with how gender is constructed, circulated and negotiated. A crucial aspect of this work is to examine how contemporary familial representations work to reproduce or contest historical representations of sexual difference. As Modleski has observed, feminist criticism now has its 'pieties and routines'.[15] This is particularly true of feminist cine-psychoanalysis which, in its very complexity, has obscured many of its basic assumptions. Nevertheless, using such methodologies demonstrates how both conventional representations and assumptive theoretical approaches were beginning to unravel.

Theory is but one purchase on reality. Reality will always exceed it. Only by adopting a range of theoretical positions can we show where that occurs and attempt some approximation.[16] The use of orthodox theoretical routines will therefore indicate failures and fissures in the theory as well as in the texts themselves. Thus, for example, while agreeing with much recent work on the inadequacy of a simple Oedipal trajectory to the complexity of maturation, particularly (as Freud himself admitted) to female maturation, it still has a purchase on narrative construction and in film theory. Its adoption does not, therefore, signify unproblematic endorsement, merely that it is an appropriate tool for that circumstance. In tackling these films, I am assuming a complex relationship between text and reality, text and spectator, seeking new perspectives through traditional tools and a irreverent approach to their combination. Patriarchy both constrains and creates; a fusion of theoretical approaches can seek out moments and traces of resistance. In this search, I have drawn primarily on cine-psychoanalysis, structural narrative analysis, sociology, structural anthropology and semiology as the most appropriate tools, both in isolation and combination, for analysing these texts.

Feminists have been deeply critical of the family as Tania Modleski's withering criticism suggests: 'The family is the structural unit keeping women economically and physically dependent on men; separating women from other women; and in extreme (but by no means uncommon) cases, providing the space in which men may abuse women with impunity.'[17] However, such categorical and universal damnation is insufficient and ignores the strong purchase familism has on popular imagination and affections. It is indisputable that women particularly have suffered within

familism – especially those outside a family unit. As wage labour drove
a wedge between the domestic and work spheres, women were precari-
ously positioned between two highly volatile marketplaces which were
mutually inimical to them, the marriage and labour markets, while remaining outside was equally damnable. However, assigning blame to the
family itself is to miss the point. We have a society and a culture which
oppress and marginalise specific social groups, including women. The
problem is that we organise society, and the cultural forms which address
it, as if it were a family. Thus the family becomes a convenient vehicle for
celebrating or denigrating sociocultural organisation and for hiding such
oppressed groups within it. By displacing our attention to the family, we
risk occluding broader social and cultural issues, the very sleight of hand
essayed by familism and familialisation. We have to look at how the
family functioned to secure other mythologies, mythologies which attempted
to resolve contemporary social panics, in order to identify the structuring
dilemmas and the alternatives. Popular films of the eighties demonstrate
how problematic the nuclear family really was and the spaces that were
beginning to emerge for other possibilities. As Elizabeth Traube optimis-
tically noted in her study of eighties Hollywood, 'I also caught glimpses
of an emergent ideal, partially blocked by the movies themselves, yet also
present in them as a utopian possibility that viewers can abstract and hold
in their imagination.'[18] This book points to the utopias and dystopias that
Hollywood cinema rehearsed throughout the decade.

Part 1:
Society/Culture/History –
Families in the Eighties

1 Britain in the Eighties

There is no such thing as society, only individual men and women and their families.

Margaret Thatcher, 1983

An era of unprecedented uncertainty ... shuffle for shuffle's sake

Tom Peters, *Thriving on Chaos,* 1987

Uniformity has given way to broader choices ... Mass markets have splintered. Size has lost its significance as it becomes increasingly clear that a company's rank in the Fortune 500 is of limited importance.

Martin Davis, Chairman, Gulf + Western, *Fortune*, December 1985

What was it about the social and political climate of the 1980s which rendered it so susceptible to familial ideology? One hundred, perhaps even fifty, years ago, one could safely anticipate living in a world that would look and function roughly like that of one's mother, if not one's grandmother. During the latter part of this century, that certainty changed but perhaps most quickly and radically, in the eighties. It was a period of great sociocultural dislocation and upheaval.[1] Drawing on a Barthesian concept of myth, we can see how contemporary mythologies functioned to explain and resolve change and paradox; social phenomena which were, in reality, insoluble.[2] In the eighties, such myths depended for their anchorage on the ideology of the family. While the family is a material entity meeting real people's needs, it also meets needs which are socially and culturally constructed. The family annealed the gap between social crisis and political mythology, mythologies which were in themselves riven by contradiction. This chapter examines the historically specific nature of these turmoils and the myths in circulation.

CRISIS AND THE POLITICAL AGENDA

Britain and America have always enjoyed a close, if turbulent, relationship from the time of the early pioneers through to the contemporary 'favoured nation' status. However, the eighties represented a time when political and social events brought the two nations into greater proximity and symmetry than for very many years. Elected Prime Minister in 1979, Margaret Thatcher gave her name to a political ideology which wedded the individualist politics of the American Dream to British neo-monetarism. A historical moment combined with a powerful personality to give focus to a radical right politics which looked very different from the Labour–Conservative consensus of the postwar period. 'Thatcherism' looked to America rather than to Europe in the enterprise of 'making Britain great again' and the 'special relationship' between Mrs Thatcher and Ronald Reagan was explicitly and publicly cultivated.[3] During this period in particular, the political and social concerns of the USA and Britain were perceived to be almost identical, mobilised through the intimate relationship played out around the heads of government. The old certainties of consensus government, state intervention and international alliance against a common enemy began to fall apart. In addition, solid manufacturing bases, which had once led industrial revolutions across the world, became vulnerable to foreign competition. Countries once dismissed as 'Third World', such as Taiwan, Malaysia and Hong Kong, competed aggressively in a global marketplace very different from the ones western countries were accustomed to. New commodity forms, particularly information, and the technologies created to circulate it, seized strong positions in commercial traffic. In the process, the bourgeois, humanist values of America and Britain were challenged. The cost of labour had been steadily driven up in the western world as welfare systems developed and individuals were protected from absolute hardship. Developing countries with little allegiance to such values began to compete in capitalist markets in which, ironically, traditional capital-rich nations had disadvantaged themselves. Ideological conflicts were inevitable in such a climate. Torn between loyalty to long-held beliefs in individual rights and the need to reverse economic decline, both America and Britain embraced a radical political agenda which incorporated and rehearsed these insoluble dilemmas.

This political agenda was itself highly paradoxical. It took the form of a reactionary utopianism driven by leaders who were innate pragmatists. Rejecting the current reality as unsatisfactory, it proposed the reconstruction of a golden era which, in reality, had never existed and never could. This vision was based on a version of the American Dream in which just by working hard enough and observing moral conventions based on nation and family, individuals would succeed. Thus, in perfect circularity, the vision looked both forwards and backwards, relying for its justification on a mythical past. In both countries, familial ideology lay at the heart of contemporary political rhetoric. There were, of course, key differences in the political maps each country followed. In America, for example, the church was a major player in carving out the political scene, while in Britain the state and the church diverged more sharply than ever before.

Church leaders openly criticised the antisocial agenda as directly contravening their spiritual mission. However, the broad political project was the same: to rein back state intervention, fuel enterprise and promote individual responsibility. The politics of the right served as the seedbed and, in many cases, the pollinator of these myths, but a broader social consensus was essential to their growth.

This consensus was built against a perception of crisis, particularly in the arenas of nationality, the economy and society. Both America and Britain were coming to terms with themselves and their history, with the loss of international power and the globalisation of capital and labour. The myths constructed to address these anxieties were particularly urgent in the domains of nationhood, the economy and social cohesion. The following is an attempt to map these crises against the cultural mythologies which attempted to contain them, mythologies which were not autonomous but overlapped with, and reinforced, each other.

THE CRISIS OF NATIONALITY AND THE MYTHS OF NATIONALISM AND HERITAGE

One of the anxieties at the core of the political project was Britain's relationship with America and their joint and separate status in the global arena. While commentators had pointed to Britain's decline on the world stage since the end of the Second World War and the breakup of the Empire, it was not until the eighties that the reality really began to bite. As Sir Anthony Parsons observed, 'By the end of the decade . . . our influence was based on the wasting asset of past glory rather than on present performance, in which we were being outstripped by the majority of our European partners, not to mention Japan.'[4] Events such as the oil crisis in the seventies and emerging economic power of Pacific Rim countries signalled radical shifts in the international marketplace and threw Britain's position as a major player into question. America was still recovering from the humiliations of Vietnam where its claim to global and military supremacy had been seriously challenged. The economic challenges from the Pacific Rim heightened nationalist anxieties, threatening to reprise military defeat at an economic level.[5] The NATO alliance, in which both countries played a leading role, began to break up as the threat of Communism receded and a common enemy, so essential to resolving the upheavals of the fifties, was less easily identified. Nuclear technology, which had buttressed American and British defence policies, was now being developed across the globe. At the same time, Commonwealth members, the last vestiges of Britain's empire, found alternative trading partners, disenchanted with Britain's attention to the United States and Europe. As the European Community struggled to establish itself, Britain hesitated over the extent and nature of her commitment by looking to America rather than Europe in the enterprise of 'making Britain great again'. Old trading and military partners were leaching away, leaving both countries prey to nationalist anxieties.

However, it was the globalisation of capital and information which perhaps most undermined the concept of nationality itself. The insoluble dilemma which the western world had to resolve was how to maximise its own access to global markets while restricting the entry of competitors, most notably those countries which it had traditionally colonised and exploited but which now threatened its own economic stability in a world where national boundaries were only virtual. The traditional weapons of cultural imperialism only increased international aspirations and fuelled economic migration. Multinational companies were both willing and able to move their production sites around the world to reduce costs just as financiers were able to shift investments almost instantaneously from one continent to another. Decisions were taken in multinational headquarters and national governments now lobbied for commercial favours as well as vice versa. National boundaries everywhere were being challenged by the steady erosion of legislative, trading and technological barriers. The concept of a country itself was in doubt. With greater access to information but paradoxically distanced from global power bases, individuals demanded greater political autonomy at local levels. The world was now a more accessible place. People travelled more and to more exotic destinations, making tourism the fastest growing industry of the decade, and borders more difficult to regulate. Cultural and intellectual products became internationally available via satellite, cable and database technologies. It was not that technology determined change, but that technology, culture and society together created an environment ready for, and susceptible to, its inventions and penetrations, in turn prompting, and contributing to, the crisis of nationality.

These anxieties were displaced into the myths of nationalism and heritage. Nationalism was staked out against the threat of the other, the foreigner. When Argentina staked a claim to the Falkland Islands in 1983, Britain used the opportunity to wage an old-fashioned war over territory and sovereignty, triggering extreme nationalist sentiments across the public domain. Similarly, despite negative net immigration statistics throughout the decade in the UK, immigration was represented as a unifying, normative 'problem', fuelling an endemic racism which surfaced in a series of riots during the decade and created an underclass of disaffected black and Asian youths. The myth of nationalism obscured the ugly reality of what was at stake and the terrors of a truly global economy by appealing to a mythical inheritance which guaranteed future security. In Britain, it was a tradition of cultural supremacy, breeding and inherent superiority in which difference was entirely effaced. In America, it was the American Dream and the myth of the frontier: the myth that anything could be achieved by a pioneering spirit and hard work. Both invoked a national confidence through a mythical past. This was epitomised in Britain by the mythic slogan of 'Victorian values', which ignored the realities of the Victorian age to propose an era of domestic and colonial bliss in which social inequalities were erased by charity and private wealth-generation. The Victorian era, noted for its celebration of the domestic and presided over by a strongwilled, but family-oriented matriarch, was constructed as a Golden Age peopled by individuals who were independent, self-reliant and enterprising.[6] Margaret Thatcher herself was constantly compared to Churchill and conceived as a successor of Boadicea. Indeed, the National Heritage Act of 1983 attempted to secure this utopian myth by creating a cultural 'command economy' promoting a seamless, teleological high-art tradition of cultural production. Key institutions were gradually appropriated by a heritage ministry which operated them on a more commercial basis.[7] Increasingly, cultural forms and productions were polarised between an 'Establishment' representation of unified homogeneous cultural heritage in which any form of difference or dispossession was firmly suppressed, and oppositional, atomised forms of production which emphasised the diversity of experience.[8]

The social Darwinism of Victorian values was also signified by a new puritanism over health and the body. The female body had long been paraded as synonymous with female virtue and value and was emblematic of all that is rolled into femininity but this physical display was now extended to men. This revelation of male flesh represented something fundamentally different to the spectacle of female flesh. On the one hand, it can be understood as a powerful display of the masculine body, signifying the power of the male in a traditionally female space. On the other, it can also be seen as also a response to the pressures of feminism and new reproductive technologies, marking increased anxiety over the definitions and nature of masculinity. What is not at issue was the importance and signification of the body in the decade, particularly the normative young, white, male body.[9] This obsession with the normative body and its indicative health was registered in the pathologising of 'deviant' behaviour through the metaphor of AIDs which was represented in moral rather than

epidemiological terms. In a decade which wedded virtue to health and
fitness, illness itself was morally deviant. Many diseases, including cancers, were represented as preventable and therefore the fault of the
sufferer. Underpinning this mythical heritage of healthy, self-reliant
entrepreneurialism was, of course, the nuclear family, which was characterised as typical of nineteenth-century English Victorianism and was invoked as a model for economic and social organisation.

THE ECONOMIC CRISIS AND THE MYTH OF THRIFT

The fifties and sixties were characterised by a sense of economic abundance. Even in the seventies, this discourse of sufficiency persisted, with
a focus on the distribution rather than scarcity of wealth. However, by the
eighties, resources were perceived as finite. Headlines of fossil fuels ending, welfare systems exhausted and long-established industries collapsing
were routine. As public spending escalated and productivity slowed, the
size of the national debt forced its way up the agenda in both America and
the UK. Although economists continue to debate the merits of increasing
or decreasing national borrowing, governments on either side of the Atlantic attempted to reduce the debt by leveraging expenditure out of state
responsibility and into the private sector. Public spending was a heated
political issue and the role of the state in supporting the individual was
continually challenged. Rather than tackling the underlying issue of how
global resources were distributed, as the Brandt Report had essayed in the
seventies, policy shifted to concentrating wealth in the hands of those
deemed most deserving. 'Wealth producers' were perceived as autonomous agents, indebted, and responsible, to no one for their success, their
tax being structured accordingly.[10]

Privatisation and the free market upset the certainties of corporatism.
There was a great rush to commodification for artefacts and services which
were formerly regarded as being outside circuits of value and exchange.
Some of these, such as water, had been regarded as a basic right. Others,
such as the prison service or even the Westminster cemetery which was
sold for a pittance, had been perceived as inalienably in public ownership.
The biggest surge in earning power was perceived to be commanded by
those who dealt in money itself – particularly in futures on the stock
exchange; a business in which there was no product at all, only the probability of one. Factored by the deregulation of the financial markets, commercial debt spiralled, leading to increased emphasis on short-termism and
huge bank losses later in the decade. This was mirrored in the widening

gap between personal income and assets, fuelled by spiralling property prices, growing unemployment rates and a credit boom. Individuals, lured by the rapid economic growth of the second half of the decade following hard on the heels of the bitter recession of its early years, were tempted into home ownership, increased spending, the use of credit cards and facilities and consequently weighed down by debt.

One mechanism for evading the dilemmas of the macroeconomic debate was to talk of the national economy as if it was a household budget. This displaced responsibility for the economy from a national to an individual level and supported the values of personal enterprise and entrepreneurialism. It also justified accusations of fecklessness against the dispossessed, blaming the unemployed not only for their own plight but for the economic problems of the nation. Yet the myth of domestic thrift obscured massive paradoxes. The economy did not behave like a family. Cuts in one area produced massive costs in others. Thus, cuts in social benefits contributed to the escalating costs of policing and healthcare. Creating a health system closer to the American model not only replicated its extravagant administrative burdens but ensured that the cost of training private-sector nurses would be carried by the NHS. Public spending continued to increase during the decade, but it was also far less accountable. Elected bodies were increasingly replaced by publicly funded, non-elected committees whose appointees were recruited by, and directly accountable to, ministers.[11]

Moreover, the domestic budget myth hid the realities of international finance. The pound could be traded just like any other commodity and the traditional economic levers of interest rates and taxation were powerless against disinterested financial traders whose allegiances were to their employers and their own wallets. The myth also hid the realities of individual aspiration. A Gallup poll carried out for London Weekend Television in 1986, for example, demonstrated that far fewer Britons were interested in being wealthy than their counterparts in Japan or America and many were pessimistic about, or not interested in, their financial prospects.[12]

THE CRISIS OF SOCIAL FRAGMENTATION AND THE MYTH OF INDIVIDUAL CHOICE

The decade was characterised by social disintegration. In the mid-eighties, Mrs Thatcher coolly announced that 'There is no such thing as society', displacing social responsibilities to the level of the individual. In opposition to the governance and protection of the 'nanny state', Thatcherism proposed the jingoistic nostalgia of a Britain which would be made Great again through the entrepreneurialism of individuals driven by an uncomplicated desire for wealth, power and commercial success who were (largely) unsupported by the safety-net of a welfare state.[13] The erosion of a manufacturing base, the decline of trade unionism and introduction of new technology resulted in fewer people working longer hours and becoming increasingly mobile as companies moved out of urban areas to new towns or green-field sites or were bought out by multinational concerns.[14] As we have seen, one of the political projects of the decade was to 'roll back the frontiers of the state', which left many vulnerable and exposed. As the public sector declined, charities proliferated, replacing central resources in areas which the government no longer chose, or could afford, to support. This shift from collective, to voluntary, financing of the disadvantaged and needy was exemplified in the growth of charity 'events' in the mid- to late eighties such as Band Aid, Live Aid and the newly urgent fundraising tactics employed by such institutions as hospitals and schools raising money for essential equipment. Unless performed within the home, the duties of dependency and caring were increasingly denigrated and those in receipt of such care were vilified. Social divisions rested less on class, the traditional barrier in Britain, than on money. Society divided into the 'haves' and 'have nots' and was represented as increasingly aspirational. Such aspirations were signified by the privileging of high earners and the reemergence of popular discourses savaging the disempowered, dispossessed and poor who relied on state benefits for survival. New social categorisations emerged which were now associated with behaviour rather than breeding or background. Each of these types was implicitly, or explicitly, contrasted with the virtues of the bluff, driven, self-made entrepreneur and marked the shrinkage of the old working class and the growth of different strata of the middle classes.[15] Neglected by the mainstream political parties, opposition coalesced in bitter, grassroots conflict, mainly between disempowered or disadvantaged groups (such as strikers, ethnic minorities, the homeless and travellers) or those who were struggling to erect a specific political agenda (such as environmentalists and antinuclear protesters) and the police. No longer were these conflicts resolved across a table. The cultural polarity and material repression of the decade forced open battles of increasing intensity and violence, right up to the bloody poll-tax riots just prior to Mrs Thatcher's resignation.[16]

In this social fragmentation, lifestyle and identity politics were foregrounded and commercial companies developed niche marketing techniques to target new social groupings for their products, particularly youth and lifestyle segments. Some identified groupings benefited and others lost out in the new social climate. Despite, or perhaps because of, the AIDS panics, gay groups actually established a firmer foothold in political and cultural arenas, although this was truer for gay men than for lesbians. By contrast, the women's movements were discredited, feminism blurring into a 'post-feminism' which, by its very title, suggested that so much ground had now been won that there was no longer any need for active campaigning. Blacks and ethnic groupings found a higher profile, particularly in sport and music and largely through direct, personal action than organised political movements. However, the real power in identity politics was with the new youth subculture. As in the sixties, it was fashionable to be young and the cult of childhood and adolescence was promulgated. Youth had the necessary attributes and energy for the enterprise culture and could present the requisite looks and appearance with considerably less effort.

One of the myths which addressed this social atomisation was that of individual choice. The breakdown of social cohesion was represented as a healthy displacement of power and freedoms to an individual level. Individuals could now select from a hugely diversified range of lifestyles and products, from breakfast cereals to education and pensions. Yet the myth of choice also cemented divisions and hid three unresolvable paradoxes. Firstly, the inequality of opportunities afforded to individuals. Choice cost money and access to it depended on personal wealth and the knowledge of what was available. It was no coincidence that marketing budgets spiralled during the decade while a new underclass developed. Secondly, this myth of choice obscured the high costs of competition as the costs of diversity and innovation forced many companies out of business. Thirdly, the myth hid a contradiction at the very heart of the Thatcherite enterprise. While the individual was celebrated in opposition to the corporation and the state, power was centralised to an unprecedented degree. The government used all the mechanisms at its disposal to exploit the lack of a written constitution in order to install the praxis and 'choices' of free-market doctrine, extending the tentacles of central government and patronage further than ever before.[17] The powers of local government, for example, were gradually appropriated, notably in the controls imposed on their expenditure and disposal of capital receipts, but also in the curtailment of their responsibilities for education and housing. Thus the state increasingly arrogated power while abrogating responsibility to an individual level. This was obscured by the myth of individual choice which actually privileged the family as the primary vehicle for social responsibility and control.

CONTEMPORARY CULTURE: CRISIS AND CHANGE

Crisis also ruptured the cultural realm. The general climate of instability and proliferation of communication channels enabled radical ideas, which

had been latent or confined to specialist domains, to be more widely circulated and to gain greater purchase in public discourse than before.
Building on the enormous scientific challenges to established concepts of
time and space in quantum physics, structural approaches to society and
culture and the challenges to the Enlightenment notion of the individuated
subject mounted by psychoanalysis, postmodernism claimed to offer new
ways of looking at the world. Public tolerance of these new ideas was
indicated by the popularity of writing as diverse as the popular fiction of
William Gibson, the science of Stephen Hawkins and the postmodern
aesthetics of Baudrillard and Jameson. Underpinning all of this was the
unprecedented circulation of information and its accretion of value from
traditional commodity forms. The development of personal computers put
individuals in a very different relation to information and to physical space
than was previously possible. The era was increasingly represented as a
period in which the physical world was in crisis, where one could not
locate oneself in an unmappable world, but only slide endlessly through
relative issues and images.[18] Postmodernism represented a theoretical attempt to engage with the new technologies and formations of contemporary capitalism, in which reality now appeared to exist only through images,
in which there were too many images and too much information to process
coherently and in which the categories of subjectivity, distinctions between reality and cognitive activity, subject and object, signifier and referent, began to break down.[19] Much debate has been expended on how
postmodernism in its actual forms differs from the output of high modernism and how it can be distinguished since it depends upon the recycling
or pastiching of found material, but the term itself entered the popular
vocabulary in the eighties and was used aesthetically to describe many of
the newer experiences generated by new technology and media forms,
particularly architecture, music, video and advertising. In this climate, it
was the aesthetic of novelty itself that was privileged and underpinned a
general climate of turbulence and change.

SUMMARY

The social crises and dislocations on both sides of the Atlantic were addressed by mythologies which attempted to secure guarantees of stasis and
fixity, particularly around nationality, the economy and society itself. More
overtly than ever before, economic and cultural discourses were harnessed
within a clear political formation. Adherence to a neo-liberalist mone-
tarism established a shifting, often contradictory framework in which

centralism was derided in theory but espoused in practice and in which the family was a constant signifier of social responsibility in opposition to the state.[20] Electoral support was sought through the reduction of taxes and, therefore, public spending. The pressure to find some way of making good the gap between public need and government expenditure pushed the family into the foreground of public attention. 'Proper families' were encouraged, and expensive, ideologically unsound 'non-families' were discouraged through the mechanisms of familial ideology. The strength of familism was epitomised in the foregrounding of the Royal Family and the popularity of family-based soaps during the decade. Across the pages of all the tabloids the narrative of the Royal Family unfolded, a drama that was explicitly and selfconsciously referred to as a soap opera, conflating fact, fiction and ideology. The royals participated in a discursive formation which circumscribed the anxieties of social upheaval by invoking a shared heritage and the apparently unchanging construction of a nuclear family, stories which focused specifically on their roles as family members rather than as public figures.[21] Both the narrativisation of the Royal Family and the regeneration of the soap opera afforded intriguing opportunities to circulate and contest dominant familial representations which almost certainly accounted for their popularity at a time when the family held such a stronghold in the public and political imagination.[22]

The family thus operated at a social level to organise reproduction and resources, but also mythically, at a cultural level, to anneal social crisis. In a decade characterised as a period of upheaval and division, the mythologies constructed to resolve those tensions needed to be correspondingly powerful and the family offered the necessary potency. When politicians pointed to a 'crisis in the family', it was rather to a public anxiety over the family's continuing power to obscure social tension. However, the question in itself served to secure that power.

2 Hollywood Cinema in the Eighties

The exhibition of motion pictures is a business pure and simple, originated and conducted for profit.

American Supreme Court, 1915

Hollywood is a place you can't geographically define. We don't really know where it is.

John Ford, 1964

The upheavals which characterised commercial interests throughout the world inevitably affected Hollywood although predictions that cinema was an outmoded industry were persistently confounded. Hollywood had long proved itself able to accommodate both its industrial profile and its products to a volatile marketplace and the industrial maelstrom of the eighties merely proved its enterprise and flexibility. Hollywood freely adapted itself to the nationalist, economic and social crises which confronted it during the decade and both its industrial and textual forms bear the imprints of their circulation within the turbulence of contemporary commercial and cultural transactions.

THE HOLLYWOOD LANDSCAPE

Hollywood's industrial landscape was an intriguing paradox in the eighties but typical of other contemporary commercial enterprises.[1] Up to the divorcement arrangements in 1947–48, Hollywood studios were defined by their vertical integration, owning the production, distribution and exhibition mechanisms for their films, a factor largely responsible for cementing industrial and film-style conventions. At that time, the 'Big Five' studios (20th Century Fox, Paramount, MGM, Warner Brothers and RKO) were supplemented by the 'Little Three' (Columbia, Universal and United Artists) which had no theatre chains and relied on the big studios for exhibition of their product. By the eighties, the industry had fragmented within a highly conglomerated structure characterised by diverse and fast-changing ownership patterns. This followed the widespread trend in industrialised nations of spreading capital assets across a wide range of international markets while meeting consumer demands for diversity and choice at local level. This apparent diversification, however, frequently masked the increasing concentration of ownership.

The major studios, with the exception of RKO, still dominated the marketplace although the industry profile now included mini-majors such as Orion, Tristar, Cannon and Dino Di Laurentiis and neo-independents such as Carolco, Morgan Creek, Castle Rock, Imagine Entertainment and Largo. Although the latter retained their film rights since they could produce pictures without needing major studio finance, they were tied into the majors by distribution deals for domestic release. The defining characteristic of a Hollywood film, therefore, was its production or distribution by one of these studios. Alongside the Hollywood system were the true independents such as Troma, New World Pictures, Vestron and Atlantic who financed and distributed their pictures entirely separately from the major system but usually to specialist niche markets. The majors further increased their stranglehold on the marketplace in 1985 when the legal decision which forced studios to sell off their theatre chains was reversed and they began to acquire exhibition outlets during the latter half of the decade.

CONGLOMERATION: THE GLOBALISATION OF CAPITAL

Hollywood's industrial productivity and export capability has always represented a significant contribution to the US economy.[2] Throughout the eighties, earnings from foreign distribution (most notably in Europe and Canada) equalled or exceeded earnings from domestic distribution. In addition to commanding a leading position in the world's cinemas, Hollywood routinely financed films made abroad, particularly in the UK.[3] By the eighties, however, Hollywood's engagement with global markets was no longer one-way. As international markets opened up, Hollywood became increasingly attractive to foreign investors, notably Japan.[4] Studios strengthened their international position either by buying into or being bought by, multinational conglomerates.[5] These were either true conglomerations, in which the business was widely diversified and involved in various, autonomous industry sectors and markets, or companies whose interests remained in leisure and entertainment.[6] Studios were a prestigious purchase for many conglomerates who, in some cases, changed their own titles to become more closely associated with their subsidiary company.[7] America's flagship product was increasingly owned by foreign interests, a fact which contributed to one of the key social anxieties noted in the previous chapter, that of nationalism.[8]

Manufacturers and developers of hardware and distribution technologies saw the value of investing in software to guarantee their own futures. In the 1950s, this had been limited to the purchase of film libraries by television companies. By the 1980s, video and TV manufacturers such as Sony (purchasing Columbia in 1989) or media barons such as Ted Turner (MGM, 1985) or Murdoch New Corporation (Fox, 1985) saw the potential of owning the studios themselves. Hollywood developed a more interactive relationship with both manufacturers and distributors, enabling new commercial synergies. Capitalising the dependence of new media forms and distribution channels on its product, Hollywood began to plan for television, video and satellite income (and to regret the low-cost sales of their libraries in the fifties). With increasing competition between networks and other technologies, the majors were able to regulate supply and increase their profits. The video market grew to represent a significant proportion of projected and actual revenue for film producers. By the mid-eighties, for example, nearly a third of those households which owned a video in the Britain were renting tapes – mainly of feature films. The sale of video tapes was also established as a growth market during the decade and most theatrical releases planned for video income. Films which were not expected to do well at the box office frequently went straight to video where, if the production budget was low enough, they could still be expected to recoup a reasonable profit. In many respects, the theatrical release of a major feature film became part of the marketing strategy for the video and, even more importantly, of the tie-in merchandising which was a particular feature of eighties movies. While other media forms were radically disrupted by new technologies and distribution patterns and critics predicted dire consequences for cinema, Hollywood accommodated, and benefited from, such innovations, selling its films more widely than ever before.

By the eighties, the most significant change was the studios' shift in operational activity from production to distribution. Spreading the enormous, front-loaded risk of feature film production, the big studios shed all vestiges of the old contract system and delegated the development of talent to increasingly powerful agents who created 'packages' of scriptwriter, stars and director to sell to the studios. By the end of the eighties, most of the prominent directors, producers, screenwriters and actors were represented by just three agencies: International Creative Management, William Morris and the Creative Artists Agency. With the advent of the package, the studios were able to maximise their investment, still controlling production, as banks would not finance a picture unless the production company had a distribution deal, usually through a major studio, but able to devolve the initial (and most risky) research and development expenditure to the production company. Since all financing was tightly controlled and dependent upon the achievement of certain production conditions, such as content and timescale, since completion money (usually from other sources and a condition of bank funding) specified running time, MPA rating and even editing rights (such as for television and foreign distribution), these distribution deals consolidated the studios' control.

While at first sight, therefore, analysis of production company credits in contemporary US-produced films suggested a proliferation of independent companies, these were often established merely for the production of a single film and were manifest expressions of the package system. Independent production company titles commonly carried a star's name, usually the producer or director, and were often formed for one film. The oft-repeated truism, 'You're only as good as your last picture' became particularly apt as both banks and distributors frequently based their investment decisions on the capital of an individual's name and most recent performance.[9] This tendency, had, of course, been exhibited since the 1940s when the fall in studio output and the tax advantages encouraged many star names to form their own independent companies. In the eighties, however, it became the norm rather than the exception. The major studios thus buttressed themselves financially through complex patterns of conglomeration, diversification and delegation while maintaining their control over production. This industrial base also served them well in hedging against social fragmentation.

FRAGMENTATION: THE PRIVATISATION OF LEISURE

The Supreme Court's decision on divorcement signalled the public's changing engagement with the leisure and recreation industries and the position of Hollywood in particular. It is a complex picture and one that cannot be summarily treated. However, it is possible to say that after the upheaval of the Second World War, patterns of social organisation changed to privilege an ideology of individual self-realisation, alongside increasing resistance to authoritarianism, central control and corporatism. This trend paralleled an increasing focus on the home and domestic entertainment reflected in spending on home-ownership, domestic appliances, TVs and commodity goods of all kinds which escalated during the decade. The divorcement of the major studios was a part, neither simply cause nor result, of this anti-corporatism and retreat into the home. However, films need audiences and, with the increasing 'privatisation' of leisure after the war, attracting large audiences into the cinema was increasingly problematic.

At the height of the cinemagoing boom in the thirties and forties, the most profitable production strategy had been mass production. Faced with the double challenge to their corporate structure and their status as producers of public entertainment, the studios rallied, changing their exhibition, production and distribution practices to consolidate and create new profit streams. By the eighties, the studios talked about demographics and niche marketing.[10] Among the strategies developed for this changing marketplace were the blockbuster and the multiplex.

In the seventies, the studios recognised the marketing value of the 'blockbuster', single, high-budget films such as *Jaws* or *Star Wars*, in capturing a potential audience and delivering it to other products such as tie-in merchandising or sequels. The blockbuster became an industry standard and spawned a trend for sequels and prequels which continued throughout the decade as studios attempted to capitalise on their successful investments.[11] In contrast with previous marketing tactics, characters, rather than the stars themselves, were promoted across serials. Indeed the decade's most successful director, Steven Spielberg, was noted for casting relative unknowns in his films. Production costs increased dramatically from an average of around $7 million at the end of the 1970s to around $12 million in the mid-eighties. Blockbusters such as *Ghostbusters* ($32m), *Rambo III* ($58m) or *Batman* ($50m) could cost several times that amount. Marketing budgets also escalated, often matching the entire negative cost as studios decreased their volume of output, concentrating on aiming for 'film hits' to attract the more occasional audience. As *Variety* put it, 'There's just no getting around the fact that the film hits draw the available business like magnets. When there are several strong films, a mediocre picture becomes a box office dud, and a weak release is a box office bust.'[12] When these films were successful, the profits were phenomenal, funding the conglomeration and diversification being so aggressively pursued by the majors. Where they were not, the studios lost large amounts of money. As the risks increased, so industrial and textual experimentation was less likely, again influencing both the content and delivery of what was screened.

If audiences were reluctant to leave the domestic space, then cinema had to penetrate that space. We have already seen how this happened via video and broadcast channels, but cinemas themselves began to replicate the privatised, domestic environment. Multiplexes fragmented audiences, giving greater choice of programmes and providing more intimate auditoria. Continuous programming not only increased product choice but also timing, while creating economies of scale for exhibitors.[13] Garth Drabinski of Cineplex neatly summed up the economics of exhibition in 1981: 'When the movie starts . . . the income from any empty seats is lost forever.' Britain lagged behind America in the development of exhibition spaces but by the end of the decade, multiplexes had penetrated the UK market and the increase in the number of screens was closely correlated with audience growth.[14] By the end of the decade, multiplexes represented a quarter of the total number of screens in the UK and many of these sites developed into broader entertainment and leisure venues in which the film was just one of a number of attractions. The segmentation of distribution sites in this way mirrored the broader marketing trend towards consumer individuation and targeting differentiated 'lifestyle' niches. Cinema owners invested massively and more cinemas were being built in the UK at the start of the nineties than at any time since the 1930s.

The average audience profile changed, becoming much younger, with higher disposable income, reflecting the rise in ticket prices and indicating a niche audience with fewer commitments still looking for extra-domestic entertainment. By the end of the decade, the average cinemagoer in the UK was likely to be male, middle- or lower-middle-class and in their late teens or early twenties. This profile in itself determined (and was determined by) production and marketing strategies during the decade. It is likely that the high proportion of action films, for example, was geared to this market segment, just as the growth of multiplexes offered a greater opportunity to solicit more than one visit per week from an individual who had fewer financial or domestic commitments. Audience fluctuation thus clearly influenced the management and marketing of the product.

HOLLYWOOD STYLE: CONTINUITY AND DIVERSITY

So what did this product look like in the eighties? Hollywood must be documented as much in its mythic, symbolic terms as its empirical forms. As David Bordwell points out in the introduction to an exhaustive study of classical Hollywood cinema, 'We all have a notion of the typical Hollywood film. The very label carries a set of expectations, often apparently obvious, about cinematic form and style.'[15] Hollywood's hegemony has both benefited and hampered its stylistic development. As an industry it must establish a strong brand in the marketplace, a brand which, in cinema, is created in the very relationship between the text and its audiences and depends, in part at least, upon the ephemeral formal properties of diverse film texts. To sustain its commercial success, Hollywood therefore has a vested interest in maintaining stylistic continuities and consistent mechanisms for soliciting spectatorial attention. However, in the eighties, it also had to innovate sufficiently to sustain differentiated marketing strategies and maintain its audience niches. The ways in which Hollywood constructed its branding through industrial and stylistic practices would repay further investigation than there is scope for here.[16] What we are concerned with is how this balance between similarity and difference was exhibited in contemporary texts, particularly at the level of the narrative.

Justifying the enormous investments in the blockbuster, production values soared and the results could be seen (and heard) on the screen. Specific formal features will be considered in greater detail in the textual analyses which follow, but it is useful to offer a broad summary here. As we have seen, Hollywood's industrial and financial base mitigated against radical experimentation. However, the marketing necessity of balancing similarity with difference coupled with new technologies and the novel aesthetics of competing media, forced some innovations. These were technical rather than systemic, incorporating ideas, themes and technical devices into the classical paradigm rather than altering the structure and impulse of the paradigm itself. The much heralded 'New Hollywood' cinema of the sixties and seventies had not broken with the conventions of classical Hollywood film style but merely appropriated stylistic devices from other film modes and media. In the eighties this borrowing was primarily from music video and advertising – an industry from which many contemporary directors, such as Ridley and Tony Scott, Alan Parker, Adrian Lyne and Richard Lester originated. In classical fashion, narrative was still privileged, and goal-oriented characters overcame obstacles in a psychologically and empirically coherent manner to achieve resolution. Spatial and temporal logic also remained subordinated to the demands of the narrative and was constructed through the classical techniques of continuity editing, eyeline matches and reverse angle shots, conventions which characterised the classical Hollywood text. Even such technical peculiarities as the persistent use of low camera angles, extended shot lengths and awkward cuts and transitions and the innovations in special effects permitted by new technology and blockbuster budgets in films such as *E.T.*, *Top Gun* or even the opening sequence of *Look Who's Talking* were classically motivated. However, despite conformance to the broad paradigm of classical cinema, films exhibited syntagmatic changes which drew attention to the paradigm itself. The dominant aesthetic was realist but innovations in special effects frequently ruptured the realist effect by excessive displays of super-realism. *Who Framed Roger Rabbit* and *Honey, I Shrunk the Kids*, for example, drew attention to the 'work' of the film, the labour of construction which classical texts seek to conceal. A few films, such as the close of *Ferris*

Bueller's Day Off, explicitly acknowledged the camera's presence, while remaining within a realist aesthetic. Handheld cameras, the use of different film gauges, slow motion and freeze-frame effects were increasingly common and, towards the end of the decade particularly, films such as *Total Recall* began to draw on the graphics and perspectives of computer architecture.[17]

However, these films were not only distinguished by their spectacular visual qualities but also by their narrative structures. The most popular eighties films explicitly engaged with contemporary mythologies, paring their narratives and characterisation to confront socially alienated individuals with difficult moral dilemmas. In contrast to the 'certain tendency' of classical Hollywood's 'concealment of the necessity for choice', noted by Robert Ray, these films explicitly dramatised the necessity for choice.[18] Characters were unable to 'have it all' and the films dramatised the results of their choices. These choices, in turn, determined their social status. The moral universe of these films was complex, constructed through the range of competing demands confronting the hero. Amidst this moral complexity, it was the family which located absolute moral authenticity. The success, or otherwise, of a character's choice was signified by the (non)incorporation of the hero, frequently represented as an 'outsider', within a family unit, a distinguishing feature of popular films such as *Kramer versus Kramer*, the *Indiana Jones* series or *Rain Man*. Far from being 'apolitical', as Thomas Schatz charges, the Hollywood blockbuster displaced its politics to a domestic arena.[19] Retaining the motor of classical narrative, which drove twin plot lines of heterosexual romance and an alternative 'social' activity, such as business, crime, politics or sport, the tension of these films was played between the separate spheres of family and society. These dual plots remained causally linked, but were frequently constructed in opposition to each other with familial goals. In the contemporary blockbuster, the second plot frequently represented a metaphorical family which competed against actual family representations. The primary appeal (reflected in box-office success, at least) of these films appeared to be their readiness to engage with contemporary ideologies, particularly those of familism. But their attraction also resided in the simplicity and familiarity of the narrative and core characters alongside the excessive display and heightened realism of the *mise-en-scène*.

Texts were still constructed according to generic impulses, but these were more permeable than before and, in films such as *Gremlins, Fatal Attraction* or *The Golden Child*, were frequently played off against another in order to achieve – or withhold – narrative resolution. Most of the top box-office films were comedies, and represented a significantly greater proportion than the next most popular, action/adventure movies. These were followed by science-fiction films, dramas (including domestic melo-drama), thrillers and fantasy films. No costume dramas, documentaries, epics, westerns, sex films or compilations were represented among the top box-office films in this period. Many popular films relied heavily on intertextual references or reprised earlier genres often by constructing ahistorical nostalgic spaces. We can deduce from this generic distribution that audiences expected to derive most pleasure from films which subverted convention and dominant norms (comedy, science fiction and fantasy) or had a particularly strong narrative compulsion with clear goals (action/ adventure films, dramas or thrillers). With the exception of domestic melodramas such as *Terms of Endearment* and *Kramer versus Kramer*, characterisation appeared to be less important in respect of constructing psychological depth or motivation outside formulaic narrative demands – despite the prominence of characters in marketing terms (the eponymous Rocky, Indiana Jones, ET). When we consider the dominant cultural aes-thetic of the time – the drive to action and goal orientation – alongside dominant political structures of control and repression, this is perhaps not surprising, although simple reflections are misleading.

SUMMARY

The wider social and political crises noted in Chapter 1 reverberated through Hollywood at both industrial and textual levels. In capitalising their asset base through export and conglomeration, studios became vulnerable to foreign takeover, fuelling nationalist anxieties. The hugely risky block-buster strategy made the economics of cinema highly volatile and studios were forced to alter their marketing and distribution strategies to accom-modate increasing social fragmentation.

The major challenge which Hollywood faced was soliciting an audience for public entertainment in an increasingly 'privatised' leisure industry. At an industrial level, Hollywood resolved its commercial dilemmas by capitalising its presence in a global marketplace and by diversifying production strategies and distribution channels in ways that diminished their commercial risks and which attracted a 'domesticised' audience. At a textual level, Hollywood specifically engaged with contemporary cultural anxieties. These crises were both rehearsed and obscured at the level of representation. The most popular films stripped down their narratives and characterisation to focus on their intersection with contemporary mytholo-gies. At the same time, Hollywood reverted to the cinema of spectacle, upgrading production values through new technologies and special effects. Successful films frequently constructed narratives which were epic in quality, grandly large-scale, frequently formulaic and repeated in different forms throughout a series. As a result, many critics levelled charges that Hollywood had become formulaic and banal. However, this misses the point. The simplicity of the narrative permitted greater attention to the moral and ideological operations of the text as well as the aesthetic pleasure of the spectacle. What is most fascinating from our point of view, however, is how both the classical conventions and the new stylistic imports functioned to position and represent the family. The family acted as moral barometer in a complex world where heroes were required to make difficult choices. However, as we shall see in Chapter 4, the family proved difficult to fix and films frequently failed to achieve satisfactory resolutions. Thus, although David Bordwell was entirely accurate when he pointed out that 'The New Hollywood can explore ambiguous narrational possibilities but these explorations remain within classical boundaries', these ambiguities were ever present in eighties films and many were played out across the body of the family.[20]

3 Family Representations: The Family in Crisis

> For what is the real driving force in our society? It is the desire for the individual to do the best for himself and his family.
>
> Mrs Thatcher, 1979

> But what exactly is the family? Whatever else it may be, there can be no doubt that it is a central political issue in modern industrial society.
>
> Diana Gittins, 1993[1]

As we have seen, the concept of the family played a major role in securing dominant cultural myths in the eighties. But what was this family type? How did it function and what relation did it bear to actual family forms?

There are four paradoxes at the heart of familial research. The first is that although 'the family' is frequently the object of heated discussion, not least in the social sciences, it is rarely defined in any satisfactory or rigorous way. The second is that, however defined, family units are inherently diverse and transient, yet there is huge social investment in both a universal family type and its appearance of stasis. The third paradox concerns the fact that the majority of our social institutions, our legislation, economy, workplace, tax and welfare systems, are organised for a family type that in materiality, rarely exists and, where it does, exists in that form for very brief periods of time. The fourth paradox is that the very concept and ideology of the family has functioned to obscure the social organisation of reproduction, specifically the range of interests vested in it and how these structure and are structured by existing relations of power. Let us briefly take each of these paradoxes in turn before moving to look at how individual family members fared in the decade.

THE FAMILY – DEFINITIONS AND DISTINCTIONS

Social historians and anthropologists alike have hotly debated the definition of 'a family'. This debate is complicated by the fact that theorists have routinely collapsed a universalising ideological family into its material counterparts. Consensus is broadly achieved around two defining characteristics: blood or marital relations and co-residence. At its most basic,

36

the family is the unit to which society has entrusted its reproductive function. This function entails not only the physical reproduction of our species, but also the reproduction of cultural, social and psychic norms. Once this is distinguished, it is clear that 'the family' does not exist as a universal, static grouping but as a series of relationships and ideologies. As A.F. Robertson noted, 'Families in other words, are not mutually exclusive, objectively definable groups of people out there in society. They are overlapping components of a huge network of relationships which is created through time out of the basic process of reproduction.'[2] This brings us much closer to my own definition of the social family as not only a simple relation of reproduction, but also a configuration of fluid relationships, intersecting through reproduction, affection, common interest and power, constantly in process.

Of course the family does not exist solely in its material forms.[3] The family organises, and gives meaning to, a multiple complex of discursive formations. Family discourses structure our understanding of how society reproduces and manages itself and of how individuals are inserted into it. 'Familism', the ideology of the family, reached a specific historical form in the 1980s, a form which exhibited many continuities with its past but also particular discontinuities. This ideological family type was indubitably the nuclear family: white Anglo-Saxon Protestant heterosexual parents with an average of two point eight children. The maintenance of this ideology depended upon, and helped to create, the concept of home and workplace as 'separate spheres', a concept which had supported the introduction of waged labour in the Industrial Revolution and the ideals of personal freedom and self-realisation inherent in post-Enlightenment Western thought.

Contemporary demographic data showed that, although over half the population lived within a nucleated family structure (defined as a married couple with children who may be dependent or non-dependent), at the end of the decade this proportion was shrinking and an increasing number of people were living alone. Family breakup remained closely correlated with the life stage of the core unit but was primarily caused by individual election rather than mortality or even economic circumstances, as in the past. The individual's choice to leave the family was both enabled by, and a reason for, such factors as easier access to divorce, increased access by women to the labour force, an ageing population and more efficient contraception. In addition, increasing longevity resulted in increasing numbers of lone widows and widowers. These factors, coupled with the concentration of capital, increasing mobility of the workforce and the drive to own property resulted in a growing number of people living alone.

What distinguished the eighties from earlier periods was the ageing population profile and the renewed emphasis on the individual. With life expectancy growing and parents living considerable periods of time after their children left home, marriage bore a heavier burden of companionship and care. Divorce rates rose but serial monogamy became far more common as individuals continued to look to the family to provide romantic, sexual and social fulfilment. Families broke up by choice rather than through death as individuals lived longer and looked for more satisfactions over a longer period of time than a single spouse could provide. In an increasingly secular and sexually permissive society, these families were not necessarily legalised by marriage contracts, although most were. While the incidence of cohabitation and live births outside marriage increased dramatically through the decade, the majority of children born outside wedlock appeared to be born into a stable relationship.[4] There were significant gender differences in these patterns. Research showed that men were the main beneficiaries of marriage and certainly men proved keener to enter and stay within the marriage bond.[5] Women increasingly postponed or avoided marriage altogether, the demographic data confirmed by a range of qualitative surveys which confirmed that women were happy being single.[6] Similarly, while the number of divorces increased across the decade, seven out of every ten petitions were filed by the wife.[7]

These statistics cannot, unfortunately, identify geographical, class or even ethnic differences to any cogent degree and such detailed study lies outside the scope of this book. What they do clearly demonstrate, however, is that the stable, universalised, ideological nuclear family had even less purchase on its material referent during the decade. Particularly crucial to this study is the fact that the privileging of individual freedom and fulfilment, prized since the Enlightenment and foregrounded in the individualistic values of the eighties, directly undermined the family unit.

INVESTING IN STABILITY

By its very nature, the family unit is always in process, always changing. It exists in multiple forms and practices in any one moment and place. It is therefore inappropriate to speak of the *family*, in talking of its social form, only of *families*. Familial ideology, by contrast, insists upon a universalised, ideal type, and considerable cultural, political and economic investments have been made in it. As we have seen, the dominant discourse of the eighties was that of change and crisis. The ideological family represented a mythical vehicle for denying the necessity and reality of change or at least finding a refuge from the turbulence of the social realm.

The investment of the social unconscious for stasis was therefore made in familism. If, to paraphrase Jameson, the function of the media is to relegate the present to the past in a postmodern world, then the function of familism is to fix the present in the future in a time of crisis.[8] The moment of representation – the imaging of the family – was thus a temporal elision which collapsed past, present and future into an always-already, has-been and ever-shall-be, model for social organisation. Not only was the family a mechanism for reproducing the present via an imaginary past through the myth that the nuclear family was a universal, natural and desirable form, but also for reproducing subjectivity, specifically gender, through a series of 'perpetual presents' in which the past could be invoked as a heritage, and therefore as a justification for, social actualities and inequalities. The family thus stood in for essential, timeless values and a guarantee that basic social frameworks would remain the same in denial of the stark realities that faced most individuals in the decade.[9] As A.F. Robertson put it, 'We seem to cling stubbornly to the idea of the family as durable and stable, perhaps because we are uncomfortably aware of our transience as individuals.'[10]

The phrase 'family values' was therefore routinely apostrophised as part of a highly organised political campaign to return to a mythologised repertoire of Victorian ethics and morality. Familial ideology therefore functioned in two pivotal areas: to obscure the negotiations between state and individual responsibility and to sustain dominant power relations through a claim to timelessness.

THE FAMILY AND SOCIAL INSTITUTIONS

Functions which have always oscillated between state, family and individual, such as education, the socialisation of children, the care of dependants or the maintenance of dominant norms of subjectivity and sexualisation, were fiercely contested in the decade. As Diana Gittins so cogently points out, 'What actually goes on in families is conveniently dismissed as "private" until it becomes "public" by creating a nuisance or a financial responsibility to the State.'[11] What became more public in the decade was the scrutiny to which 'private' family activity was subject and how previously public functions were, in effect, privatised. Mrs Thatcher's speech denying that there was 'any such thing as society' signified a reduction in discourses surrounding social organisation to the level of the family unit, an ideological family which was increasingly at odds with its material referent. With increasing pressure on national resources, one political strategy was to construct a unit of consumption and income receipt which held a powerful purchase on the common imagination and desire and could be construed as subsuming all individuals within its remit. It was certainly in the interests of the prevailing economic system (and the political party which most strongly advocated market capitalism) to construct a social unit to replace the safety-net which the welfare state and political consensus could no longer provide. As a result, many areas of policy-making moved under the familial umbrella. A Family Policy Group was set up specifically to shift responsibilities from the state to an assumed nuclear family. Its call for policy initiatives on the family (assumed to be the ideological, universal nuclear form) established the platform for such legislation as the 1988 Education Reform Act and the 1986 Social Security Act, in a legislative tradition which has always been concerned with protecting and buttressing the family as guardian of society's most fundamental resources: people and wealth. State provision began to make assumptions that the family was responsible for matters such as the care of the elderly, the mentally handicapped or the sick. However, the diverse family forms which characterised the decade were frequently unable to manage such duties. Carers were largely women, often single, who devoted their lives to disabled, sick or elderly relatives which frequently – and ironically – prevented them from starting families themselves.

This conflation of social organisation with the ideological family type was elided still further to the level of a particular individual type, a type which was again ideologically and culturally constructed: the adult male of the household – white, middle-class, father, husband, breadwinner. A clear statement of this position was offered by one Conservative MP when he stated that 'The Conservative Family Campaign aims to put father back at the head of the family table. He should be the breadwinner. He should be responsible for his children's actions. He should be respected by those who teach his children. He should be upheld by social workers, doctors and others who may professionally come into contact with the children.'[12] Although tax laws changed during the decade, most other social provision, legislation and commercial remuneration practice was predicated on a male breadwinner who represented his family in the workforce.

However, another ideological compulsion which is crucial in analysing cultural representations of the family is that of 'familialism' which constructs social phenomena *as if they were* families.[13] As Barrett and McIntosh argue, 'we need not merely an analysis of family-as-institution or family-as-socialization, we need an analysis of the utterly hegemonic status of the familial perspective and familial ideology'.[14] Not only were social activity and management displaced to the level of the family in the decade (and a specifically ideological family type) but other forms of social activity and organisation were conceived and structured as families. We have already seen how Mrs Thatcher persistently spoke of the national economy as if it were the household budget, ignoring both its comparative complexity and, more importantly, the advice of eminent economists who have argued for the efficiency of maintaining a sizeable national debt over the long term. Hollywood itself was represented in familialised terms.[15] Familialisation also extended to the organisation of institutions as diverse as boarding schools and the highly gendered hierarchy and distribution of labour in most workplaces.[16] Thus key institutions have been understood as if they were families while, at the same time, families were constructed as replacing or effacing many of the same institutions. Whether this expressed an unconscious desire for direct communication between government and its denizens through the mediation of authoritarian father-figures is a contestable point. What is clear is that many tendencies of the 1980s, such as the removal of intervening layers of organisation and line management, the autocratic governance of Cabinet and Parliament, the refusal to negotiate with 'unofficial' representations and so on, all point to a strengthening of familialisation within such a model. Familialisation thus raised the stakes for familism. The ideology of the nuclear family type sustained a universal resonance for domestic and social forms of organisation and secured the political project being implemented throughout the decade.

THE FAMILY AND FORMATIONS OF POWER

Theorists from Engels through to Althusser and Laing have been concerned with the ideological function of the family, specifically in how the ideology of the universal, 'natural' family reproduced existing distributions of wealth and power at a social level via relations of production, reproduction and consumption. The family, understood as a method of organising public resources, personal time, space and desire within a social framework and always politically charged, raised its public profile in the eighties. In an inverse move, politics intervened more explicitly within its privatised environment. As feminist sociologists Barrett and McIntosh advocate, 'We have to engage with the ways in which the supposedly private sphere of the family is in fact better analysed as anything but private.'[17] Whereas women have always been particularly subject to medico-legislative scrutiny and surveillance, it is only very recently that the state has become concerned with legislating what goes on *inside* families and even now only on a very limited basis, as in cases of marital rape, the sectioning of mental health patients and, most recently of all, child abuse.[18] This is not to say that such legislation was uncontested. Generally policiticians on the right wanted less intervention, seeing the nuclear family as the perfect self-regulatory mechanism for social and ideological reproduction and its breakdowns, inversely, the cause of many social problems. Paradoxically, though, its maintenance required constant vigil and legislative attention. On the left, the family was perceived as regressive and oppressive, a *cause* of social dysfunction. In a material sense this repression could be seen in the subordination of women and children to the adult male, who still controlled the power relations, aspirations and organisation of the family through his superior earning power and legislative status. As a vehicle for the domestication and socialisation of its members, therefore, the family functioned to replicate hegemonic ideologies, reproduce broader social power relations and contain antisocial desire. At an ideological level, the left could not conceive of the family as a vehicle for change or transformation. However, they also could not account for its pleasures and irrepressible purchase as a rhetorical figure. All political parties, therefore, have wrestled with paradoxical and shifting perspectives on the family unit.

Rather than a simple left/right dichotomy, these positions are best explored along a continuum which polarised state and family. These positions shifted according to the differing ideological imperatives they were expected to satisfy and were not always located within a single political grouping. The first of these positions proposed that society is an anarchic, dangerous place from which the family was a refuge, protecting, socialising and educating its members. In this model, the family was essential to the smooth operation of state and economy and its guardians, usually women, a great (unpaid) resource. The second position assumed greater interdependence between state and family. The family was perceived as vulnerable, normally due to the failings of one of its members, and professional agents of the state, such as social workers or police, must intervene to contain and reform the wrongdoer and reinforce the family unit. The family member who fails is ideologically and culturally specific at different historical moments but has most frequently been the mother. A third position assigned society the moral high ground as arbiter of both private and public behaviour. This model assumed that the family was a site which replicated the worst forms of social and ideological practice and actively oppressed specific social groups. Economic regulation, social policy and legislation have historically been distinctively organised according to the prevalent model. Positions shift quickly, however, and often in contradictory movements and one can trace mutually incompatible policies even within the Conservatives, the self-styled 'party of the family' in the 1980s.[19]

These social and ideological shifts in position are not easily segmentable or logically sequenced. Instead, like changes in families themselves, they overlap and are often contradictory. As we have seen, the material variances in actual household composition posit a direct challenge to such universalisation and propel contesting representations of family form and functions into public discourse. I have not, therefore, attempted a chronological history of familial ideologies through the decade. The focus of this analysis is to look at how different forms of familism intersected with the social family and to identify some of the discursive formations within which they were operating. These become clearer when we look at how individual family terms were addressed during the decade.

FAMILY MEMBERS

Fatherhood

Masculinity, in particular, was represented as being in a state of crisis in the 1980s. Given that fatherhood is a more explicitly social category than motherhood, which is overtly biological, it is unsurprising that the role of the father is one that is constantly challenged and hotly contested. What is interesting is the intensification of these anxieties during the decade and the foregrounding of specific narratives which rehearsed them across the public, rather than the private, domain. The reasons for this have been attributed to several factors. Feminists such as Susan Faludi pointed to a backlash against the inroads made by feminism in the seventies. Others emphasised the increasing numbers of men who were unemployed and now relied on women for an income. Traditional 'men's jobs', in industries such as manufacturing, coal-mining and shipbuilding, were fast disappearing and being replaced by the newer service-related jobs, often done by women and often part-time. In manifestation of one backlash to feminism, 'men's groups' sprang up in the United States and quickly spread to Britain, orchestrated most notoriously by a figure going under the rubric of 'Iron John' who advocated a return to one's father and the archetypal essence of masculinity epitomised in a mythologised 'wild man' heritage. Sexual politics now embraced the social and cultural role of masculinity alongside its analysis of femininity, postulating a politics of difference and 'post-feminism'.[20] While entrepreneurial politics challenged the existence of a welfare state and laid the burden of care on the shoulders of individuals (usually women), it also challenged the corporate institutionalisation of many working men and delivered competition in the form of women entering the workforce in far greater numbers. Meanwhile, the cultural elevation of the child fed into paternal anxieties, reinforcing the urgency of the father–protector role but also directly challenging the role of father–possessor.

In common with the familial paradigm, patriarchy is socially and historically specific, shifting from the principle of 'good lordship' in the fifteenth and early sixteenth centuries to the puritan construction of the father as spiritual substitute for the parson and agent of state control within the family sphere in the sixteenth and seventeenth centuries, shifts which have left their residues in contemporary ideologies. The construction of the male breadwinner emerged with the rise of the middle class in the late eighteenth century and was reinforced in the nineteenth century when greater distinctions were made between public and private spheres in the interests of established hierarchies of gender and class.[21]

Women and children, constructed as spiritual, pure and in need of protection, were increasingly excluded from the workforce and their care and provision entrusted to the male adult of the household. Paradoxically, the dependence of middle-class family members on patriarchy was contingent on the exploitation of the labour of women and children in the lower classes. This problem was partially resolved by redefining acceptable categories of work for different status groups and incorporating many into the domestic labour force as servants. In reaction to the advent of industrialisation and the proletarianism of the majority of the workforce, men in craft or skilled industries organised themselves into associations or unions. These groups laid claim to the privileged masculinity of the middle classes by demanding a 'family wage'. The concept of the family wage coincided with patriarchal and familial ideologies and became a primary goal for trade unions. Even in the nineteenth century, few working-class families could survive on a single wage yet the concept of one male breadwinner per family has been one of the most powerful family discourses of the modern era, and one that has had dramatic effects on constructions of fatherhood, masculinity, motherhood, femininity and family life.[22]

This ideology was deeply embedded in both Conservative and Labour party policies, the former with its vision of the economy fuelled by the pitstop of the family and the latter driven by the emulative goals of a patriarchal trade union movement. Maintaining the ideological conception of the nuclear family was thus not far from the agenda of either. The dislocation of ideology and actuality is highly visible here. Despite the ideological insistence that the father remained the breadwinner, women were increasingly entering the workplace in both America and Britain, and many of these women were mothers.[23] Increasingly fervent calls for better childcare and the provision of crèche facilities in larger organisations testify to this. The rising rate of male unemployment in the early and later years of the decade point to the fact that women were often not only significant, but frequently the sole, contributors to the household budget. In addition, increasing numbers of the population were not living in a nucleated family framework and thus were either not serviced by the family wage or were overcompensated, accumulating rather than distributing wealth. It was, at least in part, this increasing disparity which occasioned the crisis of masculinity.

The father's role, being the most explicitly socially constructed of the family terms, rested primarily on dominant conventions and codings of masculinity which were, as we have explored, a site of fierce contestation in the decade. These contests were fought through social, cultural and psychic realms. Central to them were issues of possession and power. Paternity itself has been traditionally safeguarded by a series of social and legislative controls. Marriage and punitive penalties for adultery have been the primary instruments for guaranteeing the integrity of the patriarchal lineage. With the weakening of the marriage bonds (fewer people marrying, fewer people staying married) and the slackening of the divorce laws since the sixties, these social and legislative guarantees began to be replaced by other forms of legal and social imperatives. The search for biological proofs of paternity gained impetus, fuelled by research into DNA sampling and more sophisticated techniques for blood-typing. Paternity was even more severely tested through the development of reproductive technologies which triggered public debates over women's new-found abilities to reproduce 'without men'. The position of father as patriarch was thus rendered far less stable, scrambling to reestablish itself in the guise of the 'new man' and the outbreak of public images (particularly in advertising) of men caring for children and sharing domestic chores. It seemed vital to assert the male imperative in reproduction, frequently usurping the role of women in the anxiety to appropriate potency. Paternal representations began to usurp conventional maternal images in the most visible domestic spheres: child care and purchasing.

The field in which the paternal role was most clearly repositioned was in the relationship between father and child, effacing the male–female relationship scrutinised in the wife-battering discourses of the seventies. It was here that the father most strenuously asserted his authority and struggled to re-establish the role, albeit in modified form, of the patriarch. The most intense family debates during the decade focused on the effects of removing the father from his family and the deleterious outcomes this was claimed to create, particularly with regard to the maturation of young boys. A simplistic and largely unacknowledged Freudian account of maturation was simply assimilated into public discourse and rehearsed as evidence to substantiate the claim that children needed fathers for their proper development – however abusing or violent those fathers might be. In the most serious and traumatic child-abuse cases of the mid-eighties, every effort was made to prevent fathers being removed from the family home.[24] Alongside this elision of biological males with domestic masculinities, Phyllis Chesler has documented the ease with which men retained custody of their children, when they chose to fight for it, in the United States.[25] A further instance where the hysteria of patriarchal redundancy surfaced was in the fraught arena of abortion. The case having been won – legally – in both the UK and the US over a 'woman's right to choose' abortion, the precise nature of that right was repeatedly challenged. As the number of abortions rose, attention focused on a woman's obligation to seek permission and agreement for the termination from the natural father before exercising her choice. The choice, it was argued, extended to the choice to seek permission. Heartrending stories of fathers 'losing' babies (foetuses they frequently knew nothing of, being estranged from the woman they had impregnated) through abortion without their knowledge or consent were widely publicised, carrying dire warnings to women contemplating abortion. Men were frequently featured pleading with women to bear the foetuses to term, like some lifesize test tube, upon which they would undertake to rear the baby. Paradoxically, this severed the cherished conflation of the biological and social roles of mothering, a rupture which had not served dominant interests until that time. The 'right to life' movements in both the UK and the US became more vociferous and violent, resulting in injuries and even death to medical practitioners who carried out abortions and to the women involved. Control over contraception, and therefore of reproduction, also reverted in part to the male and the Pill was increasingly discredited (often on unproven medical assertions) as the advent of AIDS insisted on the revived use of condoms.

The role of the father, and most particularly the father's control of patriarchal authority and lineage, was therefore challenged by new technology and medical advances as well as by social and cultural change. The paternal response was framed within moral and ethical formations as the father was forced to seek new forms of legitimacy and to claim different territories and powers. That the male investment in the retention of the nuclear family form was greater than for any other family member is attested to by research which shows that men benefit far more from remaining within a family structure than women. They live longer and are healthier, whereas the reverse is true for women. Men also suffer far more from mental illness as a result of divorce.[26] As American social scientist Jessie Bernard put it, 'There are few findings more consistent, less equivocal and more convincing, than the sometimes spectacular and always impressive superiority on almost every index – demographic, psychological, or social – of married over never-married men. Despite all the jokes about marriage in which men indulge, all the complaints they lodge against it, it is one of the greatest boons of their sex.'[27]

Motherhood

At the close of the decade, a new poster in the series of controversial Benneton advertisements was splattered across the world's urban hoardings. In it, a newborn baby was held, dangling and bloody, in mid-air, umbilical cord still attached, by the surgically gloved hand of some invisible deliverer. Yet the umbilical cord stretched away, out of the frame. The mother's presence was neither seen nor acknowledged. As a metaphor for motherhood during the decade, this image was stridently accurate. However, the debates it prompted concerned its relevance to knitwear rather than the absence of the mother. That had become too routine to question. While many feminists struggled to establish motherhood as a defining role in which to recover women's psychic, social and cultural power, the role itself was being popularly denigrated, evacuated or altogether occluded.[28]

At the beginning of the decade stood the surrogate motherhood and in-vitro fertilisation (IVF) debates. Succeeding to the tense abortion controversies of the previous decade, these looked forward, Janus-like, to an increasing concern over maternal obligations as well as backwards to the pro-choice campaigning over women's rights in the seventies. In the middle of the decade, and heightening in intensity towards its declining years, were the child-abuse controversies which played out an eroticised version of intrafamilial violence represented in the sixties through baby-battering and in the seventies through wife-beating. The represented victim of intra-family violence had swung away from the mother and back to the figure of the child. A predatory representation of male sexuality was once again rampant and was frequently excused on physical grounds, much as many rapes continued to be. Women, as conventional guardians against, and recipients for, such excess, were damned by their partners' actions and, although not generally represented as actively abusive themselves, were constructed as abusive through their negligent passivity. The autonomous, independent status of women as distinct from the social roles of wife or mother which had been so bitterly fought for by seventies feminists was absorbed into their familial responsibilities. Women once again disappeared into the role of wife and mother, hidden in the frenzied debates over child abuse and childcare. Surrogacy and IVF were viewed with more ambivalence but equal anxiety. On the one hand, they introduced an active demonstration of sisterhood and a capacity for female economic and reproductive independence. On the other hand, they were predicated on highly gendered capabilities. Women were once again conflated with their ability to reproduce and then rewarded for it. Social and cultural anxieties, particularly around masculinity, were projected on to the ability of women to reproduce without the biological agency of men. While tensions over 'real' motherhood have always presented themselves in adoption cases, the new reproductive technologies created opportunities for representing different categories of motherhood, and the press frequently inveighed against it, particularly when homosexual and lesbian couples, pejoratively termed as 'pretend' or 'unnatural' families, chose to have children.

The representation of the maternal figure has conventionally been starkly polarised along a good/bad, madonna/whore axis. The most persistent maternal paradigm of the modern period emerged with Rousseau's conception of the mother as a guardian and educator, a purveyor of Christian moral values and this has remained the ideal for the nuclear familial ideology. Feminists have acknowledged that, while limited, this ideology at least represented an opportunity for women to gain domestic power through motherhood. However, the mother's moral function has complicated this revisionist position. The maternal figure has traditionally only been represented positively if complicit with patriarchal regimes, entirely focused on the domestic sphere, passive, subservient and asexual. A 'bad' mother was active, often domineering, seeking to disrupt or usurp conventional patriarchal power relations.[29] In the 1980s, the role of motherhood was still primarily mapped out between such oppositions although with different inflections. It was the bad mother who was passive, who failed to act, in direct contravention of a core contemporary virtue. Such maternal neglect was most frequently rehearsed around the issues of work and children. Despite the desperate need of many households for a maternal wage, mothers were continually pilloried for working and research on the supposedly deleterious effects on childcare was routinely publicised, the dubious basis of much of which was incisively exposed by Susan Faludi in America.[30] The mother was also regularly represented as failing in her role of protecting her child, both born and unborn, not only from the external environment, but also from the excesses of its parents. Harrowing images of babies born with AIDS or drug-dependent competed with statistics concerning the low birthweight of babies whose mothers smoked. Cultural and political debates raged in both the US and the UK over the rights of a mother as against those of her unborn child, urging mothers to place the foetus's interests above her own. This pressure was most intense in the United States where child-abuse legislation was deployed on behalf of foetuses. In 1988, half of those surveyed in an American Gallup poll felt that pregnant women who drank, smoked or refused obstetrical surgery should be held legally liable.[31]

This burden of maternal liability is demonstrated by two heavily publicised cases in which the demands of mothers were publicly weighed and adjudicated. The first, in Britain, concerned Wendy Savage, a practising obstetrician in Whitechapel, who fought her male colleagues for the right of pregnant women to choose the time, place and method of delivery. This was a direct challenge to the authority (and convenience) of her colleagues who frequently induced births to suit hospital schedules rather than in the interests of the mother. The second concerned the case of 'Baby M' in America, who was carried to term by a surrogate mother under a contractual arrangement with its adoptive parents. On changing her mind, the biological (or 'natural') mother was subject to a long legal battle which first wrested the baby from her and finally (three years later) granted her rights of access.[32] The issues in both these cases revolved around the biological and social categories of motherhood, categories which until the advent of contemporary technology had been universally conflated, and around who was entitled to create the definitions. In both cases, contractual obligations were invoked in an attempt to secure obedience to patriarchal structures. Neither woman accepted these and fought instead for a 'natural' maternal right. Both analysts and protagonists have suffered from an over-essentialist construction of women-as-mothers, but the issues focusing on women's power, or the lack of it, were acutely identified. The professional (Wendy Savage) won her case, but the 'natural' mother (Mary Beth Whitehead) did not.

In the 1980s, the interest lay less in what mothers were, than in what they did, or did not, do. Such a shift is symptomatic of this materialist, action-oriented decade in which secular puritanism reigned. The two extremes now were between the do-it-all, have-it-all Supermum and the do-nothing, have-nothing drudge. This was exemplified by the publication of Shirley Conran's *Down with Superwoman* in 1990, a successor to the two most famous female guides to personal achievement.[33] In the intervening decade, even this super-optimist was forced to acknowledge the disappearance of many of the social-welfare props which buttressed her overachieving heroine in the seventies. As reviewer Deborah Philips put it, 'Superwoman

Mark Three is firmly back in place servicing her family efficiently ...
Superwoman now has to do an awful lot of campaigning to keep her
creche open, to get those workplace nurseries in operation and to keep her
evening class viable.'[34]

Childhood

The category of childhood is a comparatively recent one. In mediaeval
times, childhood ceased at the age of seven and children were entirely
their father's property – to the extent of being sold as objects of commodified
exchange.[35] The sexual possession of the child by the father, namely incest, was itself legal until 1908 in the UK. Up until the Reformation, a
Renaissance celebration of childhood purity prevailed. This representation
was violently crushed in the late sixteenth and seventeenth centuries by
Puritan repression and the emergent concept of the post-lapsarian child
who was born sinful and had to be corrected. In the eighteenth century,
this Calvinist construction was in turn succeeded by Locke's conception
of the child as a *tabula rasa,* a position midway between these extremes.[36]
Romantic Utopianism competed with Victorian neo-puritanism in the nineteenth century, with the latter slowly giving way to a view closer to Locke's
mingled with new scientific understandings of genetic, psychic and cognitive development. In our own century, ideologies have continued to
oscillate between these positions which formed the basis for childhood
representations in the eighties.

Sociologist Diana Gittins identified seven reasons commonly given for
having children, which offer some insight into the social and cultural
functionality of contemporary childhood. Parents generally cited one or
more of the following justifications: as an heir to property; as a source of
labour; to achieve immortality; to bring status; to form a permanent loving
relationship; to introduce a new power relationship or as a source of security in old age. All of these confirm the individual's investment in the
family as a source of personal fulfilment. However, the desire for children
should not be seen as 'natural' but as culturally and socially constructed
and, by the eighties, there was a powerful additional reason for procreation: the access to new epistemologies and forms of power. Children were
constructed as a privileged group, vessels of innocence who required protection. They were particularly privileged by their access to specialised
forms of knowledge, particularly in relation to popular culture and new
technology, and by their highly prized vigour and energy. This was the age
of the teenybopper and teenage supermodels. Correspondingly, children
steadily gained in power during the decade – both as consumers and as a

social category. The distinction between child and adolescent (the omni-present 'youth') was increasingly blurred while many adults re-presented themselves and attempted to establish their credibility by aligning them-selves with youth. Although the vilification didn't fully gain momentum until the nineties, single mothers were often represented as having children merely to gain both status and material benefits, an almost axiomatic paradigm of the child's power to bestow privilege. Certainly the demo-graphic bible, *Social Trends*, assumed that the only way to become a family (as opposed to a household), with all the social and cultural cachet that carried in the decade, was by having children, implying that adult relationships were only legitimated by reproduction.[37]

Power balances, traditionally weighted towards the father, now tipped towards the child and the most heated debates in the 1980s revolved around the rights of the latter. These ranged from adolescents' rights to contra-ception and sexual relations, foregrounded in the Victoria Gillick case in the UK, to the rights of children to 'choose' their parents, highlighted in divorce cases on both sides of the Atlantic. These rights were always represented as being won at the expense of the parents, particularly the father, mothers being marginalised in such contests. Although children gained unprecedented legal rights during the decade, these were never accorded to their mothers who have historically had little legal power over their children, an interesting paradox for daughters to deal with as they matured.[38] The 1989 Children's Act signified how comprehensively the child was identified as a special body for intervention and legislation. The Act enshrined childrens' rights to be protected from the excesses of their parents alongside their rights to speak and make demands. The debates around this legislation, and its enforcement, highlighted the inevitable conflicts inherent in protecting the innocence and vulnerability of the child while forcing it into the public domain and foregrounding its discourse.

Children were paradoxically constructed as both innocent and 'know-ing', embodying truth while ignorant of its applications and consequences. Thus children indicted their own parents as visible evidence of neglect or abuse; their words and their very bodies being used *against* their parents in court actions where the state adjudicated on standards of parenting.[39] What was really on trial in the eighties was the form and content of 'proper care' and the rights of the parent versus those of the professional in nurturing and socialising children. The construction of childhood had moved, in some senses, close to the formulations of Rousseau, but instead of exalting the mother's role as protector and educator, the debate focused on the threat posed by the father and the weakness of the mother to withstand him, requiring external assessment and intervention. In such instances, the evidence of familial breakdown was pitted against the normative ideals of familism, which privileged the solidity of the family unit and which were rehearsed as frequently in the courts and case meetings as in the media and in which the child was required to serve as moral index. Ironically, therefore, the family was often found to be the solution to, as well as the cause of, child abuse and it was the child who was the cause and justification of both.[40]

Alongside this extraordinary potency was constructed a paradigm of the child's dependence and vulnerability. In 1985, for example, the National Children's Home launched its campaign 'Children In Danger' to tackle 'rising poverty, increased drug misuse, deteriorating housing, escalating family breakdown, a continuing high level of physical and sexual abuse, and cuts in services for children' and the popular television presenter, Esther Rantzen, launched Childline, a telephone service offering advice to those children who felt themselves to be under threat, normally from intra-family abuse.[41] However, children also needed to be protected from exposure to cultural representations of which the government disapproved, particularly in film and video. Thus, in 1989, the British Board of Film Classification introduced a new 12 category for film which had the unintended consequence of enabling 12-year-olds to view films they would previously been barred from while it was seeking to protect them. A further example of acute public concern was indicated in 1982 by the submission of a Private Members' Bill seeking to protect children from violent videos, the so-called 'video nasty'.[42]

The case is instructive as it exemplified all the discursive anxieties circulating around the social and cultural category of the child and its location in the family in the eighties. Although the Bill failed, it prompted the formation of a Parliamentary Group Video Enquiry in July 1983. The remit of the enquiry was to examine the effects of video film violence on children. The ensuing report was inflected throughout by familism and overtly rehearsed prevailing ideologies on culture and the family, its findings being mainly anecdotal and deductive. The report's assumptions that video viewing was a passive activity, that viewers were unable to distinguish fact from fiction and that identification is unproblematically located with the perpetrator of violent acts have all been cogently analysed and refuted by theorists.[43] Suggesting that 45 per cent of children aged between 7 and 17 have seen one or more 'video nasty', the report somewhat arbitrarily concluded that the material had a definite and measurable effect on its young spectators.

Of paramount importance to this study was the suggestion that 'the influence of family example and parental control have been waning in highly developed countries for some decades, while the effect of models set outside the family exert a proportionately far greater influence' and that 'the viewing of "video nasties" by children correlates highly with the amount of viewing by their mothers'.[44] This tension between mother-blaming and the reduction in family influence was, of course, blatantly paradoxical and highly instructive. Mothers were implicitly blamed for the corruption of their children and, by extension, the decline in social standards. A correlation between violent or abusive families and watching violent films was interpreted as 'one of the major sources of the growth of a syndrome of violence as a social phenomenon'; video nasties would have more harmful effects in 'bad' families, those whose mothers 'let' them watch videos.[45] The report also found particularly disturbing the fact that not only were the perpetrators of such violence frequently women but that they were represented as physically attacking men, a judgement which fuelled its criticism of mothers.[46] Finally, it is particularly instructive that the Report identified rapid social change as predisposing individuals to feel less secure in established 'foundational social values', illustrating the deep-rooted anxiety over social change and the importance of the family, specifically the child, in anchoring mythologies which sought to mask it. Thus the health of present and future families depended upon the moral health of the child, and mothers were primarily responsible for monitoring this and ensuring they were not exposed to corrupting cultural influences. As a result of this report, the Video Recording Act of 1984 classified video material for home viewing to protect the child viewer. Alongside this, the Local Government Act (Section 28) stipulated further material which was illegal for classroom use, resulting in the toughest censorship restrictions in Europe.

The major signifier of the anxieties over childhood in the eighties was, of course, the explosion of child abuse cases which hit the popular agenda. Investigations such as Elizabeth Ward's in Australia, a welter of professional research, alongside the advent of self-help groups and more anecdotal explorations in talk-show formats such as the Oprah Winfrey confessionals, demonstrate that such abuse was not a new phenomenon, but that it was being permitted into public discourse for the first time.[47] One explanation for the entry of sexualised child abuse to the public domain was the contest over the nature and construction of the child within the private and highly determined familial space. The eroticisation of the parent–child relationship created a discourse in which power relationships could be confessed and resolved within the public space. The most frequently adopted solution to instances of such abuse – the punishment of the mother and removal of the child – attests to the power of patriarchy to reinscribe a traditional familial possession firmly within its grasp. The fact that familial relations are particularly highly saturated with this eroticisation also explains some of the medico-juridical reluctance to intervene in domestic violence. In the 1970s when women were making some inroads into structures of patriarchy, this violence was predominantly represented and managed as wife battering. In the 1980s, the focus shifted to the abuse of children – a form of assault which was highly sexualised.[48] It is crucial to understand the reality of sexual abuse on a child and the discourses that construct and contain it in the public realm within the context of power relations – the child within the hierarchies of power within the family and the family within social power hierarchies.

In the mid-eighties, a single event occurred which was to focus familial anxiety and reverberate to the end of the decade. The Cleveland child abuse cases concentrated primary anxieties over the responsibility and role of the father, the accountability of the mother, the breakdown of the family form and the levels of intervention permissible for external social agencies. Over the bodies of the children, a complex interplay of discourses competed for ideological dominance.[49] At stake were the ideological integrity of the father, the moral integrity of the mother and the physical integrity of the child. The father's role of guardian and protector of the family unit was thrown into crisis by the extension of his absolute authority to its logical conclusion – the right of access to the bodies of his children. At the same time, the mother was transfixed by paradoxical duties of care to her child and obedience to her husband. In a desperate attempt to narrativise the event to a satisfactory resolution which would clear the father of blame, the mother's very passivity was problematised. Narrative resolution was secured, in this case, through the vilification of the doctor who identified the abuse – doubly guilty through her gender (a woman who challenged patriarchy) and through her active intervention into the family space. Throughout the eighties, highly contradictory and controversial discourses circulated around the child who was represented both as sophisticated and autonomous, given far greater legislative rights and privileged access to certain forms of knowledge than before, while being simultaneously represented as increasingly vulnerable to extra- and intra-familial penetration and loss of integrity.

SUMMARY

What is clear from this cultural overview is that social anxieties were displaced to the level of the family in a more urgent and explicit way than ever before. Indeed, the panics that were exhibited around the family on both the left and the right in the 1980s can be seen as proceeding from the sharpening divergence between the ideological family and its material referent at the same time that both its material and ideological forms were bearing the burden of a radical social programme which the integrity of the family was vital in securing. Not only was the private space of the family being forced out into the public domain and under political scrutiny but it increasingly became a discursive formation through which all popular mythologies were filtered and assessed. The crisis in the family stemmed from anxiety over the family's ability to carry such a burden. Whether the diversification of the social family itself was a problem is not really at issue. It has been consistently demonstrated that only its variety and versatility have been constant throughout history. The features of that diversification are important in that they point to broader developments and dislocations in society itself and are historically specific. The key problematic lies in conflating the material variances of society with the ideological family – specifically with a culturally constructed head of household – and basing the development of social and economic policy on that understanding. Diana Gittins put it most succinctly: 'An ideology that claims there is only one type of family can never be matched in reality, for it presents an ideal to which only some can approximate, and others not at all. It is this attribute of family ideology which makes people believe there is a crisis in the family when the real problem is the gap between the ideology and reality'.[50] What was clear throughout the decade was the broad ideological pressure to conceptualise a universalising family type which could occlude or pathologise material deviance while attempting to secure deeply reactionary political and cultural discourses.[51] Our interest in analysing film representations in this context is to understand better how these representations work to expose, displace or anneal the gap between lived experience and cultural forms.

Part 2:
Film Families –
Family Films

4 Family Fortunes: Key Representational Paradigms

All happy families resemble each other, each unhappy family is unhappy in its own way.

Leo Tolstoy

So how did the family function in mainstream Hollywood films – films which held a purchase on an international marketplace – in a decade which was obsessed by defining its morality, politics and practice through the lens of the 'happy' nuclear family? If we assume Hollywood cinema to be deeply implicated in circulating and engaging with contemporary ideology and that familism was an important discourse within that, how did Hollywood represent the nuclear family?

The *Indiana Jones* trilogy included three of the most popular films of the decade and offers some paradigmatic examples of familial structures. These films shared stylistic characteristics with many other top box-office films of the decade – a focus on action, excessive male specularity, rampant individualism and the ability to sustain a narrative thread (however simplistic) across a sequence of discrete texts, notably through the agency of a male hero. Yet it is the familial scene invoked by the trilogy which is of primary interest here. Across the decade Indiana Jones pursued an arduous quest for his father – a father who represented the solution to fascism, to the conflicts and rivalries of Indiana's profession and to his own personal inability to form lasting relationships. The father's absence both motivates the narrative and disrupts his son's professional activity, activity which is consistently represented in familial terms. To appease the two patriarchs, Brody and Marion's father (the father substitute with whom Jones had quarrelled, splitting the archaeological community) Jones competes with arch-rival Belloq for the film's object of desire: the Lost Ark, symbol of spiritual regeneration.

However, Jones's exploits are constantly crippled by his desire to appease these fathers and be reconciled with his father. All else is subordinated to, or thwarted by, this quest. In common with many of the films of the eighties, his mother is totally absent, evacuated from the text and unnamed. Women generally are marginalised in the trilogy, relegated to being reluctant helpmates who become more alienated and devious in each sequel. The final sequence of *The Last Crusade*, in which Indiana, his father and his two sibling-substitutes ride off into an archetypal desert sunset in masculine celebration, recalls the fate of the outsider hero of the Western and typifies a powerful discursive paradigm of the eighties; the alienated hero who is socially and morally positioned in familial terms as a result of the choices he makes.[1] Jones's choice is to subordinate himself to the patriarch, rather than seeking autonomy and sexual maturity. The final celebratory reunion does not hold the promise of a future family in the privileged nuclear sense. These men remain separate, alienated from their society. They have destroyed a group of fascists, but only as a result of their individual acquisitive and affiliative desires, rather than as a political act. Their bonding is sterile, in both a reproductive and transformational sense. Social dislocation and loss is collapsed into the representation of the family and projected on to a desire for the ambivalent term of the father. The solution is sought in restoring the father, but this does not fully restore the family or resolve the social problems.

THE THREE-DIMENSIONAL FAMILY

The failure of the family either to support itself in nuclear form or to sustain a successful professional and social structure is a central theme in the popular eighties film. By mapping familial paradigms in three narrational dimensions we can see not only the fragility of the familist ideology but exactly where and how these familial breakdowns occur. These dimensions examine the *narrational relationship, outcome* and *modality* of the family within the text. The resulting paradigms expose a complex relationship between actual and representational family forms in which the hegemonic nuclear family was contested and where accommodations to actuality can be detected in mainstream, popular Hollywood films.[2]

The first of these dimensions concerns the family's *relationship to the narration*. This identifies the importance of the primary character's family(ies) to the narrative flow. Familial representations are clearly inflected by whether they are foregrounded, present or absent as a narrative term. Foregrounded families are the subject of the narrative and clearly structure the narrational and discursive field. While still providing a background of familial assumptions against which any central (non)families can be compared, present families are less dominant in the narrative structuring of a film. By contrast, absent families are never fully achieved or are missing entirely from the narrative although the absence itself is frequently a primary narrative motivation.

A second dimension maps the *potential narrative outcome* represented by the family – the family as possibility – and is located by all the families represented in the film through their textual sensibilities as well as empirical forms. The dimension of family-as-possibility concerns its ability to close the narrative and achieve its potential as a nuclear family unit. The outcome dimension offers a lens through which to scrutinise the family's ability to resolve the narrative and make good any sociocultural inadequacies. In this dimension, families are either utopian or dystopian. A utopian family structure locates the family as the solution to the narrative hermeneutic and its obstacles. In these films, for example, *Rocky IV* or *Honey, I Shrunk the Kids* or *Look Who's Talking,* a utopian family is fully achievable and represented within the text. Within dystopian films, such as *Rain Man* or *Private Benjamin*, the family is itself the problem, whether in full, fractured or absent form, and can neither be achieved, represented or even desired. Families which need a great deal of external intervention to maintain them are also represented as dystopian. In this dimension, the family frequently enters an intriguing loop, in that the *family itself* is the inadequacy which the narrative strives to liquidate and to which the family is then universally proposed as a proto-solution. This loop will be explored in greater detail later in Part 2, when we look at films such as *Top Gun, Pretty Woman* and *The Jazz Singer.*

Finally, I have examined the *modality* of the family, a dimension which turns on whether a family is actually or metaphorically represented in the text.[3] A significant proportion of popular films are not immediately susceptible to a familial analysis based on the representation of an 'actual' family, that is, literal family characters bound together by blood or marital ties. Yet they represent powerful social communities in which a familial structure can be discerned. Their core characters play out the dramas and obey the determinants of the reproductive unit within other social or cultural spheres. As I proposed in Chapter 3, one response to social fragmentation is to make social structures like families, the trope of familialisation. The family functions as a social unconscious, structuring cultural and social institutions within these texts, most frequently within professional hierarchies. These metaphorical families are explicitly organised on a familial structure both at an empirical level (they contain metaphorical 'mothers', 'fathers' and 'children') and at a psychic level (they obey psychic determinants and strictures in the formation and maintenance of subjectivity).

As Virginia Wexman has conclusively demonstrated in her book on the Hollywood couple, many films achieved closure through incipient families – closures on the conventional Hollywood coda of the heterosexual romance to indicate a potential generative unit.[4] I have termed this type of closure the Final Romance. As a large proportion of these texts represent 'rites of passage' movies, charting an Oedipal trajectory for the maturing hero, this form of closure carries a good deal of narrative weight. However, unlike previous generations of classical Hollywood texts, in which the Final Romance was in and of itself a resolution, these romantic alliances are generally coded as highly unstable. Closure is sometimes undermined by our knowledge of the characters' own instability (in, for example, *Terms of Endearment, Tootsie, Airplane!* or '*10*'). In other cases it is problematised by the scale of social fragmentation (such as *The Untouchables* or *Any Which Way You Can*) or even by subsequent revelations in sequels such as the *Star Wars* series, which substantially undermine the spectator's knowledge base. The first two *Indiana Jones* movies, for example, close on a Final Romance yet their sequels make no reference to them until the final film in the trilogy indicates the real nature of Indiana's desire, which is for his father. Thus to predicate a utopian family resolution on the promise of the Final Romance would be unsafe, as *The Last Crusade* conclusively proves. In these popular films, the Final Romance was no longer a guarantee, in and of itself, of resolution.

FAMILIAL PARADIGMS: PICTURES OF PESSIMISM

The mapping of these three dimensions forms a complex matrix of narrational paradigms which are distinct and unique from each other and reveal some intriguing familial operations.[5] The decade's most popular films present an overwhelmingly pessimistic view of the hegemonic nuclear family which is unable to achieve a successful resolution at either an actual or metaphoric level.[6] Where films manage to represent the nuclear family form successfully, they need to focus all their narrational energies on constructing and maintaining it and on excluding the social realm. Reciprocally, successful metafamilies can only be represented in the absence of the domestic arena. Most films which represent the actual family either foreground it or represent it as an absence, but an absence which drives the narrative forward, usually in the form of a quest. These quests, however, are rarely successful since the realm in which the quest occurs is necessarily social and absorbs the narrative energy required to build an actual family.[7] As most films foreground familialised social affiliations or communities, there are very few utopian outcomes.[8]

These metaphorical family structures are characterised by strong parent figures and dependent children organised within a hierarchical structure which conforms to psychic familial imperatives of power and desire.

However, this familialised organisation cannot solve, and indeed frequently causes, the inadequacies or problems which the narrative attempts to liquidate. Nor is the actual family indicated as a potential solution to the problems of the social grouping. The family and the familialised community are represented as opposed and mutually exclusive and both are the root cause of textual anxieties. Thus these films indicate a deepseated cultural pessimism about the hegemonic family form in both its actual and familialised variants. At their best, they hint at alternatives to the nuclear family which lie between the social and private realms of nation, race, society, profession and individual and which might represent a constructive approach to imagining alternative forms of social organisation. However, none of them can fully realise it and represent it within the text. At their worst, they are deeply pessimistic about the success of any form of social organisation or emotional intimacy.

Such analysis therefore identifies exclusive relationships between the domestic and social spheres. Successful nuclear families appear to be unrepresentable within a successful socioprofessional framework. As Zaretsky has noted, 'Far from the state "invading". or "replacing" the family, a certain kind of alienated public life and a certain kind of alienated private life have expanded together.'[9] Certainly in these representational modes, the family inhabits an impregnable space which depends upon its isolation and inviolability for its success and hegemonic survival. The nuclear family form cannot be utopian within a space in which a social structure is also foregrounded and successful. Therefore, to be utopian, the actual family appears to require a metaphorical family structure which is dystopian and/or absent.[10] The sole exceptions to this are the *Rocky* films in which the metacommunity of first boxing and then, in *Rocky IV*, entire nations are represented as successful familialised communities (that is, they are able to generate, to be transformed and to nurture their 'offspring').[11]

Alongside this separation of public and private space, there is a strong vein of absolute pessimism about the broader social fabric. There are very few utopian metaphorical families.[12] As we have noted, the *Rocky* films are the only texts to represent both domestic and public spheres functioning successfully within a nuclear family framework. It seems clear that the represented family cannot stand alternative patterns of relationship outside the domestic scene if it is to be successful. Inversely, those films in which the actual family is absent and dystopian also represent dystopian metaphorical families.[13] A reading of these films suggests that, despite the separation of domestic and social, the nuclear family requires a sympathetic, but discrete, social environment in which to flourish. In other words, the nuclear family form requires social structures which mirror its own for its survival; a constant 'shoring up' of its own construction by the repeated reflection of its own image. By a reciprocal move, the social communities which are represented in these films rely on strong, foregrounded families for their own success. Thus, the Final Romance trajectory is most heavily represented in those films which foreground a utopian actual family and either do not represent, or represent as dystopian, any external familial organisation. The actual family unit must consequently be divorced from external structures in order to enact successfully its own reproductive mechanisms: the Oedipal journey, romance and regeneration of a new family unit.

A small number of films represent a successful metaphorical family but a dystopian actual family. These achieve closure by creating alternative family structures (such as *Who Framed Roger Rabbit, Ghostbusters* or *Star Trek – The Movie*) or professional hierarchies (in *Pretty Woman* or *Top Gun*) which compensate for the absence or impossibility of the actual family. The most common alternative form of affiliation is an exclusive male relationship which is inevitably represented as incompatible with an actual family resolution. As we shall see, those films which incorporate a close, frequently homoerotically charged relationship between men, must sacrifice this to achieve familial resolution, although such bonding patterns are perfectly compatible with a metafamily paradigm.[14] Generally men are represented as most comfortable in an exclusively male environment – either within a domestic scene from which women are excluded or marginalised (such as *Three Men and a Baby, Tootsie* or *Look Who's Talking*) or in an all-male relationship in the extra-domestic sphere (*Lethal Weapon* or *Beverly Hills Cop*). There is no comparable female bonding in these films, the only possible exception to this being *Private Benjamin*, although Judy quickly surrenders her peer recruits' fellowship (symbolised in their chorusing of 'We are Family') for the lure of the elite male Thornbirds.

Those films which are least susceptible to any kind of familial analysis are those set entirely outside the domestic scene and where the foregrounded social structures are dystopian (the actual family is absent, ceding to a foregrounded metadystopian family). These texts typically represent an autonomous, lone hero in a predatory external world. These heroes are neither inside nor outside a social structure and, even where social groups threaten to coalesce into a family structure, they constantly fragment or contest it.[15] It is as if the American Dream has turned sour. The social fabric, constructed in a familial image, has begun to fragment. The family, when isolated from it, remains a triumphant vehicle for reproducing the nation's citizenry but as soon as the two realms coincide, the family collapses, unable to sustain itself or to make the world in its own image. The only hedge against this deterioration is the activity of the enterprising male, either as a new entrant to the Dream, and therefore proof against social corruption (such as the eponymous Rocky) or by having to win his spurs as 'Good Father' through personal transformation (*Three Men and a Baby, Honey, I Shrunk the Kids, The Golden Child*). Such endeavour frequently means he must isolate himself from the social realm to focus upon the domestic as Ted Kramer does in *Kramer versus Kramer*, as Wayne Szalinski does in *Honey, I Shrunk the Kids*, or as Dan Gallagher does in *Fatal Attraction*. Inversely, he may need to isolate himself from the domestic realm to achieve social or personal success through which, as in *Rocky IV* and *Coming to America*, he may also achieve social transformation. In transforming the social sphere through personal endeavour, he must frequently reconstruct it like a family (as in *Star Trek – The Movie, Top Gun, Lethal Weapon, Beverly Hills Cop* or *Return of the Jedi*). To achieve domestic bliss, however, he must isolate himself from society and, as we have seen, specifically from the obsessive comradeship of men.

If, as Peter Brooks suggests, 'the sense of a beginning . . . must in some important way be determined by the sense of an ending' then posing this question of these films provides interesting material in terms of familial representation.[16] Using Brooks' inverse view of narrative, that the ending invokes 'the beginning and transforms it', then contradictory or, at best, ambivalent readings are triggered. For, in so many of these films, it is the *destruction* of the ideal family that is figured, and the motor of the narrative, *against which* resistance is offered by other characters, is towards the obliteration of other, similar families. The potential for 'transformation' proposed by Brooks – in this case, the restitution of the destroyed family – is frequently overwhelmed by the excess of the representation and by the flaws in all the other represented families. There is, therefore, a twin motor to the narrative, generating conflicting spectatorial returns. The first motor drives the pleasure to be found in repetition and familiarity, the chain of destruction endlessly repeating itself, fulfilling its own prophecy. The second drives the pleasure to be derived from narrative closure, the restitution of the family and conventional happy ending.

This duality is, of course, common to any text which shows the moment of disequilibrium to the spectator. However, these texts are additionally complicated by the ambivalent positions taken to their 'heroes' and their villains and by the conjunction of oppositional generic modes. For example, *Terms of Endearment* cannot effect a transformation because, in effect, the beginning and end are synonymous. The father is a present-but-absent term, attempting to move the mother into the law of patriarchy and failing, the desire for fusion with her child overwhelming. My analysis of this film in Chapter 6 illustrates that, while there is a powerful case for reading this final segment of the film as the mother's admission to the symbolic, there is still no established patriarch and no guarantee that the narrative cycle of fusion and inadequate oedipalisation will not be repeated. The only available patriarch is endemically flawed. This scenario is echoed in *Ghostbusters*, where our desire for the subversive antics of the team to continue is played off against our desire to maintain the *status quo*, including the unity of the team itself. The representation of adults-as-children device permits the team to stay together and be subversive but it is at the cost of their subjectivity and sexuality. Thus those films which depend upon a familial breakdown for their narrative hermeneutic already contain within them the fatal seeds of a dystopian paradigm. In dynastic tradition, they carry it through to the end, perpetuating familial pessimism sewn deep into these texts. Although the narrative goal is almost universally to establish a specifically nuclear family as a fixed and stable point amidst social adversity and fragmentation, the texts rarely resolve this. They may (occasionally) be successful at establishing alternative forms of family, but this is not the resolution to the nuclear paradigm.

FAMILY PARADIGMS AND GENRE

Family paradigms do not appear to be heavily inflected by their generic field or vice versa. There are some indications that where actual families are present or foregrounded, the utopian paradigm prefers action-adventure or comedy genres. The former privileges the active male necessary to a classical resolution. The latter is perhaps less significant due to the high proportion of comedies in the top box-office films. However, it does appear that comedies specifically rely on a utopian familial resolution, normally through the Final Romance, in order to contain the subversions, panics and crises triggered by the text. On the other hand, dystopian families are also most heavily featured in comedies, suggesting that comic conventions can overwhelm the familial representation which is then unable to close the text. A significant number of dystopian paradigms also appear in action-adventure, drama or science-fiction films. Actual families are rarely represented at all in action-adventure or comedies, which tend to be set in professional or social milieus. This pattern is similar for metaphorical families: utopian metafamilies feature predominantly in action-adventure films while metadystopian paradigms are most frequent in comedies. Metadystopian paradigms are also fairly heavily represented in action-adventures, dramas and science-fiction films. Science-fiction films and dramas are the preferred setting for dystopian families, whether actual or metaphorical and do not feature utopian families at all. However, these proportions largely correspond to the generic proportions appearing across all popular films and would need broader analysis than lies within the scope of this book to identify minute and precise generic inflections.

As noted in Chapter 2, what is particularly interesting is the way in which these films juxtapose or combine diverse generic impulses to organise and subvert familial representations. For example, the narrative compulsion in *Fatal Attraction* is to consolidate the family into its ideal form, yet the ending is rendered deeply ambivalent by the recruitment of the iconography and narrative suspense of two other genres, horror and thriller, to close the narrative initiated by the melodramatic impulse of the first half. This reinforces the mistrust created around the hero and poses the question whether his adulterous 'other half' may have been destroyed, or, in the true nature of horror, can be regenerated, hydra-like, as his mistress herself is from the bath. This ambivalence is further consolidated by our extra-diegetic knowledge of the rejected alternative ending to the film which was widely publicised and positioned the film within a melo-dramatic mode. Other popular films followed suit. While *Lethal Weapon* frames its narrative trajectory within a police investigation, the definition and regulation of the family is central to its investigative project. *Ghostbusters* is organised somewhat differently, but its mode of address assumes a familial discourse, particularly by its reliance on the child–adult opposition for both its humour and its identificatory mechanisms while combining comic, science-fiction and horrific generic elements to achieve closure on the Final Romance.[17] *Out of Africa* uneasily combines elements of melodrama within an action-adventure field, organised around the fig-ure of the 'loose woman' who cannot be contained and bursts the narrative apart. The closure of *The Golden Child* is similarly compromised by the extraordinary competition of thriller and fantasy discourses woven into the Manichean fabric of a horror text. While family paradigms may not have determined genre, it is clear that the generic modes of the most popular films proved susceptible to their development and deployment.

FAMILIAL ICONOGRAPHY

The iconography of the ideal nuclear family is shared by all these films, whether or not it is fully realised and is constantly reinforced through such devices as character's testimonies, photographs, home movies and even answerphone messages. These ideal family types are authentic inheritors and embodiment of the American Dream – white, middle-class, affluent, beautiful, mid-American, affectionate, permanently laughing/happy, untouched by external events and upwardly mobile. As representatives of the ideal family, their function is to provide some form of marker, a standard against which to measure other families and alternative forms of social organisation. They are neither urban nor rural dwellers (both groups heavily marked in cinematic terms as affected and 'de-natured' by their environments – a reason for the mother's urgency to move her family out of the city in *Fatal Attraction*). They belong to the suburbs, the sunlit suburbs of *Terms of Endearment* and *Honey, I Shrunk the Kids*, earthly paradises where the sordidness of history and politics cannot intrude, where picket fences are kept intact, lawns mowed and dogs kept on leashes. They are the insulated fortresses of middle Americans privileged to concentrate on their own affairs rather than those of others. Even where the urban milieu does intrude on the domestic scene, it is carefully regulated, maintained outside the front door by wealth and conspicuous security. In the dystopian films, however, the domestic fortress is unable to prevent the penetration of the urban environment, and even the suburbs, the perfect family space, are corrupted. Anxiety over the suburbs, a locus previously problematised only in the horror genre, itself foregrounded a horrific mode which inflects several of these films.[18]

The distinctions and nature of public and private space are crucial to establishing the stable, universal nuclear family. Untouched by the passage of social time, the domestic sphere can remain the inviolable, unalterable domain of the patriarch. Fathers may span the public/private divide (between job, social and family roles) without mishap or discomfort, although they may bring dislocation back into the family through such interpenetration. Mothers, however, may only cross internal, private boundaries (between family roles and generations) while their transgression of public space is severely punished. In *Terms of Endearment*, for example, Emma enters her husband's workplace and is punished by her diagnosis of cancer; in *Fatal Attraction* Alex wants children and a job and dies violently and in *Kramer versus Kramer* the woman seeking fulfilment is denied access to her child. If fathers transgress, the family is punished; if women transgress, they are personally punished and the punishment is conventionally wreaked upon their bodies.

RESPONSIBILITIES AND RELATIONSHIPS

Individual family members contribute in very specific ways to the narrative paradigms and are accorded very different narrative weight. The most successful type of family requires fathers to be present within the text although, as we shall see, every represented father fails in some way. As we have noted, it is through the transformation of the father that the utopian family is generally created. Conversely, a significant number of successful families function without a mother although the family is significantly less likely to be dystopian if she is present. The mother also does not possess the transformational power of the father. Although the mother's presence is important to the success of the family, she cannot create that success; she is merely a necessary condition for it. It is by the father's effort that the family will succeed. In other words, both parents must be present to enact a utopian paradigm, although the *quality* of presence required is quite distinct. Most fundamental of all is the fact that, even in utopian films, the dystopian must be staged in order for it to be resolved and just the staging of the dystopia admits it as a possibility. In almost every case, it is the father who admits that possibility.

Responsibility for the failure of the family appears to have shifted from the mother, the historic vehicle for carrying the guilt of family failure in earlier melodramas, to the father. This does not mean that the mother escapes censure, but it is usually a sin of omission rather than commission, and it is the role of the father that is most closely interrogated. In so doing, the father actually opens up the text to oppositional readings. Absent fathers, by their very absence, structure the narrative and, in marking an occluded or repressed discourse of patriarchy, can afford access to another point of view, making space for more progressive and subversive readings than the text itself privileges. In all these films, the real promise of utopia lies with the child. In Romantic tradition, these films privilege children as innocents, born into a world of corruption and vice. Cassandra-like, they have access to truth but are marginalised, exploited and suffering. Sons receive the law and the word from the father and have more opportunities to develop both themselves and their parents. Mothers are generally marginalised and access to their viewpoint is extremely limited. They react to, rather than initiate, narrative development and their status is defined and legitimised within the text by their relationship to the family and their function as mothers. The function of wife is but a transitional stage on the way to motherhood. Siblings' relationships with each other and the grandparental role are generally discreetly marginalised as attention is focused on the vertical intra-family relations.[19] Meanwhile 'non-family' individuals threaten familial stability and must be incorporated or displaced. Whereas women are physically punished for their existence in the public sphere or absorbed into a Final Romance, 'non family' men enter or create 'alternative' families, bonding with another man or a metafamily.

The family cannot tolerate external competition and familialised communities cannot coexist with a utopian family.

What is crucial to the drive and resolution of the narrative is the father–child relationship. The father's failure rendered the maturation process problematic for both sons and daughters. Daughters, always other within the symbolic realm, must search outside the Oedipal process for their development or remain passive and marginalised. Sons, who benefit most from oedipalisation, only inherit the symbolic mantle if their fathers remain unflawed. Sons are therefore represented as suffering far more from the failure of the father than daughters who can not only benefit from, but whose interests may be best served by causing, that failure. However, in these films, paternal failure is generally motivated by external penetration of the family rather than internal sabotage and is typically motivated by the father's transgression of symbolic or actual boundaries. Furthermore, it is impossible to distinguish between the cause and its effect, whether the father's failure is caused by the family or vice versa. Mothers or daughters have the power to heal the family but the recreated family is a different family, either marked by transformation in the persona of the father (a new utopian form) or by its divergence from a posited ideal (the dystopian family). They have the potential to create new family forms. Thus mothers may neglect but they can also heal. Fathers may manage and delegate the symbolic/public realm, but they also damage and destroy. Sons and daughters, however, have the power to reproduce (by their passivity) or to transform (by intervention) the dystopian family form.

SUMMARY

Successful representation of the dominant ideological family form depended upon a complete separation of public and private spheres. The most popular films of the decade could not accommodate foregrounded representations of the social realm alongside the private world of the family without either one being severely damaged by the juxtaposition. Paradoxically, it was the father, the individual with most to gain from a utopian family structure, who, as traveller between the two, was frequently the harbinger of cross-infection. The phenomenon of the nuclear family disintegrated unless constantly represented and reinforced and its absence was correlated with the dystopian representation of all other familial forms. Thus the normative structure of the nuclear family could not survive in other social communities unless strongly represented in the private sphere of the text. The familialised social institution which predominated in the absence of an actual family was the professional world of the police, the other representation of law and order outside the specifically patriarchal family sphere. Both police and family hold a similar relationship to sociocultural structures, through their respective roles in upholding social and psychic regulation. However, utopian families could not coexist with utopian familialised institutions, revealing social, cultural and psychic regimes in direct conflict with each other. If the family's role was to anneal social crisis by endorsing popular mythologies, it was unsuccessful. The representation of families and familialised social structures as solutions to crisis, created contradictions which overwhelmed the very representation and resolutions they proposed.

This dystopian view of the family appears to endorse critic Michael Medved's claim that contemporary Hollywood has an 'anti-family agenda', but that statement does not explain these films' huge success at the box office.[20] In fact these films intersected in very specific and complex ways with broader cultural discourses to interrogate both the actuality and the rhetoric of the nuclear family, producing representations which reverberated with the anxieties of a fracturing social unconscious and polarising political project. It is impossible, because of the industrial nature of the product and the endless diversity of spectatorial readings, to assert any simple tendentiousness in these texts. To suggest any kind of 'agenda' is therefore specious. In direct contrast, in tension with these structural dimensions, there were prominent pro-family discourses circulating throughout these texts which, for individual spectators, may be sufficiently powerful to anneal the fractures. Many texts worked hard to inscribe the spectator within a patriarchal relation to the narrative, inviting the spectator to identify, say, with Charlie in *Rain Man* in his quest to appease his father and bond with his brother. Yet oppositional positions are possible, and even encouraged, by textual lacunae created, in this case, by the breakdown in language signified by Raymond's autism and the marginalisation of Susanna, thereby jeopardising any kind of Final Romance in the endeavour to bond the brothers. Such competing readings further undermined the failures of hegemonic representations, highlighting prevalent social dislocations.

The most popular films fell squarely between those discourses which posit the family as problem and family as solution; as site of abuse or restitution. All the films analysed here oscillated between these two poles. However, they also drew on dominant contemporary discourses of the academic and professional realms whereby the family has, rather than is, its problems and which has transferred many of its pre- and early-modern functions to social institutions. In this model, its true purpose is still in the process of being negotiated between the public and private realms with an entire army of professionals required to monitor and manage the process. Suspicion of this latter was clearly marked in many of these films, notably *Kramer versus Kramer, Terms of Endearment, Rain Man* and, at a different level, *Ghostbusters*. It was rare, however, for any external intervention to be successful and the utopian family was largely unrealised at a representational level during the decade.

To see how this happened in practice, we must look in greater detail at how the individual family terms – mother, father, child – contribute to these paradigms.

5 Backlash Patriarch or New Man? The Role of the Father

Susan Faludi has rigorously documented the backlash against feminism which dominated the eighties and was symptomatised by the parade of the 'new man', a figure who both reacted against, and occupied, traditional female spaces. The most obvious of these spaces was the domestic scene. The final chapter of Elizabeth Traube's book on eighties Hollywood film, asks, 'Who will do the caring?' and this was certainly the most pertinent question in examining masculine representations. The 'new man' gained his credentials by adopting 'feminine', nurturing, affective qualities and the terrain in which he staked them was the domestic scene traditionally associated with the mother. Yet had the patriarch really converted into the new man? How were these oppositions represented in Hollywood cinema within the family circle?

In examining the most popular box-office successes across the decade, we can see that the transformation was neither absolute nor simple but highly paradoxical. As its greatest beneficiary, the father had the greatest investment in maintaining the family yet it was most frequently the father who posed or introduced a threat to it. The paternal role was itself unstable, jeopardising familial stability and the nature of this instability frequently triggered the narrative, often through the motif of a journey which mirrored an Oedipal trajectory. The destination of the journey was figured as the restitution of a nuclear family and the mythical serenity of a domestic space. However, such a destination was, as we have seen, rarely reached, and where it was, it was so shot through with contradiction that it was either unrecognisable or unconvincing. Thus the father failed in his project to fix the family as a sustaining power base from which to maintain his social role.

What is clear from an analysis of all these films is that although the father motivated the narrative, the actual trigger was the father-as-problem. Even apparently successful fathers were marked by failure and it was this from which they tried to save the family. The problematic of the father dominated popular narratives, occupying the space that the woman once held in the *film noir* as a central focus of investigation. This problematic can best be characterised as a paternal failure. Taking some of the top box-

office films as exemplars, we can identify the tensions inherent in this
failure and the ways in which it drives and shapes the narrative.

CORE PATERNAL TENSIONS

Central to paternal failures are two core tensions: the problems of patriarchal succession and individuation. The former concerns the age-old tension between father and son, in which the father is caught between a desire
for his progeny's success and a fear of being superseded, most obviously
represented in the failed male films, *Back to the Future* and *Total Recall*.
The second tension addresses the boundary between individual and society, a fraught division throughout the decade, represented in *Rocky IV* and
The Jazz Singer. To fully understand the particular forms of failure, it is
important to analyse these tensions.

Patriarchal Succession

Two films in particular, *Back to the Future* and *Total Recall*, show how
issues of succession undermined the stability of the family. Both chart the
liquidation of an inadequate father by an initially innocent and unwitting
son. Both employ the trope of travel: *Back to the Future* through time and
Total Recall through space. Both struggle to deploy the conventions of an
Oedipal scene to bring the hero to psychic and social maturity. Yet each
film addresses specific paternal anxieties prompted by such maturation,
specifically those arising from sons who challenge, and seek to obliterate,
their fathers. Both are therefore unstable in their resolutions. *Total Recall*
cannot overcome the fact that its hero, Quaid, was sired by the villain,
Hauser, who are one and the same. Although its closure posits a potential
utopia through the Final Romance and the revitalisation of Mars, this
closure is marked by the collapse of the 'father'-'son' dichotomy. Not
only were father and son one body but they were born from the perverse
and sterile imaginings of Hauser, thereby transgressing psychic, cognitive
and psychological boundaries. The film subverts the Oedipal scene, loop-
ing reproductive anxieties into a focus on male subjectivity and succession. *Back to the Future* also points to the volatility of the father–son
distinction. This film invokes the taboo latent within oedipalisation, that of
incest, the risk of the son's accession to the mother supplanting the father
entirely. Both films raise a material anxiety that these and the other top
box-office films work hard to suppress, the instability and inherent transformational character of the family itself. While rendering the paternal

role less stable, the time/space journey also ironically insists on the permanence and ubiquity of the paternal function. *Total Recall* strives to displace anxieties over familial transience into the permanence of the refertilisation of the planet Mars and creating the father/not father dimension. *Back to the Future* posits an omnipresent, omnipotent proto-father, Marty, who is able to intervene across generations, thus creating a timeless and therefore 'permanent' solution. The film also creates a metafather in the figure of Dr Emmet Brown, a magical mentor, who gives Marty access to his omnipotent status. In each of these two films, the proto-fathers (Quaid and Marty) achieve their procreative status through the liquidation of their own fathers and an eroticised relationship with their mothers; feats for which Oedipus was blinded. The apparent rewards of the Final Romance are undercut by our awareness of this contradiction: Quaid has suppressed Hauser but has also incorporated him; Marty has transformed his inadequate father but was sired by him in his incompetent incarnation. Lori was implicated in the reproduction of Quaid and then moves in with him; Marty's mother attempts to seduce him. Latent punishments lie literally below the surface, buried in the unconscious, as psychic triggers. These proto-fathers cannot simply create new families – they are scarred by generational history, which cannot be relinquished and the sins of the fathers may be revisited upon the sons.

Individuation

Paternal anxieties around selfhood and subjectivity are key features in these popular films. The most extreme example of this can be seen in *Rocky IV* where the assertion of Rocky's own fatherliness rests upon his claim to the American Dream of achieving success through one's own efforts, signified in the excessive trappings of wealth displayed everywhere in the first half of the film. However, it also depends on his moral and subjective integrity, to which even wealth must be subordinated and which he demonstrates in the Siberian training camp. Drawing on America's Cold War heritage, Rocky is pitted against the Russian fighter, Drago. This polarisation of western affective individualism and eastern scientific collectivism is signified by a family/non-family dichotomy. Drago's wife is part of his training team and they are represented as childless, focused on building a consummate fighting machine, Drago himself. Thus Drago is both father and son, creating himself and being created while his wife supervises in sterile, clinical devotion. Rocky's trainers, on the other hand, are part of his family, joining him in the family home, intimate and affectionate with him. His wife is located in the home, resisting Rocky's desire to avenge Apollo, his buddy, and only joining Rocky's training effort when she realises that the family itself is at risk.

Rocky's relationship with his son is the vital one, promoting his aspirational capacity, wanting more for his son than he himself had. In opposing the collectivisation of the Russian camp, connoting transformation from outside and the intervention of science, with the individualism of the American camp, conversely connoting transformation from the inside and belief in oneself, it is the individual's own ability to transform himself which is at stake. Rocky continually insists that people can change, Apollo dies insisting they can't. Substantiating the Dream of individual transformation, is the evidence of self-advancement. Rocky identifies this in his final victory speech over Drago, personalising the Cold War to the level of their own battle, 'During this fight, I seen a lot of changing. The way I felt about you and the way you felt about me. Two guys trying to kill each other. But I guess it's better than 20 million. I guess what I'm trying to say is that if I can change, you can change. Everyone can change.' However, such change was in itself the root of contemporary social panics and Rocky's appeals to the next generation stimulated the anxieties of succession, the challenge of the next generation.

In films such as *The Jazz Singer*, it is the father's very insistence on integrity and paternal logic which is resisted by the child. The imposition of paternal authority conflicts with the individualism promoted by American culture and by the child. This can be interpreted as the extreme patterning of an Oedipal trajectory in which the absence of a mother on whom to project desire requires the father to impose alternative sanctions upon the child in order to force separation. However, the loss, enacted as 'natural' in the Oedipal scene, forces a rupture which becomes the very subject of the film and causes the son to lose 'himself'. In this film, it is the son's point of view which is privileged. The father's observance of strict, 'imported' religious and cultural conventions pull against the individualistic American culture and threaten to suppress the talent of the child, jeopardising his sense of self and status within the value framework of the indigenous culture. As in *Rocky IV*, the narrative is strung between collective and individualistic values and played out through a rehearsal of transformation – the individual's ability to transform himself in isolation from any social foundation. In extreme cases, the father's inability to change may drive the child away completely, as in *Private Benjamin*, a film in which metaphorical, as well as natural fathers bully and betray the child. Thus, fathers who cannot accommodate contemporary cultural aspirations, adapting themselves and their families, will be rejected or supplanted. The dilemma here, of course, is that one of those cultural aspirations was the very fixity of the familial form itself. Fathers were caught in a perfect vicious circle of being forced to change, but jeopardising themselves and the social organisation in which they had most invested by so doing.

PATERNAL FAILURES: THE FIVE PARADIGMS

All the represented fathers fail in some capacity. There are five specific nuances to this failure, each of which inflect the narrative structure and familial representations in different ways. The five types are: the absent father, the failed father, the failed patriarch, the failed male and the betrayer.[1] Within each of these categories, I have selected films which typify the themes running across the majority of box-office successes, to examine both actual and metaphorical father-figures. *Rain Man*, the *Indiana Jones* trilogy and *Top Gun* are paradigmatic examples of the father who failed the family by his absence while *Kramer versus Kramer, Private Benjamin* and *Beverly Hills Cop* typify failures of paternity through negligence or authoritarianism. The failed patriarch structures *Beverly Hills Cop II, The Untouchables* and *Good Morning, Vietnam*, destroying both actual and metaphorical families. The failure of the male, the masculine category itself, is highly complex and is figured by increasing textual neurosis. *Back to the Future* and *Total Recall* are excessive examples of the schizophrenic text while *Airplane!* and *Tootsie* are both hysterical, able to achieve some level of closure, but still highly ambivalent. *Rambo: First Blood Part II, The Empire Strikes Back* and *Pretty Woman* demonstrate the familial damage wreaked by the treacherous father, although *Pretty Woman*, at least, is able to suggest a less dystopian outcome than most contemporary successes. These films also explore the role of the potential father, heroes constructed as proto-fathers through their agency in the narrative and their incorporation into a Final Romance. In these films, as we noted earlier, the Final Romance stands in for the reproductive process and subsequent generation of a family unit. This form of closure casts its shadow into the preceding narrative in retrospectively constructing the hero as proto-father while portending actual fatherhood in some extra-diegetic future space.

The Absent Father

In a significant proportion of these films, a father structures the narrative through his very absence, whether this absence is actual or metaphorical.

This absent father is usually, but not always, dead and the narrative struggles to make good his lack. The absence of the father forces a quest for restoration or substitution, disrupting all other narrative lines. These films, for obvious reasons, are recounted from the child's (normally the adult son's) viewpoint and rehearse traumatic scenes in which the family is usually foregrounded as the subject of the narrative and in which any familial resolution is represented as impossible. Thus the absence of the father triggers a quest which involves the hero or heroine in a desperate bid to create a new family unit, but one which ultimately founders on, or is destabilised by, the structuring absence. The anxiety generated by the father's actual or potential absence is the hermeneutic for narratives which explore what happens when the father isn't there. Thus the father's role is defined through its very absence, locating a space for the father to inhabit but which is never filled. The space is further defined through the activity of the child, usually the son, who often invests affection and moral energy into a metaphorical familial structure either as a framework, or substitution, for familial restructuring.

Rain Man charts the impossibility of personal fulfilment either in domestic or social terms, against the conjunction of paternal failure and loss. In struggling to leave the father behind, however, the son merely repeats his failures. The film narrates Charlie Babbit's quest to recreate his parental family, destroyed by the failure of his father to keep his sons together on the death of his wife. Charlie, a driven, risk-taking entrepreneur, returns to the family home on the death of his estranged father to learn of the existence of his autistic brother, Raymond, who has been bequeathed the bulk of his father's estate. Charlie abducts Raymond and travels with him and his girlfriend, Susanna, across America. This quest, ostensibly to hold Raymond hostage against the iniquity of his father's will, metamorphoses into an attempt at reconciliation as Charlie slowly learns to love and value his brother. Raymond, literally valued at $3 million at the start of the film, is coveted purely as a brother by the end of it. Charlie attempts to reconstruct the paternal relationship through the resurrection of his brother and, in doing so, has to become both child and father. To prove himself equal to the role of Raymond's protector, he must strip away the social and cultural persona he has created for himself while assuming the role his own father was never able to fulfil. The narrative is thus constructed along an axis running between knowledge and emotional authenticity. At the beginning of the film, Charlie clearly 'knows' everything, mirroring the controlling father-figure he strives so hard to reject. His first admission of ignorance on any subject comes when he talks to a doctor about Raymond and is forced to engage in a different register of professional language to which he has no access. Once he admits to his business associate that he 'doesn't know' what to do when his business is failing, Raymond and Charlie become 'connected' and Charlie learns about his brother through emotion rather than cognition. Touch and jokes, Freudian indices of the repressed, are constantly deployed to indicate fraternal bonding. By the final scene these are highly charged devices through which Raymond's 'joke' ('KMart sucks') and his caress of Charlie's face signify the emotional coldness of the doctors and the authenticity of the sibling relationship. The poles have reversed: Charlie's new emotional self-knowledge is counterposed to the doctor's invalidated professional knowledge.

A pivotal textual dimension is the incompatibility of family and workplace. The family scene is privileged but unattainable, due to the father–son breakdown. However, Charlie's attempts to substitute his business for domestic fulfilment also fail. His obsession with money-making gives way to 'family business' as he draws closer to Raymond, signified by the phone-calls to his firm which are gradually replaced by calls to Susanna and the doctor as the journey begins. However, in struggling to succeed his father, Charlie mirrors his failures. Charlie devotes his time and emotional energy to his business, paralleling the way in which his father showered attention on a beautiful vintage Buick, the car he described as 'his baby' and in which Charlie abducts Raymond. It was Charlie's and his father's shared perfectionism and stubbornness which led to their estrangement, and the suppression of Raymond. The loss of the father (first through estrangement, then through his lonely death) was caused by his insistence on knowledge at the expense of emotion, an insistence inherited by his son. His father's last words to Charlie in his will were reminders of the 'value of excellence and possibility of perfection'. As Charlie says, 'Nothing I did was good enough for this man.'

This failure of communication and subsequent alienation is literally represented in Raymond's autism. The text constantly stresses that Raymond is autistic rather than suffering any other form of mental disability; Raymond is 'alright' – he just can't communicate to express emotion, a trope which symbolises the failure of the father–son relationship. Raymond's doctor succinctly states the plot to Charlie just before the abduction, 'I think you feel cheated out of your birthright by a man who had difficulty showing love', invoking an epic Jacob and Esau struggle which can only be resolved by the recreation of the family. Charlie has to both become and exceed his father to 'win' Raymond, but he has to do it against the scientific knowledge of the medical community and the cultural and social grain of the legislature. He also has to combine this with the affection his father was unable to show. His girlfriend Susanna, who left him in their first motel stop on learning the covetous motives for the abduction indexes his transformation. She later becomes a temporary reward when Charlie sees the 'real' motive for his quest, by returning to the new family unit in Las Vegas. However, in the end, his emotional 'connection' to Raymond is not strong enough for him to take possession and he is left alone on a station platform, significantly donning his sunglasses to re-enter public life and mask out his private failure. Susanna is again sidelined by the end of the movie, the dominant focus being on the male siblings, rather than any Final Romance. The absence of women is both problem and solution, but subsidiary to the overarching motivation: the relationship and dynamics of the father–son, brother–brother relationships. Although the death of Charlie's mother was the original motivation for rupturing the family and his oedipalisation, this is entirely displaced to the father's absence. *Rain Man* cannot resolve its double paternal failure and loss through conventional strategies. Although morally centred by his rejection of the social realm for the values of the family, Charlie cannot achieve a satisfactory resolution. The family breakdown is too severe to permit a substitute and Charlie's social affiliations are represented as morally suspect. The only resolution at the end is Charlie's self-knowledge, a different form of narcissism from that depicted at the beginning. At the end, he is still alienated and still cannot communicate with his brother.

Although many of these absent-father films (such as *Raiders of the Lost Ark, Any Which Way You Can* or *Top Gun*) do close on a Final Romance, it is signified as volatile and temporary. Indiana Jones's alliance with Marion in *Raiders of the Lost Ark*, for example, is not only undermined by his previous treatment of her but, most importantly, by his preoccupation with resolving the loss of both his real and adoptive fathers. Jones is recruited by Brody, the Museum's curator, and Army Intelligence to hunt down the Ark and prevent its seizure by the Nazis. The film unravels Jones's complex and ambivalent relationships with both metaphorical and actual patriarchs. The events mapping Jones's search for, and subsequent loss of, the Ark parallels the train of events triggered by the loss of his own father (who is missing, presumed dead), the betrayal by a father-substitute, Ravenswood, and the consequent procession of gifts he must offer to propitiate his new father-surrogate: Brody, and the state. In an even more complex loop, the substitute-father with whom he feuded was Marion's own, and is also dead by the opening of the film, a feud which also ruptured Jones's earlier romance with Marion. Jones's own development has thus been consistently undermined by paternal failure and loss, paralleling the compound alienation and loss suffered by Charlie. The film's ending thus points back to a history of quests in which Jones has resisted any social ties or community, in which he fetishises archaeological artefacts, using women as the currency in his battles for possession of priceless historic objects. The ending looks forward to a repetition of that history. The invitation to a drink which Marion extends is juxtaposed with the subsequent image of Jones's latest, and ultimate, trophy (the Ark) being incorporated in a graphic symbol of his worst anxiety, bureaucracy, in the form of a huge, anonymous warehouse. This 'stifling' of Jones clamours for a sequel – a sequel which cannot integrate a wife or family but invokes the unreliability of familial ties, his lost parent and his betrayal by the state and his professional community.

Jones himself is the eternal child, constructed in *Raiders of the Lost Ark* as unable to achieve maturity and signally having failed to consummate his relationship with the brittle, vapid Willie, he transfers his fickle affections firstly to the gritty Marion then to the treacherous Dr Schneider. His representational volatility is made even clearer in the film's prequel, *Indiana Jones and the Temple of Doom*, in which, as surrogate father to Shorty, he not only fails to protect him but has to be rescued by him before he can rescue the children he is seeking. By *Raiders*, he has apparently abandoned Shorty to whom there is no reference. That the solution to Jones's alienation can only be found through the real father is made apparent in *The Last Crusade*, where the quest for the father is equated to that for the Holy Grail. Jones cannot become either a responsible adult or a father until he has found a way of entering or creating a new community or by achieving full oedipalisation himself through successful creation of, and transference via a surrogate patriarch and the forging of a Final Romance. However, the final bonding of father and son is entirely self-sufficient; all the women have been lost along the way. The entire series is thus constructed as a quest for the father, awakened in *Raiders*, but not satisfied until *The Last Crusade* and in which the sole solution to the absent father is his full restitution which, in turn, denies any other familial possibilities. Unlike *Rain Man*, Jones is restored to his father, but both are so flawed by the choices they have made, that they are further from the familial moral centre than even Charlie is. The father, although represented as the solution to social alienation, cannot be relied upon to achieve it.

Perhaps the only one of the absent-father texts to invest any degree of reliability in the paternal role and the stability of the Final Romance is *Top Gun*. Despite the impossibility of reconciliation with his dead father, the son is able to redeem him and find a positive paternal role model in Commander Metcalf. Again the quest theme dominates. The aptly-named test fighter-pilot, Maverick, strives against the ruined reputation of his father and, in so doing, is able both to reclaim his father's name and claim

the girl. Unlike the previous films, various models of paternity are represented: his Commander, the patriarchal, knowing Metcalf; his co-pilot, the
nurturing, sympathetic Goose (whose family is not only shown but also
characterised) and his actual father, the dead but noble Mitchell, disgraced
in a tragic loop by his own sacrifice. Through the models, Maverick is
offered a composite range of possibilities, which together might form the
perfect paternal role. Despite struggling against them, lost in his narcissistic desire to substitute professional success for familial fulfilment, Maverick is finally ready to hear of his father's nobility and accede to a Final
Romance.

However, the family is also fetishised in the film and occupies a problematic space in relation to the narrative. The film constantly references
and celebrates it but only in snatched glimpses as some unattainable ideal.
Every time it is represented, it is destroyed or displaced. The photograph
in Cougar's plane is the object which causes him to lose control and flunk
out; a classically conventional family scene around the piano, frozen in
time and space, is the final sequence before Goose's death and Maverick's
own death-wish results from his obsession with his dead father – suggesting that too great an investment in family (even the creation of a natural
family) will result in death or disgrace. The family, constantly referenced
as the narrative goal, is unstable and potentially dangerous. The narrative
is actually constructed around twin axes of law and safety. Maverick (whose
name suggests his imperatives) must break the laws (of flying, of engagement, of forces discipline) to satisfy the Law of psychic maturation by
redeeming his father. Yet in doing so, he risks the safety of his new family
– his incorporation into his co-pilot Goose's utopian nuclear unit. 'You're
the only family I got. I'm not going to let you down', Maverick stresses
to Goose, after nearly killing him in a mock dog-fight but it is a promise
he cannot keep since, in his Oedipal quest, he must redeem his own dynasty, taking his place in the generative cycle by proving his skill as a
pilot. His relationship with Charley, his androgenously named girlfriend
and ex-instructor, is built around the same axes. Maverick must observe
the Law by controlling their relationship, which threatens to swing out of
control through her autonomy and professional standing. It is not until he
does that, overturning the dynamics of power and displacing her hierarchy
of theoretical knowledge with his own, which is practical and experiential,
in the dinner-scene at her house, that she falls in love with him. His
symbolic disposal of Goose's dog-tags – Goose is the 'false father' and
buddy who has come too close – is the final act required to win Charley
and the right to become an incipient father himself. Although Maverick is
incorporated within a Final Romance by the end of the film, the resolution

is highly problematic. He has not renounced his career, a career which forces him to take risks, nor has he therefore contained the riskiness of, and to, the family structure. His girlfriend is similarly implicated and a safe familial future cannot be guaranteed by their coupling.

The Failure of Paternity

The majority of popular 1980s Hollywood films feature the failure of paternity itself – the breakdown of the represented paternal role in the the family. This is signified in behavioural terms by being negligent or, most frequently, overly authoritarian. While both types of film follow a conventional Oedipal paradigm, the failure of the father fatally inflects it so that the films rarely achieve satisfactory or complete resolutions.

Neglectful Fathers
Neglectful fathers represent the opposite end of the authoritarian spectrum but share the same continuum. Their neglect is a function of their attention to external exigencies which, in these films, are likely to be professional rather than social or cultural. While authoritarian fathers try to impose external constraints within the family, neglectful fathers are distracted from the family scene by external demands. Both sets are outward-facing, utilising different strategies to construct their paternity. Murtaugh, for example, in *Lethal Weapon 2*, allows his crime-fighting activities and buddy relationship with Riggs to imperil his family, to the extent that he is finally reconciled with Riggs rather than with his 'natural' family. Even *Indiana Jones and the Temple of Doom* proposes that the village fathers attending to the demands of agriculture 'allow' their children to be stolen from them and the state's patriarchs are, of course, the instrument of this theft.

Kramer versus Kramer, one of the most celebrated family films of the decade, plays out the consequence of familial neglect, charting the progress of redemption through the father–son relationship. Here the external distraction is again professional. Ted Kramer has concentrated on his career at the expense of his family. On his wife's departure at the beginning of the film, he must learn the true priorities of fatherhood and take on the role of both father and mother, eventually winning the moral, if not the legal, case for custody. The film also explores the family's role in instigating, and rewarding, individual endeavour. The film charts the self-realisation achieved by one man who relinquishes his professional life and embraces his paternal role. One of the many symmetries in the film turns around the competing abilities of a man's boss and his son, to hold his attention. Both

employ anecdotes to do so – a trick the heroic father himself uses at the
beginning of the film. Both withhold the ending of their tales – the boss
as a deliberate ploy to maintain his employee in his thrall, the son artlessly
as his concern shifts to whether he will be late for school. Significantly,
it is the son rather than the patriarchal boss who wins, capturing his father
within the domestic realm and providing fulfilment. The mother, of course,
has already lost the struggle to combine personal fulfilment with domestic
bliss before the film opened. *Kramer versus Kramer* explicitly deals with
a quest for redemption, the 'lost object' being the son, rather than the wife,
who remains outside the renewed family unit. A further 'lost object' which
is restored is figured as Kramer's own subjective and masculine integrity
– he becomes a 'whole person' at the end of the film, mature, nurturing
and forgiving. However, the very representation of neglect flaws the closing incipient paternal role and insists on its possibility in future. Although
designed to represent the degree of Ted's transformation, the persistent
symmetries in the film also suggest the possibility of repetition. For example, an early breakfast scene in which Ted demonstrates his inability to
carry out even the most simple domestic tasks is contrasted with a later
scene in which father and son operate in perfect synchronicity to prepare
their morning meal. However, neither speak and the son prepares his own
food. This scene contrasts vividly with the labour that the mother performed on behalf of her son and proposes that neglect may still be the
extension of such apparent ease. The mother remains alienated at the close
of the film and Ted's subordination of lovers to his growing intimacy with
his son suggests a familial resolution which excludes women. Although
the film has been widely interpreted as a misogynistic text on the dispen-
sability of the mother and celebration of the father as all-powerful, it is
important to remember that the narrative is motivated by the mother's
action, by her search for an extra-familial identity, albeit one that finally
closes with the conventional maternal sacrifice paradigm. Only by the
mother's departure is the father pushed into action in the domestic sphere;
the father does not initiate change, but it is his transformation which
achieves resolution.

Pursuing the theme, the actual and surrogate fathers of *The Blue Lagoon*
both sin by omission, distracted by worldly concerns. Emmeline and Richard
are in the care of the latter's father when the ship catches fire and they are
cast adrift with Paddy, the ship's cook, who then drinks himself to death.
The absence of his paternal instruction leads to their failure to care for
their baby adequately and their exposure to human sacrifice. This is a
contradictory and unstable film, eroticising the teenage characters in its
exploration of sexual maturation and establishing uneasy resonances with

contemporary anxieties over child abuse. Its poor critical reception cannot undercut the massive box-office appeal of a film which represented a volatile mix of different family forms inadequately incorporated into a conventional structure by the end through the serendipitous rescue of the children by Richard's father. At a metaphorical level, in *Star Trek – The Movie*, Captain Kirk returns to his starship family after neglecting them at the behest of the authorities. The rewards for such neglect are reaped in the challenge of a usurper son, Dekker. Kirk must win back his patriarchy by force of right and affective ties rather than his technical skill or ability, forcing Dekker out to create his own dynasty. Kirk might jeopardise his family by his age but he has the right to do so. Kirk thus recreates his metaphorical family, but only by the exclusion of a natural one. Less dystopian than the absent father paradigms, neglectful fathers can restore their families by rejecting the distractions in the social realm (Kramer returns to his family, Kirk returns to his ship, Richard's father devotes his life to searching for his son). However, as we have seen, a familialised social structure cannot tolerate an actual family and Kirk must expel his 'son' from the ship.

Authoritarian Fathers
The ability of the authoritarian father to restore his family is also dependent on a separation of public and private spheres. While oedipalisation is dependent on the child's challenge to the father through bonding with his mother, in this paradigm, the father's behaviour can be too excessive for the child to identify with him and reject the potential castration signified by the mother. The child may thus remain bonded to the mother, unwilling to accept his father as model for maturation. In this paternal paradigm, the father's excessive behaviour is offset against the contemporary privileging of the child and mitigates against utopian resolution. This tension between father and child resonates with the lingering discourse of intergenerational conflict films, popular with young audiences since the fifties, which solicited spectatorial investment in the child's rebellion. The core opposition aligning father against child sets the domestic, in which the patriarch rules supreme, against a social realm which demands a new patriarch and new values. The extreme position of the father, signified by behavioural or cultural extremes (such as in *The Jazz Singer, Arthur* or *Coming to America*), initiates the child's rebellion and challenge to the father, obviating the need for affective transference from the mother who is either absent (as in *The Jazz Singer* or *Arthur*) or actively assists in the rebellion (as in *Coming to America* or *Back to the Future*). The child therefore cannot fully separate from the mother and achieve maturation and the mother is effectively

effaced or elided with the child. The Final Romance signifies the child's successful maturation through the defeat of the father as well as bestowing familial and social status.[2] Thus paternal authoritarianism is paradoxically punished (by the temporary loss of the son) and rewarded (by the success of the father in achieving his son's maturation and independence).

These mechanisms are given a new inflection when the child is female. *Private Benjamin* charts the maturation of Judy Benjamin and represents the failure of both actual and metaphorical fathers. Judy is driven into the army first by her failed marriages and the treacherous blandishments of the first surrogate father-figure, later by the authoritarian strictures of her real father. Her parental home is unfavourably compared to her army unit in which the women form a close-knit sisterhood, a family without fathers who signify their threatening, alternative familialisation by singing the contemporary hit, 'We Are Family' in celebration of their triumph over their superiors. However, Judy is again seduced into reliance on a father-figure, Colonel Thornbird, who betrays and attempts to rape her. Escaping from the army into a new romance, she is further stifled by her fiancé's transformation into a new patriarch who infantilises and diminishes her. 'Am I making sense?' she asks at one point. 'No, that's what I like about you.' As a gynaecologist, he holds privileged knowledge about her sex by which he demeans her gender and her words. Judy successively rejects all the family forms presented to her, the Goodmans, the Benjamins, the familialised Army (the women's squad, the authoritarian elite Thornbird squad, the bureaucracy at SHAPE) and finally the creation of a family with Henri. Although her struggle for individual fulfilment follows the patterns established by contemporary male heroes, because she is a woman she cannot sustain individual integrity and be part of a family. The fathers suffocate or betray her, perhaps explaining her symbolic longing for 'up-holstered balls', a metaphor for an alternative formulation of power, in the opening pre-wedding sequence. The series of paternal abuses sits even more uneasily with a female heroine. The essential problematic here is the impossibility of converting the Oedipal quest of the son oppressed by his father into a correlative resolution for daughters. A utopian family is unachievable, even undesirable. The succession of authoritarian fathers means that Judy cannot fully enter the symbolic realm. At the end of the film Judy walks away from any form of social organisation or personal intimacy that has so far been available to her.

Authoritarian fathers feature prominently in metaphorical family films such as *Beverly Hills Cop*. Stunned by the murder of a close friend, Foley decides to investigate on his own initiative, following the trail from his own base in Detroit to Los Angeles where he is persistently warned off by his own and the Angelean police chiefs. Finally winning over Billy and Taggart, the two policemen assigned to guard him, Foley uncovers a criminal ring and solves the case. *Beverly Hills Cop* thus confronts and attempts to incorporate its structuring anxieties of race and sexuality through a metaphorical family plot which draws heavily on, but also subverts, the generic conventions of the police thriller. Utilising the classic figure of the renegade but brilliant cop, the narrative constructs authoritarian patriarchs (Lt Bogomil, Inspector Todd and Chief Hubbard) against which the rebellious son can battle. The plot dimensions are thus represented as the conventional dilemma of a cop who must bend the law in order to uphold it. Yet the laws which get bent are psychic and cultural as well as social. The otherness of Foley ruptures generic conventions which the narrative struggles to contain through the creation of familial motifs. Foley is not only black but sexually ambiguous. The explicit motor of the narrative is the murder of his buddy, Mikey, who has drunkenly declared his love for Foley at the beginning of the film. This undercurrent of homoeroticism is persistently echoed throughout the film in Foley's language and behaviour. He strikes an immediate affinity with the excessively camp characters he encounters and whose mannerisms he mirrors unhesitatingly; he poses as arch-criminal Victor Maitland's boyfriend in order to gain access to him; he discusses the rigidity of his fellow cops' Billy and Taggart's 'dicks' in the highly charged strip joint and he repeatedly tells fellow cop Billy that he loves him. The rebellion which the patriarchs struggle to curb is therefore that threatened by Foley's race and ambiguous sexuality, which constantly threatens to burst the narrative apart and is inadequately contained by the end. The police patriarchs' overly rigorous attention to the bureaucracy of statutory law directly conflicts with the hero's attention to the symbolic Law, the integrity of the metaphorical police family and a wider ethical order of the conventional *policier*, but it also conflicts with his volatile allegiances to race and gender. The extremity of the patriarchal representation pushes the son's to excess and neither is adequately contained at the end. This structure prompts a version of the rite of passage movie which enables the hero to achieve his object – in this case, the creation of a nuclear subgroup, the buddy triangle.

The film thus treads a risky path between explicit homoeroticism and the male-male officer relationships while negotiating its racial terrain through the trope of a journey – both actual and aspirant – from Detroit to LA. The opening sequence representing a montage of Detroit, spills over with images of a black population, mooching and slouching on street corners. By contrast, LA teams with glittering golden-haired white people, mainly in cars and all busy, going somewhere. The film displaces race on to Foley's iterations of how-we-do-this-back-there versus how-you-do-things-here, comparisons which are never fully resolved and are rendered more ambiguous by Foley's own lust for the high life of LA. The racial anxieties are thus elided into the universalising police family (paradoxically both 'here' and 'there') and contained within the central familial oppositions of police/sub-group/criminal groupings. However, both the racial and homoerotic tension constantly threaten to rupture any resolution. The black Foley cannot end up with the white girl marked out for him – he marginalises and exploits Jenny, who was also Mikey's friend, diminishing her loyalty and bravery. Instead, the internal psychosexual dynamics revolve around Foley, Taggart and Billy. Foley must recruit both cops into the new buddy family, by first seducing Billy and then confronting Taggart in front of Maitland's house. The alliance is sealed by Taggart's contribution of an oversized phallic gun which signifies the possibility of resolution at both actual and metaphorical levels. This new 'family' is created within and, largely in opposition to, the larger metaphorical context of the police force. Only by creating two containers for this explosive mix, the police 'family' and its buddy nucleus, can the narrative posit closure. Yet the closure itself is a journey – pointing forwards to a sequel and to further quests for resolution. In *Beverly Hills Cop*, there are no families outside the metaphorical affiliation structures (police, buddy sub-group, criminal clan). As we shall see, the film's sequel attempts to create just such an external 'natural' family structure, for its own safety.

The Failure of the Patriarch

A further failure of the father represented in these films is the failure of the patriarch, the failure to uphold the law and the symbolic order. For obvious reasons, most of these texts explore the role of the father in metaphorical rather than actual form. *Beverly Hills Cop II, The Untouchables* and *Good Morning, Vietnam* specifically enact this paternal problematic.

The Untouchables is particularly interesting in that it combines two forms of failed father. Eliott Ness fails in his paternal role, jeopardising his family by his attention to crime-fighting, while the Chicago authorities fail to uphold the statutory laws, colluding with Capone in his stranglehold on the city, accepting bribes and condoning violence. Although it is superficially the threat to the family which motivates the narrative and Ness's own intervention through the death of the little girl in the bar and her mother's appeal, Ness must expose his own family to danger in countering the crime. Ness's family physically represent the ideal he is fighting for, yet he risks his own place in it by his action. He jeopardises them in two ways, firstly by attracting the physical threat posed by Capone's man and secondly by the recruitment of his own rival 'family'. Ness creates Malone as his mentor-father and Stone and Oscar as subservient 'sons', a familial substitution epitomised in the 'family photo' of the group which becomes a fetish object, displacing familial values for male integrity, law and order. Physically and emotionally close to his wife and child at the start of the film (the early familial scenes are characterised by two- or three-shots showing all family members in close proximity to each other), he is increasingly separated from them. He is not present at the birth of his second child, and, following his family's removal under threat, he is only imaged once speaking to his wife over the telephone through reverse cutting rather than face to face or even in split-screen framing, just prior to the crucial confrontation and declaration with Malone. When his wife and child next appear, they are separated by the physical barriers of the courtroom and he is never shown with them again. At the end of the film, although he says 'I'm going home' in response to a waiting journalist, he is alone, his final words on the ending of Prohibition ('I think I'll have a drink'), displaying his absolute subjugation to the forces of law on whose behalf he has fought. His wife is never privy to what is going on, merely shuttled around 'for her own good'. Perhaps most crucially, he risks the life of the baby he goes to save at the penultimate climax of the film, when he allows the pram to slip from his grasp during the shootout over the bookkeeper.[3] Bookended by the murder of the child and the potential death of another, the text balances the fragility of the infant against the threat of the father. Despite his iconographic association with the family man, Ness privileges the war against crime, relinquishing the domestic burden – and terrible threat from the Capone hitmen – to his wife. Ness is the archetypal family man who nevertheless is drawn into the vacuum left by the failure of the patriarchs and, in so doing, fails his family.

Beverly Hills Cop II is also concerned with the crisis of the patriarch. The film moves away from the simple crime/law nexus of its precursor to explore what happens when the patriarchs cannot uphold the law. Lieutenant Bogomil is impotent, literally disabled by the criminals, and the Chief of Police, Lutz, is abusive and incompetent. The anxieties around race and homosexuality which bubbled furiously in the first film are more strenuously, but still inadequately, displaced. Although heterosexual relationships are given more prominence in a desperate attempt to resolve the contradictions, they are ultimately expendable. The never-seen but apparently desirable Marcie, for example, is simply passed over by Foley to Jeffrey when he leaves for Los Angeles. Bogomil's daughter, Jan, is

subsequently proposed as a potential romantic interest for Foley, the potential successor to the patriarch apparently bidding for his daughter. We
are given to understand that their relationship had warmed on Foley's first
visit, although there was no hint of this in the earlier film. 'You know if
she didn't have a father with a gun something woulda happened', Foley
announces to 'Andrew over the phone at the beginning of the film. Thus
the threat of miscegenation is apparently liquidated by the phallic father
although it is at the expense of fixing Foley's own sexuality. Further undermining any attempt to contain Foley in a Final Romance, Foley purely
exploits her in solving the crime rather than pursuing any romantic attachment – even when Bogomil is safely out of the way.

The film attempts to offset the homoerotic bonding between Foley,
Taggart and Billy by evoking other familial forms and establishing a subplot of opposing patriarchs. However, the three men's concern over
Taggart's failing marriage is quickly lost as a subplot only to resurface
conveniently at the end to fracture the final bonding. Natural families are
marginalised or trivialised – Foley uses a story of 'his kids' as a cover;
Jan's concerns for her father are quickly sublimated to the hunt for the
killer; Taggart's relationship with his wife is referenced but invisible,
operating purely as an indicator of narrative fissure or resolution. The
attempt to create an oppositional meta-police family, the evil Lutz versus
the morally superior Andrew, Todd and the Mayor, also fails to draw our
fascination from the nuclear unit of Foley–Billy–Taggart and, in a peripheral way, Jeffrey back in Detroit. Most importantly, all the fathers, whether
actual or metaphorical, fail. Andrew is castrated, unable to solve the crime;
Lutz is morally and ethically tainted, finally thrown off the force; Dent, the
crime patriarch, is outwitted by Foley and cannot save the criminal frater-
nity he has created; and Taggart puts his buddy family before his own
when he risks his job, allowing Foley to override his protests about supporting two kids on his own when he appeals to Taggart's loyalty for the
police-patriarch, Andrew. All fathers make mistakes. Only Foley, the son-
father, is infallible, but he is morally off-centre and can't be trusted by
anybody. His final parodic line in the film, as in the earlier one, is 'Trust
me' as he drives away leaving his buddies to cope with the aftermath of
his latest deceit.

The textual trope most commonly used to elide these contradictions is
that of masquerade. Foley is constantly disguising himself as 'what-he-is-
not' but, in fact, what he appears most to be. However, this double bluff
only heightens the contradictions, drawing attention to the displacements
of race and sexuality and underlining the threats posed by patriarchal
failure. The display of Foley dressing and driving his high performance

car in the opening sequence, for example, turns out to be the elaborate disguise for his latest undercover operation. Yet this disguise resonates with Eddie Murphy's own star image as well as the character established in the film's prequel to remind us of his 'flashiness', his aspirational rich, whiteness and (not least, by the metonymic cutting which is more characteristic of the camera's observation of women) his ambiguous sexuality. Similarly, when he answers the phone to Andrew with a mock blackface joke in a deep South drawl, he both displays and parodies his race. Disguising himself as Ramone, Victor Maitland's fictitious boyfriend, Foley draws attention to his sexuality and, in further (mis)representing himself as diseased, excessively confirms his transgression. This string of metamorphoses suggests the outcome of patriarchal failure; the inability to fix the son's identity and allegiance to race and sexuality. Such a failure renders the hero suspended between two realms, the social and the private, trying to recreate one within the other but unable to do so satisfactorily and with no possibility of permitting a utopian family resolution.

Finally, at a metaphorical level, *Good Morning, Vietnam* explores territory similar to that of *Rambo: First Blood Part II*. Airman Adrian Cronauer is failed by the American patriarchs, uncovering the dystopian underside of the American Dream in his exposure to the complexities of Saigon in 1965. His microcosmic battles to retain his risqué slot as a DJ on the Armed Forces Radio Network displace the atrocities of the war until he is naively drawn into the 'family' of the Viet Cong by his attraction to Trinh. Unable to fully comprehend the complexities of his position, he is defeated both by Sergeant Dickerson, who has always wanted him removed from the station, and by his own failure to rescue anything from the débâcle he has unwittingly created. Fathers who fail at a social level are unable to generate successful sons. Like Rambo, Adrian finishes the film alienated both from his own society and the one which he has been forced to penetrate and rupture.

The Failure of the Male

The failed male fails fundamentally at a psychic level, failing to maintain essential boundaries, particularly those of subjectivity and gender. This represents a categoric failure of masculinity. A failure of the male principle highlights insecurities latent in the paternal role and causes an interrupted Oedipal scenario in which either the father has failed to enter the symbolic order and differentiate fully between essential psychic and social categories or has caused the son's failure to do so. In these texts, the father has either failed to separate gendered domains fully or has paradoxically become alienated from important elements of 'him-self', failing to integrate a feminine side within a highly coded masculine persona. This paradigm mines dominant discourses of a biologically determined masculinity which collapses physical and psychic categories. Conventionally, masculine properties are hard-edged and fixed, centring on phallic power and a complete entfy into the symbolic order and the law of patriarchy, and are almost always associated with the male figure, narratively and iconographically. Men are conventionally active, possessive, aggressive and operate with absolute certainty and focus. Certain genres proved highly susceptible to the destabilisation of such characteristics. The majority of these male-failure films are either comedies or science fiction, both genres providing fertile ground for breaking down psychic, social and cultural norms, in this case those constructing identity and sexuality. Freudian analysis of verbal slips and jokes has demonstrated how humour licenses slippage between psychic categories and the projection of unconscious desires to the conscious level.[4] Science fiction also deals directly with slippages, paradoxically working hard to establish boundaries only then to collapse them. The primary anxiety of the science-fiction film is to construct other/ not-other distinctions, but these are inevitably blurred by the problem of representation: the text must be able to show something both constructible and recognisable. Thus the other must share characteristics of the not-other, just as the not-other becomes other by its very presence/absence in the film-as-medium. In its very *mise-en-scène*, the sci-fi film necessarily collapses temporal and spatial boundaries, future and past, there and here, in order to represent the fantastic as the here-and-now present.

Films in which the father transgresses fundamental masculine/feminine categories trigger a psychic breakdown in the text itself, which becomes either hysterical or schizophrenic in its narrative and narration. In schizophrenic narratives, such as *Total Recall*, the father is uncertain of any reality. A plethora of unreal worlds appear real to him and slippage between these realms is seamless. In hysterical narratives such as *Airplane!*, *Honey, I Shrunk the Kids* or the *Police Academy* series, the father apprehends such distinctions, but cannot maintain them. Some buried trauma constantly surfaces, or threatens to surface, in unbidden, spontaneous eruptions. In a key reversal of feminine hysteria, this unconscious memory is linked to the pre-oedipal mother and is manifested in womb-fear (indistinguishably close to womb-envy) and exhibited through the promotion of a strong female protagonist and ambiguously sexualised male. The drive of the narrative in the hysterical films is to surface and incorporate the repressed trauma into the symbolic realm, usually through the vehicle of successful oedipalisation and the creation of a utopian family.

Four films, in particular, demonstrate these narrational neuroses. Already touched on at the beginning of this chapter, both *Back to the Future* and *Total Recall* feature schizophrenic fathers for whom the boundaries of temporal reality and subjectivity are completely eroded. *Airplane!* provides an excellent example of the surreal schizophrenic comedy. By contrast, *Tootsie* offers a classic example of the hysterical comedy, in which gender boundaries are elided but always acknowledged.[5]

Back to the Future is a paradigmatic example of the schizophrenic science-fiction text. Through the agency of his son, Marty, George McFly and his family are rebuilt and their domestic and sexual history rewritten. In the process, George's own subjectivity is categorically divided, without his apparent awareness, between two opposing personae. The cause of George McFly's schizoid state is his son's desire for the perfect family, notably for his father to be other than he is. It is, therefore, the father's failure to fulfil the son's desire which motivates the narrative, prompting Marty's intervention. Yet in achieving a resolution, the son must *become* the father, recreating him in his own image and even pandering his parents' relationship. The unsatisfactory, weak father represented at the beginning of the film is unproblematically transformed into an assertive, healthy one by the end. In a similar way, Marty transforms his transgressively slovenly mother into a utopian model of maternal virtue and energy. Neither parent is conscious of the transformation. Thus primary intra-family boundaries are obliterated and the son's desire is privileged over the father's subjectivity. The son recreates the father, usurping his parents' own reproductive capacity.

Total Recall follows a parallel trajectory. Quaid is created by Hauser from his own consciousness to enact a bizarre counter-plot to obliterate Martian rebellion. As Quaid says: 'It's the best mindfuck yet.' Thus in a vertiginous generative loop, Hauser 'fathers' Quaid who then 'kills' his father by refusing to reintegrate with him. It is the paternal consciousness which can reproduce. Women are opposed, but peripheral, to this process. As Cohagen instructs Melina, 'You'll be respectful, compliant and appreciative. The way a woman should be.' Yet the destabilisation of subjectivity also undermines such established gendered norms. It is Melina's words which sow doubt and disrupt the closure: 'I can't believe it. It's like a dream' – to which Quaid/Hauser is forced to respond, 'I just had a terrible thought. What if it is a dream?' Melina's final words, 'Well kiss me before we wake up' reinforce the possibility that the reality on which they have staked their Final Romance may only be a different level of consciousness, one reality among the many Quaid/Hauser has created. She therefore implies the non-reality of reality, suggesting alternative possibilities which destabilise male integrity. This is a film in which nothing is secure and even at the end, Quaid cannot be sure of who he is or even which one of the multiple personalities Hauser's 'mindfuck' has spawned. As in *Back to the Future*, men attempt to usurp reproductive capabilities. Not only does Hauser produce Quaid but the rebel leader, Cuato, is actually 'born' from another man's stomach. Such usurpation, however, has terrible consequences. While this thematic is taken up in other films in the decade (notably in comedies such as *Three Men and a Baby* and *Look Who's Talking*), these two films literally inscribe this capability directly into the narrative.[6] Marty stands in for his father, nearly substituting for him in his mother's affections and is the creator of his redeemed and transformed family; he literally creates them in his own image. In *Total Recall*, Quaid is his own creator, threatening to destroy the integrity of his own subjectivity and, in the process, eliding gender boundaries – Hauser/ Quaid are both father and mother, parents and son. The creation of the new Martian climate (strikingly generated by the phallic explosion of the mountain) can be seen as a physical attempt at ensuring permanent reproduction; the founding of a dynasty, but one which rests perversely upon the subjugation of mutants and the potency of an ambiguously sexualised and integrated earthman.[7] It also attempts to reverse the destructive capability both of nuclear energy itself and of the male principle, transforming it into creativity. Neither film can achieve a stable familial outcome. The paternal crises in both films render all boundaries unreliable and send both heroes on further quests; Quaid to discover whether this is truly a dream, Marty to solve the crises of his own, as yet unborn, children.

As we have seen, the fathers in these schizophrenic films inhabit a terrain where boundaries are unstable and permeable, a feature particularly common in surreal comedies such as *Airplane!*, a highly popular genre piece of the eighties. Ted pursues his ex-girlfriend, Elaine, on to the plane on which she is an air hostess in a desperate bid for reconciliation. However, once the plane is airborne, the ensuing disasters trigger his own fear of flying, initiated by a disastrous wartime mission in which he believes he was at fault. Ted overcomes his traumatic memories to assume control and be reunited with Elaine at the end of the film. *Airplane!* constructs a romantic subplot of an incipient family unit (Ted/Elaine) broken up by Ted's reluctance to assume responsibility. Oppressed by memories of his wartime 'failure', Ted has been unable to form and maintain a mature, heterosexual relationship or hold down a job. In a version of oedipalisation, he is forced to take control (urged on by surrogate fathers Doctor Runach and Kramer) and rescue the plane to achieve a Final Romance.

However, the Oedipal trajectory is anarchically undermined. The 'fathers' themselves are proved unreliable as patriarchal models. Both are made comic by their language, by the chaos they each motivate and by the generic conventions they subvert. At the close of the film, the Doctor has become a parodic automaton repeating, 'Good Luck' endlessly as they land while Kramer rehearses clichés into the mike to which Ted is no longer listening. The Oedipal scenario is subverted through generic distortions, notably the conventions of the seventies disaster movie. The symbolic realm is volatile, words elide with visual images in which signification itself is subverted, rupturing signifier from signified or collapsing it entirely in a series of visual and verbal dislocations. Spatial and stylistic conventions are ignored: Kramer walks through the mirror he has been reflected in; a window cleaner appears at the windscreen of the aeroplane. The narrative itself has unstable boundaries, subplots are overlaid, interwoven and then lost. Characters disappear, their motivations subservient to the exigencies of the latest drama. The Final Romance itself is rent by the mirroring device of two blow-up dolls which symbolically fly off in the resurrected plane on a parallel narrative trajectory. As the couples wave farewell, they seal the collapse of real/not real boundaries and fracture the apparent triumph of heterosexual union. The comedy is caused by, and is a symptom of, infantile chaos – the eruption of the archaic anarchic unconscious into the conscious world. Ted and Elaine are relatively uncontaminated by the comic effects which erupt around them but are accepted as part of their normal schizophrenic domain, the conventional and unconventional collapsing into each other. Neither of the patriarchs are adequate to fixing these boundaries, but instead undermine them further through their very incompetence.

The hysterical comedy *Tootsie* is also preoccupied with boundaries but, by contrast, is always acutely conscious of them. The boundaries at stake here concern not only the obvious male/female elision, but also what is real/not real and what is seen/not seen through the mechanisms of masquerade. Struggling actor Michael Dorsey disguises himself as a woman (Dorothy) to land a part in a TV soap opera. Complications ensue when he falls for leading lady, Julie, and when both Julie's father and the soap's male lead fall for him/her. On revealing his 'true' identity, Michael loses both the part and the girl. He must make further confessions to win her back, both to her and, significantly, to her father, Les. His reconciliation with Les is achieved through their masculine exchange in a bar. His reconciliation with Julie, albeit fragile, is achieved by a sidewalk declaration: 'Look, you don't know me from Adam but I was a better man with you as a woman than I ever was with a woman as a man. . . . I just gotta learn to do without the dress.' This 'talking cure' is entirely consistent with classical psychoanalytic treatment for the reincorporation of a hysteric within the symbolic order, a reincorporation charted throughout the film. Michael begins the movie as a promiscuous, predatory single man, living with a male flatmate, hating children. He ends wanting a stable relationship with a woman who is already herself a single mother. It is an hysterical rites of passage movie, charting the trajectory of an inadequately oedipalised male (characterised as excessively masculine in behaviour while coded feminine in appearance) to a mature, monogamous, heterosexual male through the intervention of a surrogate-father as inadmissible object of desire. His own family is significantly absent, never mentioned while Julie's is ever-present, always talked about. The film thus tries to resolve the juxtaposition of the professionally successful Julie, able to combine work and homelife, with Michael, unsuccessful in either, by siting her firmly in the domestic sphere.

Michael overcomes his antipathy to women by becoming one. What appears a progressive recognition of his lack of emotional maturity and a search for his lost femininity can also be interpreted as undermining women through incorporation. In achieving maturation, Michael both disrupts the signifier of woman and becomes the authority *on* woman. His entry into the symbolic, although perverse and delayed, bestows him with phallic authority to speak about and on behalf of women. He is constantly sought out for advice, frequently by other women and particularly by Julie. His 'true self' is resolved and integrated by the acknowledgement and incorporation of the feminine – as he lectures his students at the beginning of the film, 'Don't play a part that isn't in you.' His transformation, through surfacing and then incorporating his repressed desires intriguingly allows him to project desire on to the mother through becoming a woman, but he is potentially able then to possess her while slipping back into the masculine persona. Throughout this transformation, however, Michael acknowledges and manages the ambiguity of his subjectivity and remains conscious of the gendered boundaries in play. In addition, all the other characters 'in the know' constantly admonish him about going too far, reining him within boundaries. His flatmate Jeff seeks reassurance: 'It is just for the money, isn't it?' His agent begs him to stop. Yet the characters who 'know' are all men. Even those who are not told, are uneasy with him, such as the director Carlisle who states, 'I don't know. There's something about her that bothers me.' By contrast the women are completely taken in and trust him absolutely. This leaves scope for two competing interpretations; that women are less sensitive to gender difference than men (and more easily fooled) or that Michael is essentially more female than male and the unease that men exhibit in his presence is no more than conventional male unease in the presence of assertive women. The film leaves both interpretations open. It thus constructs a proto-father who resolves his failure as a male through confronting and literally incorporating his fear of the female. However, his unreliability prevents him from being accepted unproblematically as proto-father at the close of the film and the ending does not posit a utopian family.

The Treacherous Father

Finally, there is the *betrayer* who is both a failed and absent father, having let his family down at both a personal and social level. The betrayer, however, is a very specific failure – his acts of infidelity or treachery represent a particular form of family tragedy and result in very particular narrative structures. Actual fathers betray actual families primarily through sexual infidelity in these films. In metaphorical texts, however, the main vehicle of betrayal is treachery, usually by desertion to an opposing side. It is as if these texts hesitate to imagine such acts of betrayal within the actual family and can only displace it to a metaphorical form. Three films, *Rambo: First Blood Part II, The Empire Strikes Back* and *Pretty Woman* serve to demonstrate the narrative outcomes of such treacheries.

In *Rambo: First Blood Part II*, Rambo is betrayed by his 'fathers', the founding fathers of the US as exemplified in Trautman, the army patriarch, with whom he strikes a deal to be released from incarceration in order to find and free American prisoners taken in the Vietnamese war. America is constantly represented as the mother country who has taken other father-lovers. However, Trautman has betrayed America's sons by pandering their mother-country to a new 'lover', the hi-tech bureaucrat, represented by Marshall Murdoch. Murdoch is divorced from the 'natural' ties between mother-country and son. The father is thus emasculated and the sons alienated. To resolve this lack of coordination and direction, Rambo must retreat from the highly organised, technologically sophisticated politics of the new order and return to a 'natural' state, a retreat which is spectacularly signified in his destruction of the command centre at the end of the film. His body is constantly specularised through intimate, extended close ups as he prepares for and executes his mission, lingered on in a highly eroticised torture scene and presented as the ultimate solution to all difficulties. He is displayed as excessively 'natural', every muscle honed and nurtured, every sinew and tendon exposed and taut. On parachuting from his plane, he cuts loose his hi-tech weaponry and returns to more primitive tools, an elemental creature who relies on the 'old ways' of wits, brawn and craftsmanship to fight an 'old war'. His mission is to release

the sons from the war that holds them still and which was the cause of his
'father's' betrayal. Vietnam shook American belief in its own infallibility
to the core. The arrogant insertion of Rambo's body into the jungles of
Vietnam where he overcomes not only the Vietnamese but also their Soviet
supporters in hand-to-hand combat, spoke to a deep need in the American
psyche and partially explains the film's phenomenal success and cultural
resonance. At a time when the Cold War was ending and the enemy was
not so easily identified, Rambo's naturalness was in stark contrast to an
increasingly complex reality. In tune with the times, the outcome of such
betrayal is represented as total alienation. Asked not to hate his country at
the close of the film, Rambo strides out into the jungle alone, insisting that
he would die for his motherland, if she would just return his love and that
of the men who died for her.

Yet Rambo is the object as well as the subject of violence and he effects
just one successful rescue. The first is subsequently thwarted and the second is only made possible following his own rescue by the girl Co. He is
an anarchic, primitive force, the pre-oedipal chaos – he cannot free himself, but is freed by others. Relying on his excessive masculinity, he finds
it wanting and it is the active female who saves him, an act for which she
is later punished by her sacrificial death. There is no resolution in the film
(at an extra-textual marketing level, this opens up, as in so many other
films of this period, the possibility of a further sequel). What is primarily
at stake in this film is the knowledge of 'where I stand'. Rambo cannot
take his place in the 'new' post-Vietnam, postmodern America, because he
does not know where he stands and because his 'father' has failed him.
Rambo is the explicit manifestation of Fredric Jameson's postmodern
'unmappable world', in which the eponymous hero, the motherland's son,
has lost his coordinates, collapsing family, nation and professionalisation
into a dystopian miasma. However, in regaining his own subjectivity through
the loss of a nation–family that is unchanged by his act, he is ultimately
alienated. Rambo cannot regain his subjectivity within the changed mother-
community and cannot cope with the loss of the unified self. The choice
is alienation or fragmentation; Oedipal resolution (emulation of the father
and appropriation of the bride) cannot be achieved. The father is emasculated, and the potential bride (the Vietcong Co), who is not only alien but
also active, threatening to eclipse Rambo's own achievements, must therefore be killed.

The Empire Strikes Back veers between metaphorical and actual betrayal. The film is centred on the fight against Darth Vadar who is revealed
as the protagonist's father and master of the evil Empire. Part of the *Star
Wars* series, the text is inevitably incomplete and the resolution open:

Luke cannot become a Jedi, cannot overcome his father and cannot achieve a romantic alliance with Leia. To compensate, Luke creates a series of surrogate fathers – Obi, Yoda, Ben – all of whom he fails or who fail him. The only resolution to the conflict is the liquidation of Darth Vadar, preferably by Luke, the hero. Yet the familial narrative mitigates against this outcome. The taboo on killing the father cannot be broken in either this film or *Return of the Jedi*. Darth Vadar is killed by accident when Luke pulls back from doing so. Although his death enables the new dynasty, it must be through Han (the redeemed 'bad son' of the freedom fighters) and Leia. The revelation that Leia is Luke's sister further corrupts Luke's heroic stature as we are reminded of the sub-thread of incipient endogamy which has run throughout the trilogy. As in *Rambo*, Luke is alienated from the new order he has helped to create through the treachery of his father. This exposes him to attempting the transgression of vital taboos, namely patricide and incest, and leaves him tragically flawed. Thus Luke is unable either to close the narrative through his own agency or to form the portended Final Romance.

The narrative of *Pretty Woman* charts Edward's quest to combine both professional and personal fulfilment, a narrative which is motivated by the childhood betrayal of Edward's father in committing adultery and deserting his family. Like Charlie in *Rain Man*, Edward compensates for paternal loss by immersing himself in his work which is represented as robbing him of his humanity and denying him a satisfactory domestic life. He first confronts, and then, through Vivian's catalysing influence, allies with, a surrogate father, James Morse. Edward's estrangement from his father is thereby resolved by Vivian's intervention as she helps him to find his affective 'lost self'. In a reciprocal move, Edward completes a Pygmalion transformation of Vivian, the archetypal whore with a heart of gold, who then escorts him along a classic Oedipal trajectory. The trope of dealmaking, similarly deployed in *Out of Africa*, elides the contradictions inherent in such mutual reconstruction, and obscures the imbalance of power in the relationship. Edward has purchased Vivian and so she is his to change and, if necessary, to reject. Vivian in turn can shed her inhibitions about retaining her own subjectivity through the motif of control and exchange. The final deal – the fairytale ending – trades the satisfaction of Vivian's desire for Edward's control. Both Vivian and Edward are redeemed, re-entering the symbolic order through a Final Romance. At the same time, the new surrogate father has also struck his deal for status and power. *Pretty Woman* demonstrates how the father's sexual treachery damages his offspring, rupturing the Oedipal transfer and splitting domestic and social spheres apart.

SUMMARY

All fathers fail in some way and their failure forces the family into the foreground of the film. Even though the father is represented as a role in crisis, it is still a role which structures the narrative. The crisis itself, in effect, is the dominant narrative driver, just as the father's absence provides the initiating narrative moment of so many texts. However, we have also seen that, if the narrative goal is to restore the father within the family, it is signally failing. The father cannot so easily incorporate competing forms of representations and narrational possibilities. Paternal failures are caused primarily by the father's inability to maintain the distinction so essential to the establishment of a utopian family, the separation of private and social spheres. Nor can the father fix the temporariness of the family unit, a structure from which he can be seen to enjoy the greatest social, psychic and cultural benefits. The father has the greatest investment in familial ideology, namely in mythologising an essentially temporary social structure as a permanent system of power and dependence. He is therefore deployed to fix the nuclear family in some mythical, idealised space. Yet in trying to impose a universalising structure on an essentially volatile relationship, the father must inevitably fail. The father is, therefore, a paradoxical figure – both in and out of time, a threat to the family and a defuser of that threat. In the very attempt to freeze the family the father also indicates the possibility of transience, working against his own project. It is, therefore, precisely those fathers who emphasise the importance of change, such as the eponymous Rocky, who are represented as successful in the paternal role, but who thereby jeopardise their own investment.

The father in these films is therefore both the desired outcome of stability, and desirous architect/subject of that equilibrium. All fathers endeavour to recreate the family type whether in actual or metaphorical form, in order to guarantee their own power base. In all these texts the fathers fail in some way, yet it is a paradoxical failure fraught with ambiguity and ambivalence. Their failure is either the motivator of the narrative and predicate to the son's (it is rarely a daughter's) success and subjective integrity or it is representative of the dystopian alternative to that which the sons strive for. These narratives track the struggle to represent the paternal role against perceived marginalisation and the problematics of masculinity. Yet this representation is merely an upgraded version of the old patriarch, willing to incorporate a more complete, integrated 'feminine' side within the old masculine codes of the symbolic. Hence the tropes of journeying and dealmaking. In permitting such incorporation, such films marked a radical shift from the hegemony of the authority–father-figure to the figure, particularly the body, of the child while the mother was edged out of the frame. However, such power shifts are often incomplete and do not go unchallenged. As we move to look at representations of motherhood, and more particularly childhood, in the decade, it is possible to see oppositional discourses emerging.

6 Absence and Loss: The Evacuation of the Mother

While many of the most popular Hollywood films of the decade questioned the nature of fatherhood, little space was made for either the recuperation or expansion of the maternal representation. Anxieties over the role of the father served to displace the mother at the centre of the narrative. The mothers in these texts are therefore far less susceptible to a structural analysis based on narrative motivation than the fathers, and their failure or success in achieving a successful familial resolution is, as we shall see, not a central issue. For, given that the mother is entirely subsumed by the family in her very definition, she can only be the object, rather than the subject, of familial failure. Her failures are those of neglect rather than of activity. Whereas the father attempts to fix the family through establishing his own inherently unstable role, mothers have an inherent representational stability and render the family unstable by any deviation from an ideological norm. While the narrative drive constantly reverts to the restitution of the patriarchal family and the obsession with the father's failure, the maternal principle is just one condition of its success, not in itself transfiguring. In these films, mothers still fail but their failures are failures of representation. They do not live up to a prescribed ideal. The maternal paradigm is strictly coded as unproblematic – mother is an assumed, always-already 'natural' category. Since all other female attributes are rendered invisible once a woman becomes a mother, the mother must stand in for, but can never become an instrument in changing, the human generative cycle. Thus the failure of the mother influences the narrative in significantly different ways to the failure of the fathers. While fathers are in the privileged position of constructing their discursive positioning and function, mothers are relatively fixed, their biological functions defining their sociocultural position. Unlike the fathers, the mother-as-mother is never the trigger for these narratives because their role is not up for question. To gain any discursive flexibility or extend their representational repertoire, mothers must actively contest their own representations. The narrative failure of the mother is therefore indexed against normative representational codings and structures.

One of the most obvious symptoms of this failure of representation is the evacuation of the mother from the text. The majority of the most popular films of the decade represent the mother as literally absent.[1] While certain of these texts, such as *Rambo: First Blood Part II*, represent the mother metaphorically, in this case as the motherland, these are not inscribed into the narrative in such an overt way as the metaphorical fathers and are so abstracted as to be effectively absent. A small number of feminist critics and radical filmmakers, arguing from a position developed from Lacanian psychoanalysis, have argued passionately for women to use silence as a weapon against the language and strictures of patriarchy and, without offering such a separatist position unqualified endorsement, it is certainly in the absences and silences that we must look for any contestations of maternal representation.[2] Just as the absent father structures many of the popular films, so the absence of the mother frequently works to displace dominant discursive codings and the primary narrative drive. Whereas the family was equated to the figure of the father in 'breadwinner' discourses, the mother was displaced to the level of the child. Defined as a mother rather than as a woman, narrative agency was denied to her.

Of the mothers who *are* present in the films, few are foregrounded. Instead, we can chart the conventional deployment of active/passive, good/bad axes running across these movies, axes which inflect representations of the mother in inverse relation to those of the father. Feminist theorists have charted how historical representations of the mother have conventionally been organised around a semiotic system which works to elide passivity with virtue and activity with wrongdoing.[3] Mothers who are active outside the domestic sphere, and therefore bad, have either to be reincorporated (as in *Honey, I Shrunk the Kids, Three Men and a Baby* or *Look Who's Talking*) or be punished (*Terms of Endearment, Out of Africa*) for their transgression. The mother's relationship to, and agency in, the narrative is consonant with her symbolic and moral integrity and correspondingly constructs her representational paradigm. Trapped in domesticity, she cannot step outside the family to change it; she can only service what-is since any extra-domestic adventure will be punished. It is more productive, therefore, to divide those mothers who are present into those who are represented as active and those who are passive and to analyse their effect on the narrative and the oppositional discourses they stimulate. The generalisation 'absence/activity equals bad, presence/passivity equals good' cannot hope to be adequate to the complexities of such representations across their social, cultural and psychic terrains. Women and mothers attended these films in massive numbers and, on generalised assumption, personal experience and anecdotal evidence, found pleasure in them. If such pleasures are not explicitly apparent within the maternal representation itself, it is to the gaps and contradictions that we must pay attention in order to identify the uses and pleasures which these audiences discovered in contemporary maternal representations.

THE ABSENT MOTHER

As the mother is intrinsically defined by the family it is perhaps a tautology to point out that her absence destroys it. Why therefore, when the family was such an integral discourse in popular Hollywood films and in wider cultural representations, was the mother so frequently absent? The majority of actual absent mothers were dead or simply unexplained, in marked contrast to the absent fathers whom the text was always at pains to explain away. As so many were absent, we have to question whether they were unrepresentable. And if so, why? All we have to go on in answering this question are the specific textual consequences of the mother's absence and how the films attempted to compensate for it – to look at the spaces in the texts. At a time when masculinity was persistently problematised and the role of the father in crisis, one attempt to reassert patriarchy was obviously through the terrain of the family. However, the mother was so firmly collapsed into the family that creating additional space for the father meant dislodging the mother. Rather than negotiating power relations within the familial space, many of these films opted simply to remove the mother from it. Rooting her out of it, however, threw the family into crisis, a crisis which most narratives found impossible to allay. These films rehearse three distinct but complementary narrational responses to the mother's absence. In the first her child is unable to achieve maturation. The bulk of the absent-mother narratives chart an Oedipal journey in which the child attempts to mature, such as *Indiana Jones and the Last Crusade, The Jazz Singer* or *The Empire Strikes Back*. However, the symbol of successful maturation, the Final Romance and the assumption of social responsibility within patriarchy is, as we shall see, frequently flawed or incomplete. The second response marks the collapse of intrafamily terms, in which the child also becomes the father or vice versa and the mother's procreative function is usurped, as in *Total Recall* and *Pretty Woman*. The third response is to privilege the extra-domestic, the metaphorical family, as in *Rain Man* or *Top Gun*, to replace the actual family within the text and mask inadequate oedipalisation.

These three responses show how irreparably the family was damaged through the mother's absence and the most dystopian films enact a combination of all three. The primary effect of the maternal absence was these films' failure to produce a satisfactory Final Romance and, therefore, any possibility of familial reproduction. Once the mother is evacuated, the narrative cannot easily be closed through the substitution of a new mother since the same anxieties resurface. Where the failure of the father combines with an absent mother and cannot be restored as in *Rain Man* or *Total Recall*, the generative prognosis was dystopian. In both these films, the final unions are highly unsatisfactory, suggesting temporary or only partial closure. The results of the maternal absence are carried forward into the next generation as the last film in the *Star Wars* series demonstrates. *Return of the Jedi* resolves the Luke/Han/Leia romantic triangle through the revelation that Luke and Leia are siblings. This manoeuvre settles the rivalry (and intense male bonding) between Luke and Han but effectively alienates the hero and excites the retrospective threat of incest. Thus the family becomes the vehicle by which Luke is excluded from his 'natural' affiliations and inheritance. Although Luke retains a delegated patriarchal authority over her, Leia is only sexually available to Han and Luke is alienated from the new dynasty. In those absent-mother texts which did not close on even the possibility of motherhood, the resolutions were even more volatile and a theme of social alienation emerged. *Good Morning, Vietnam*, for example, is destabilised by the recall of Cronauer to the metaphorical 'motherland' from which he has distanced himself through his anarchic broadcasts and unwitting alliance with the Viet Cong, just as the eponymous Rambo is alienated through the same metaphoric and psychic conflicts. In such social alienation films, the Final Romance was frequently supplanted by a male–male bonding, which displaced all other social affiliations, including the family. Films such as *Beverly Hills Cop* and *Beverly Hills Cop II* or *The Fox and the Hound* replaced a family unit with a buddy arrangement which was outside social convention but proposed as a resolution. Women, including mothers, were explicitly excluded from such an arrangement. This, in familial terms, produced an inherently dystopian outcome.

Out of Africa perhaps comes closest to representing what is unrepresented in these other absent-mother films: an alternative to the nucleated domestic scene. The narrative is figured by a deferred chain of loss, stimulated by the absent mother whose absence both motivates and closes the narrative. Home and hearth are constant themes – not the 'farm in Africa' repeated across the title sequence which Karen takes over with her husband Bror, but her maternal home in Denmark, a place of refuge when she became sterile through syphilis and again when her lover dies at the end of the film. This is the tale of a woman who is inadequately contained within patriarchal structures, forming unsatisfactory relationships, first with Bror's fickle brother, then a marriage of convenience with Bror himself

and finally with the inveterate hunter-wanderer, Denys. Independent and
rebellious, Karen is unwilling to conform to Danish, or expatriate, social
mores. She treks across the bush to join her husband, defying the colonial
community, takes over the running of the farm and finally creates a school.
However, she is consistently punished. Her slight to Bror in their wedding-
night fight, in her instruction to the servant: 'Kinanjui, fetch some wine for
my lover's brother', was immediately punished by Bror absenting himself
'until the rains come' without notice the next morning. The litany of
retribution continues through Bror's infidelities and her consequent con-
traction of syphilis, her ejection from the Club and containment during the
war and finally her divorce and the destruction of the farm. Her final act
of rebellion, the taming of the wild but conservative Denys who refuses
to accept any change in the Africa he himself exploits, is punished by his
death and she returns to her maternal home.

The plot revolves around bargains. In order to gain a foothold within a
patriarchal, capitalist system, Karen must strike deals; with Bror on the
terms of their marriage, with the Chief on the school, with the settlers on
her containment during the war, with Denys on the terms of their relationship and, finally, with the settlers on the relocation of 'her natives' after
her farm is razed to the ground by fire. The currency of these deals is both
her status and hard cash. Denys gives his friendship and the fateful pen in
exchange for her stories. Her mother's cash buys Bror his farm – and her
marriage. Her marriage buys her status, but not fertility or satisfaction.
She must in perfect circularity, trade her stories with Denys for that.
The dealmaking in *Out of Africa* recalls that transacted by Vivian in *Pretty
Woman* and is a conventional trope in which women are themselves the
objects of exchange. Those women who venture outside the familial framework, attempting to establish some social currency, must have something
to trade. At the beginning of the film, Karen trades sexual fulfilment and
procreation for social respectability and her right to farm her mother's
property. By the end, she is willing to trade her respectability for sexual
fulfilment. Vivian has nothing to trade but her body, but does so in order
to escape from her own unsatisfactory family background. Karen's mother,
by contrast, appears to offer a supply line outside the deals of patriarchy.
It was her mother's wealth that enabled Karen to enter these negotiations
and it is her mother who provides a refuge. But it is not only the maternal
representation which is problematic. *Out of Africa* constantly stumbles
against the possibility of representing a father. Bror cannot become one;
Denys chooses not to; her own is dead. The socialite settlers are depicted
as flawed, their patriarchal roles misguided and sterile. Because of the
fathers' failures, mothers are never realised either. The only reproductive

possibility resides in the indigenous Chief who, surrounded by children, is a counterpoint to Karen's sterility. His concern for their future – a future past his own lifetime – outstrips the vision of the settlers and pushes him to accept Karen's school. However, the Chief is marginalised by his otherness – his blackness, his 'ignorance' and his primitivism, signified by the iconography of mud-huts and nakedness. He is the object of Karen's attentions rather than the architect of change. Barclay's attempt to bridge the divide between sterility and fecundity through the relationship with his indigenous servant is illegitimate and covert and is punished by his death. The narrative plays with the possibility of alternative family structures, with miscegenation, with the matriarchal dynasty, with the extended family structure of the Somalis, but is unable to represent them.

The play on textual reliability is highlighted in the film's formal construction. The film is one of the few top box-office hits to be told from a woman's point of view and is assigned the contemporarily unusual convention of a voice-over. This device ironically points up the artifice of the film, since it is, paradoxically, based on Karen's autobiographical writing and the voice-over is a direct quotation from the literary text. It also points forward to the setpiece stories within the narrative which endear Karen to Denys and are rewarded by the writer's tool of a pen. This woman's story, it suggests, is but a story, a fiction of woman's telling. A space is therefore permitted for spectators to disavow a tale of fathers who cannot be whole or sustain life and who are challenged in their provider role by an absent mother. Yet the stories and the patriarchal anxieties they provoke are there and we must not lose sight of the fact that the film was one of the top box-office hits of the decade.

The very absence of Karen's mother opens up spaces for alternative articulations of who and what she might be. She is both a port of refuge, sufficiently wealthy and generous in her own right to finance Karen's farm and yet a figure from whom Karen sought escape at the start of the film. At each crisis point, however, it is she to whom Karen turns, representing a far stronger bond than any of her romantic liaisons. The absent mother, therefore, stands for something outside representation. In the spaces she leaves by her absence, there are possibilities for articulations beyond those of the text itself, permitting gaps for spectatorial projection and identification which connect with disturbances and dislocations within the text. These lacunae are a site of continual contestation. Competing discourses frequently attempt to control and reinscribe the gaps by connoting the maternal absence as negligent and blaming the mother for the consequences of her death or departure.[4] *Pretty Woman*, for example, explicitly blames the absent mother for Vivian's fate and Edward's mother for driving his father into the arms of another woman. The anthropomorphic hero of *The Fox and the Hound* suffers cruel vicissitudes as a result of being abandoned first by his natural mother and later by his adoptive one, siting the mother as responsible for all ensuing cruelties. However, the very act of mother-blaming constructs the space as active and tears the text open at the very heart of the familial representation.

MOTHERS WHO ARE THERE

As discussed earlier, the small number of natural mothers who *are* present within the text can be organised within active–passive paradigms. The fates of these maternal representations run true to type: active mothers are punished, controlled or rejected, passive mothers quietly ignored.

The Passive Mother

Passive mothers are represented as being obedient to their husbands and subservient to their families. They almost exclusively inhabit and care for the domestic space. They do not work and any glamour or sexual allure they may possess is entirely at the service of their husbands, a vehicle for his social or professional advancement. As 'good mothers', they can lay some claim to moral authenticity, providing a convenient index to the success or failure of the central character, typically a son, but they enjoy little narrative power themselves caring instead for those who do. In *Staying Alive*, for example, the mother is a fixed point, a place of refuge and reinforcement for Tony Maneiro as he carves his career from the hearts of various women. *The Untouchables* and *Private Benjamin* both feature mothers entirely in thrall to their husbands, servicing their needs by maintaining the family unit. Any activity the passive mother does undertake is entirely at the service of her family. Thus, in *Rocky IV*, Adrian initially resists her husband's decision to fight but succumbs and supports his training regime as she realises the seriousness of it and the potential threat to her family. The mothers in *Indiana Jones and the Temple of Doom* passively wait for Jones to release their children, entirely subservient to the desire to reconstitute their families and are soulfully grateful when he does so.

The Active Mother

Active mothers either dominate and control their families or seek satisfaction outside them. These mothers run the risks posed by the father; of crossing the public/private boundary and thereby compromising the family. These mothers must be reincorporated into patriarchy or expelled completely. Different measures of punishment are meted out according to the severity of the transgression and the cultural or social allegiances of the mother. *The Jazz Singer*, for example, counterpoises an active present mother with a passive, dead one. The virtue of the latter, however, is tainted by her Jewishness, representing a culture alien to the film's value structure. By contrast, Molly, the active mother, is far closer to the ideological centre of the film and can thus be redeemed through reproducing an ideologically sound family. Molly is presented in direct opposition to Jess's own dead mother, who is portrayed *in absentia* as an archetypal loyal Jewish mother and to Ruth, his steadfast wife. Molly, by contrast, is an active producer of Jess's career, finally bearing his child, for which she is rewarded by a final reconciliation with Jess and his father. It is her reproduction rather than her musical productivity which is rewarded. However, it is also possible to read the final reconciliation as a celebration of Molly's efforts at establishing Jess's career, a success which, however vicarious, still rewards her activity outside the home and, inversely, punishes Ruth.

By contrast, in a far more regressive move, the synonymous heroine of *Look Who's Talking* is reinscribed within a doubly patriarchal relationship by the combined efforts of her son and James, her future husband, as reward for her transgressions. This Molly has given birth to the voluble Mikey, offspring of an affair with a deceitful, self-obsessed married man. She compounds her sin by wilfully evading the 'true' surrogate father in a quest to find a perfect one. Her quest is doomed to failure from the start, her judgement consistently represented as faulty by her liaison with Mikey's natural father, her choice of suitors, her rejection of James and by her ignorance of Mikey's wishes as she fumbles with career and childcare. As the film progresses and she is increasingly attracted to James, she is represented less frequently in the work environment (the final workplace scene indicates her deteriorating performance) and almost entirely at home, in the company of Mikey and, finally, of James. Molly settles for a happy ending, her career ambitions sublimated to the happiness of her son and the desires of Mikey's 'real' father. Her sexual and professional activity are retrospectively tolerated because she has returned to her primary duties of chastity and care. In a similar move, Lorraine's unwitting seduction of her son in *Back to the Future* is recuperated through her transformation from slovenly, nagging mother to perfect, home-making wife. She is gradually reinscribed through her son's makeover of her persona. When mothers admit their transgression, they can be incorporated within patriarchy. Indeed, confession is a precondition for recuperation. In *Honey, I Shrunk the Kids*, Diane Szalinski 'confesses' that she has neglected her domestic duties, vowing to give up her job and return to the home, despite the fact that her children are both of high-school age. In doing so, she perversely castigates herself for the outcome of her husband's neglect.

Other mothers who transgress representational norms are dealt with more severely. Trish Murtaugh, in *Lethal Weapon 2*, is ruthlessly punished for her assertiveness at home by being banished from it. Trish is not only assertive but black, problematising her husband's submission to Riggs by her own authority. She is first seen admonishing her husband and is clearly dominant within the family circle, having access to domestic discourses and affections her husband is not privy to and which she uses to exclude or control him. Murtaugh's marginalisation within the home space is tauntingly summarised by the man constructing his 'den'. When Murtaugh grumbles that, 'A man's not safe in his own home', the builder dismissively replies, 'Well stay out of it then', implicitly reminding us that Murtaugh is not safe outside it either. The film incorporates Murtaugh's racial difference by subordinating him to the maverick Riggs, who continually risks his life, in symmetry with Trish's subsequent subordination and endangerment. Murtaugh is further humiliated by his ignorance of his daughter's boyfriend and the nature of the advertisement she is to appear in. While Murtaugh triumphs by separating daughter and boyfriend and by turning the builder's tools into weapons in his fight with the criminals, Trish's reward for her challenge to paternal authority is firstly to be tied up and threatened (significantly, in the marital bed) and then to be exiled from it – 'for her own protection'. The most transgressive mothers are banished entirely from the text. In *Kramer versus Kramer*, Joanna's rebellion against her husband's neglect is punished by the loss of her son. Yet her penalty is marginally leavened by her agency in it, her ostracism is self-chosen and her success in her new career is evident. Creating intertextual resonances which anchor these readings even more firmly, Joanna is played by Meryl Streep, an actress who suffers a similar fate as Karen in *Out of Africa*.

Active Passivity and the Family

Thus mothers are rewarded for their home-making and good wife-and-motherly skills whereas mothers who go out to work or exhibit passions or ambitions outside the domestic space are represented as fallen and are punished. If active mothers are successfully 'retrained' to passivity and family life, it is through the agency of their offspring, usually their sons. Yet these active/passive oppositions are not so simplistic – just as

Shakespeare's Katharina was tamed, so Bianca became rebellious.[5] Even the most stereotyped mothers contest their representations. In *Rocky IV*, for example, the feisty Adrian challenges her husband and is clearly an important decision-maker in the 'family business' of boxing. She flies out independently to an isolated and inhospitable region of Russia during the height of the Cold War to support her husband's training. Despite being ignored by Rocky in his victory speech, it is clear that much of the credit for the victory must lie with her. It is Mrs Maneiro who prompts the revitalisation of her son's career in *Staying Alive*. On his sole visit home for comfort and food, she angrily confronts him when he is defeatist about his career, 'I don't believe this! Your attitude got you out of this neighbourhood so you must have been doing something right.' Implicitly, she is represented as Tony's tutor – her role is that of expert mentor, knowing when to coach, when to let go. Yet her bewilderment and pain at being left behind are very real. Her poignant final words are spoken after Tony's showstopping finale, 'When did you learn to do this?' While she is a positive influence on his achievement of the aspirational resolution, she also reinforces his narcissism, his inability to change and even his belief in the undesirability of change. Her agency is entirely subservient to his desire. Without her intervention he might not have carried on.

In *Coming to America*, Queen Acacia also bends to her son's whims. She challenges her husband's resistance to Prince Akeem's girlfriend and is the architect of the final union, even usurping her husband's choice of bride and inserting her own. As well as fulfilling familial desires, mothers also act to repel invasions from outside the home. Lynn Peltzer, in *Gremlins*, otherwise a passive, homey mother, destroys an invasion of horrific creatures by liquidising them. In a film that deals directly with the underbelly of suburban mid-America, depicting a Lynchian world of horrific interiors and topographies, the weapons of the domestic are wielded upon the terrors introduced from outside by a mother who liquidates the intruders her husband brought into the home. The home itself – and its immediate neighbourhood – is far from an innocent environment needing protection from the outside world and Lynn is clearly mistress of it. Her suburb is profoundly more problematic than the cosy ideal of familial ideology. However, in all these cases, it is clear that such activity remains in the service of maintaining the family unit. These mothers are still primarily focused on the domestic and their roles are to preserve, nurture and protect it.

While these maternal representations inhabit the same discursive terrain as traditional forms, particularly their occupation of active/passive dimensions, they are also more complex in their engagement with it. It is possible to identify contesting elements of the maternal representation which do not sit so snugly in the mould. Mothers who are too transgressive are still punished, but the transgression survives in the very act of its representation.

TWO PRESENT MOTHERS: *TERMS OF ENDEARMENT* AND *FATAL ATTRACTION*

A closer analysis of two 'present-mother' texts, *Terms of Endearment* and *Fatal Attraction*, indicates the range of contradictions in play between maternal representation and narrative motivation. Both films were hugely popular and both draw on melodramatic modes. The former film permits more space for a recuperative reading. The latter, constrained by a combination of generic impulses, represents a maternal figure who is far more circumscribed. Both films draw on a melodramatic tradition directly concerned with renegotiating moral and social mores, a tradition which provided a vehicle for confronting and incorporating social problems. What the films also have in common are the problems they confront, specifically, the nature of motherhood and the mother's role within and outside the family, problems increasingly at issue as more women entered the workforce and men re-entered the home.

Terms of Endearment directly takes the family – its creation, constitution and regeneration – as its subject matter. This is signified in its representational field, its generic mode as melodrama and its organisation of time and space. The text is constructed around the rhythms and milestones of family life within highly specified domestic locations. Family events both trigger and close the narrative which encompasses the lifespan, literally, from cradle to grave, of one woman, Emma, and her relationship with her mother, Aurora. Around this duo, a matrix of other relationships is constructed, including the generation and dispersal of Emma's own family grouping. On the widowing of her mother at the opening of the film, the young Emma is charged with her care by a family friend. Emma fulfils these often onerous duties until her marriage to Flap, which her mother strongly opposes. The marriage bumps rockily over the birth of their two children, the competing demands of Aurora, Flap's constant infidelities, Emma's own brief affair and finally founders with Emma's death.

The film enjoyed phenomenal success at the box office and was nominated for eleven Oscars. It received a mixed reception from the critics, a reception which gives some indication of the film's textual contradictions and revealed both how provocative maternal representations were in the eighties and how little any film is able to control its own readings. Press reviews focused primarily on genre and performance, particularly the performances of the film's stars: Shirley MacLaine, Debra Winger and Jack Nicholson. The film was frequently described as a woman's film and, reviving the contemptuous discourses around this genre in the 1930s and 1940s, just as frequently dismissed on this basis. Women were explicitly linked with certain forms of trivialised emotion and thereby diminished. One reviewer labelled it, 'A woman's film. Gossipy, amusing, tender . . . a tidal wave of sentimentality', echoing another, 'a woman's film . . . biggest load of slush'.[6] The press coverage was explicitly gendered, conflating the female stars with the much-derided femininity of the genre, while excluding Nicholson from the same stigma. Nicholson was generally praised, even by those critics who expressed dissatisfaction with his tendency to play his star persona off against his character within a text. As one critic put it, 'He brings a sharp masculinity to the blanket femininity.'[7] A review in *The Spectator* even suggested that the film represented the death-throes of feminism while condemning it for those qualities ('caring', 'warm', 'tender', 'sensitive') that feminists have refuted as exclusively female and which were, in any case, increasingly being appropriated for masculinity.[8] The actresses themselves were criticised for being publicly active. In a highly charged summary, Vincent Canby suggested that MacLaine had sacrificed her primary duties to her public ambitions, pointing to her 'very busy private life . . . outspoken feminist and sexual revolutionary (well sort of), author, on first name basis with all sorts of people in and out of government . . . deep thinker about reincarnation, Miss MacLaine has sometimes seemed too busy creating a public character to be able to create the fictional ones that are a performer's profession'.[9] Much was also made of MacLaine and Winger's rivalry, particularly over their credits, in an extratextual attempt to rupture their intense fictional relationship.

In common with many films with a realist aesthetic, the film was explicitly measured by its proximity to 'reality'. *The Spectator* insisted that the textual rhythms of the fiction film should be those of 'real life' and confused this further by insisting that the film's adequacy to show real life was a precondition for audience identification. The underlying implication was that women's lives could not be 'real life' – and that women were not equipped to deal with it. 'Some recent American movies have been trying to re-write post-war history, others to interpret it afresh. *Terms of Endearment* – as poorly written, edited, designed, lit and acted a film as I've seen this year – pretends that nothing of consequence has happened in America over the past 3 decades. This abstract quality of the film may be at the root of its popularity.'[10] The elision of its formal competence with a failure to reflect historical events evaded debate over the nature of the 'abstract', specifically the problematic of ideology itself, and its attractions for audiences. Reviewers did not reflect on whether engaging with the 'abstract' was a valid way of approaching a knowledge of the real. Such views not only confused ontologically discrete categories but ignored the film's outstanding box-office success, thereby ignoring the long and honourable tradition of melodramatic enquiry into the fabric of culture itself, a tradition which has proved highly popular with film audiences. In a similar vein, the influential Pauline Kael bemoaned the film's representation of 'real' mothers and daughters, 'They don't have the uncanny similarities . . . of real mothers and daughters.' *You Magazine* took this reflectionist critique a stage further, featuring a mother and daughter who 'saw the film and here talk about their reaction', directly comparing the film to their own version of reality.[11]

These reviews identified the critics' huge investment in the realist aesthetic as a criterion for critical discrimination while largely ignoring the imaginative resource it provided for understanding a complex and changing reality. The purely reflectionist criticism practised by the majority of press reviewers simply conflated fiction with reality and obviated any reference to theory and, particularly to the workings of ideology. Films could therefore be praised or condemned on the critic's own 'naturalised' value system and endorsed by appeals to a commonsense, transparent reality. In a virtuous circle, it was always a version of reality which directly reflected the critic's ideological position and which took no account of how their position constructed the reality they invoked. This positivist tradition of critique absolved critics from engaging with his or her own value structure or the complex relationship between fiction and actuality while validating their own ideological positions. This practice was of particular relevance to *Terms of Endearment* as the mother–daughter relationship worked against the grain of familial ideology and thus came under close and highly ambivalent scrutiny in the press, scrutiny which generally endorsed patriarchal positions.

The relationship between Emma and Aurora mobilised particularly uneasy and contradictory discourses. *The Daily Telegraph* derided the mother for being 'So possessive of her daughter' and *The Guardian* suggested both primitivism and banality in the mother–daughter bonding, 'it must touch some primal chord in its portrayal of mother–daughter relationship . . . not very interesting'. Another reviewer in *The New York Times* also felt uncomfortable with a 'possibly smothering mother–daughter relationship' in contrast to *Time* magazine which was able to accommodate both women and emotion without derision, 'sisters under the skin, connected not just by kinship but by subtle parallels of emotion and experience'.[12] There are at least two competing readings of the Aurora–Emma bonding which can be supported by the text. Firstly, a patriarchal interpretation which proposes that Emma was incompletely oedipalised due to the early death of her father and the infantilisation of her mother. Aurora's childlikeness is heavily signalled throughout the text from the opening sequence in which she almost climbs into the crib herself. She is represented as needing care and protection by all those around her. The fetishistic, indulgent way in which she is treated by her circle of suitors, her clothing and her behaviour, all mark her as frivolous and childlike. As a result, Emma cannot fully transfer her affections from a parent-figure to her husband, Flap, who thus looks for other, adulterous relationships. By contrast, a feminist reading proposes that the mother–daughter bonding transcends romantic love. Men are important and triadic relationships are clearly possible; indeed, Aurora surrounds herself with admirers, although she scorns their approaches. However, when romantic liaisons are desirable they prove to be unreliable (Flap and Garret) and undesirable if reliable (Ed and Vernon). At the midpoint of this continuum and disrupting conventional patriarchal norms is Emma's relationship with Sam. Stamped as it is by his approval of her treatment of the children, in contrast to Flap's neglect, it solicits spectatorial endorsement. He is the father rather than the lover – Emma is immediately dependent on him financially (he pays for her shopping and he is her bank manager), he occupies the adult world, holds a responsible job and has a clear sense of morality. However, he is also married (his extra-marital activity justified by his gender and his wife's frigidity) and thus the liaison can never be fully consummated by institutional union or incorporated into patriarchy.

This desirable–attainable oscillation displays not only the contradictions of the female Oedipal scenario – the presence/absence of the father in the embodiment of the lover – but also the mechanisms of desire itself – the impossibility of desire and satisfaction in coexistence. The film thus exposes the inadequacies of patriarchy for women's psychic maturation. Women bond with, and rely on, each other (Aurora–Emma–Patsy–Rosie) and accept, tolerantly, the shortcomings of their romantic entanglements. There is, however, within this model a strict hierarchy of relationship. The integrities of blood-tie and class are strictly observed. Patsy cannot adopt Emma's daughter because she is not family and she is also a single career-woman. The only time that Aurora will acknowledge her dependence on the (unstinting and uncritical) affection of Rosie, her servant, is in crisis, when she learns of Emma's cancer. This is also, incidentally, the time at which Aurora ceases to wear her girlish clothes and frills. The Oedipal scenario of this text is played around the catalysing and redemptive figure of Emma, whose illness causes the maturation of both Aurora, her mother, and Garret, the unreconstructed astronaut. On Emma's death, Aurora is able to embrace Flap, acknowledging her daughter's own status as adult and her sexuality, and takes over the role of mother to Emma's children. While Garret metamorphoses into proto-father, the natural father fails utterly. Flap is represented as inadequate and untrustworthy right to the end when he admits his inability to care for his children and falls asleep at Emma's death. He is, ironically, a teacher entrusted with the education of other people's children, a failure he compounds by using his workplace as an environment in which to meet and seduce other women. While the film's conclusion is ambivalent about the future of Aurora and Garret's relationship, the children are definitively located within Aurora's care – they are passed from daughter to mother through the female line.

Throughout the film, it is the children who negotiate the adult world on behalf of a parent. Emma takes on the adult role, interacting with the external world, interpreting the Law and entering the symbolic realm through marriage. She is coded as a solid, sensible brunette who, particularly after her marriage, wears practical, somewhat dowdy clothes.[13] She is also measured constantly on her 'good motherliness', a quality which is used as a moral indicator throughout the film, a standard by which all women can be measured. Although it is ostensibly Emma who is assessed throughout, the judgements in turn offer assessments of her judges. Thus Emma is judged by Flap when he falsely claims that her 'paranoia' (her speculation about his infidelity) is directly due to her pregnancy; by Patsy's New York friends (who deride her role as housekeeper in contrast with their careers, abortions and divorces, only exonerating her because she has been punished by cancer); by Aurora ('you are not special enough to survive a bad marriage'); by Sam (whose seduction is directly prefaced by his praise for her motherly qualities) and by her own children (caustically by Tom, the proto-patriarch: 'You are driving Dad away' but more leniently by her younger son, still bound to her in pre-Oedipal fusion). Their sympathy to the spectator is in direct proportion to their endorsement or condemnation of Emma. Tom also assumes a maturity beyond his years and psychic status. When Emma and Flap move away from Houston, Aurora instructs him to 'look after' his mother. He takes this role very seriously, becoming a constant commentator on, and critic of, his mother's behaviour, assuming the patriarchal role of assigning familial responsibility to his mother while his father's increasing irresponsibility is marginalised in the growing urgency of assigning blame. Emma is consequently accused of 'driving Dad away', after Flap has again uprooted the family and is in the middle of a series of affairs. Tom and Aurora thus become opposing analysts of the family's state of health, their concern justified by the official, institutional diagnosis of Emma's sickness.[14] Tom, for example, appears to be vindicated by his mother's cancer and his subsequent harsh treatment of her does not contradict this. However, Emma is able to convince him that he really loves her, undermining his patriarchal succession and drawing him back into their pre-Oedipal scenario, but also absolving him of blame. It is Garret, in the final scene, who is delegated the task of supervising Tom's maturation, a process which Aurora shortcircuited by her injunction to care for his mother. Reciprocally, Garret is empowered to take on the role of adult–father in this process of exchange.

Maturation is, therefore, the currency of the text. It is less sexuality which is at stake, than the ability to form appropriate relationships within a patriarchal order. Yet, because the construction of subject positions for the spectator proposes identification with the mother–daughter dyad rather than with either of the two men, the irresistible drive throughout the film is towards fusion, bonding with the mother and the denial of regularity and normative, patriarchal boundaries. With the diagnosis of Emma's cancer, however, the narrative thrust shifts and drives towards a very different resolution. While a matriarchal narrative may be traced to this point, it is necessarily more open-ended and cannot achieve closure. The pressure in the mainstream, fictional feature film is towards resolution, however unsatisfactory. Emma must be punished for her adultery while Flap, according to the ancient patriarchal 'double standard', is excused his.[15] Aurora will enter patriarchy through her renewal of motherhood, repressing her anarchic womanliness; Tom can become a child again and Garret can become a father. From an exuberant display of female assertion, all the women are safely incorporated or expelled. These metamorphoses are specified in the film's titling. By the end, the 'terms of endearment' of affective bonding become the terms and conditions of relationships within patriarchy; the Law. The handwritten title in the opening credits (with scrawled kisses underpinning them) are translated into sans-serif block capitals at the end. The film thus achieves an uneasy resolution by punishing one 'loose' mother and substituting one who is punished and reformed by the loss of her daughter and responsibility for the children she resented. It cannot, however, obscure the representation it suppresses: the active, sexual mother.

Fatal Attraction charts the fate of the passive mother. Its UK release was heralded by a storm of controversy in the US which invoked both sexual-political and familial discourses. As one critic noted, the film was 'pre-sold as the movie which set America arguing. Both parable against permissiveness and searing thriller'.[16] Directed by Adrian Lyne (*Flashdance, Nine and a Half Weeks*) the film boasted two major stars, Glenn Close and Michael Douglas, and had grossed $130 million by its UK release-date in mid-January 1988. Scriptwriter Dearden claimed that the story had been inspired by a real-life case and, as with *Terms of Endearment*, press reviews routinely conflated the stars with both their characters in the film and their 'real-life' personae.[17] Close was particularly targeted as synonymous with her character, Alex, and therefore the subject of vitriolic abuse. As the *Daily Mirror* asserted, Close had become 'the most hated woman in America. She's not here for the opening. She had gone off to Connecticut to sort out her own tangled love life. She is expecting a baby by the man she had an affair with before she married her second husband.'[18] A reciprocal, and mutually damaging, relationship was thus established between the behaviour of the star and the character she played. The same article purported to analyse whether the film would deter men from adulterous one-night stands and interviewed various professionals for their opinions. As with *Terms of Endearment*, this realising tendency enabled critics to expound their own beliefs in the guise of reviewing the text which, in turn, confirmed its status as a reference point for opposing sides in contemporary familial debates.

Like *Terms of Endearment*, *Fatal Attraction* takes the family as its point of narrative momentum. The opening pan takes us over the city at night into the family home, a flat in a huge condominium, both unique and typical, refuge from the terrors of night-time New York. There we witness the initial equilibrium of the Gallagher family, Dan, Beth and daughter Ellen, all enjoying the fruits of their affluence, the products from Dan's labours, as the two parents prepare for a party. However, there are already indications of the dynamics and fissures in this ideal family. Beth is shown doing manual domestic labour, under pressure, as Dan works with pen and paper lying on the sofa, the division and hierarchy between intellectual/ manual and public/private work being drawn right from the beginning. Both are working in a space and time reserved for leisure. While Beth's domestic work is culturally sanctioned and continuous, Dan's introduction of public work into the private space is more transgressive. They are also isolated by the pressures and conditions of their lifestyle. No one hears the telephone ring or can speak to each other, separated in the private spaces of the home and drowned out by the television. Dan wears headphones to insulate himself from household and technological interference. This is a family squeezed in the stress and pressure of city life, crowded yet isolated.

These fissures escalate in the events leading up to Dan's illicit weekend with Alex. The party where he first meets Alex is a work-related event happening at a 'family time' – Friday night. This is a party where both sex and achievement are privileged, what conversation there is revolves around one or both topics. Its disruption is also connoted in the otherness of the Japanese, in whose honour the party is held. The text attempts to contain this sense of estrangement and difference by the shots of nodding, bowing and sushi-eating which are both framed and commented on (by Jimmy, the commonsense voice of the 'ordinary man') to emphasise difference, and understated ridicule, from the American way of life. Alex is an intrusion from the world of difference who makes a demand to be taken seriously. In meeting Alex here, Dan has clearly strayed outside the realm of the known and the domestic. Beth's subsequent departure for her parents over the weekend removes the domestic regulation of his sexuality and leaves him exposed to external temptations. The Saturday conference which heralds their second encounter marks a further intrusion of public affairs into the private space. These mergers of public–private spaces and times allow the entry of the disruptive woman and mark Beth as contributor to the event – even if only by her negligence. The affair itself, veering between soft-focus romance (the sequences in the park, the meal) and violent passion (the aggressive lovemaking, the final wrist-slashing, Alex's proximity to the meat market), code the liaison as highly dangerous.

Dan's transgression disrupts established hierarchies of power and gender. When the family are reunited, to Dan's clear relief, both women compete for his subjugation. Beth is the 'natural' winner by virtue of her maternal status. Her goal is to extend the family, moving them nearer her parents to a 'safe place' in the country, Alex's is to rupture it. It is a battle fought over the very spaces and claims of the family. Recognising the terrain, Alex attempts to secure her sexual desire through a claim to maternity, first by asserting her own pregnancy, then by abducting Ellen. This chain of events – triggered by the threat of Alex's confession which prompts his own and his subsequent expulsion from the family home – leads Dan to break in and assault Alex in her flat. Dan's extreme reaction exposes the danger that women pose to patriarchy by speaking. Alex's speech must be repressed, even at the cost of the breakup of the family, the event Dan is ostensibly speaking to prevent. As he strangles her, we have an extraordinary subjective shot of Dan's face from Alex's point of view. His face is so twisted with venom and hatred that it is almost unrecognisable. In this scene, dressed as she is in white, Alex appears innocent and virginal, and so a bizarre juxtaposition has taken place. Although Dan stops before he kills her, he is now doubly marked as

aberrant – a potential killer as well as adulterer. By this stage, Alex has
achieved the literal dismemberment of the family. Her final crusade is to
remove Beth and take her place. In the fight, Dan fails to kill her – twice.
It is Beth who shoots her and reunites the family for, in killing Alex, Beth
also kills her 'baby' – Dan's illegitimate offspring. This is a family whose
inequalities and fragilities are all too easily exposed by the entry of an
assertive, determined woman, a crime for which she is hideously punished.

As in many eighties films, there is no other family to compare the
Gallaghers with. They bear the burden of representation for all families
within the text. The father is depicted as weak, easily tempted. He must
be guarded – specifically at those moments when the public intersects with
the private life of the family. He must also receive adequate sexual stimu-
lation to be rendered safe.[19] He is, however, unable to keep the family
together or defend it appropriately. Unlike Beth, who musters her resources inside the family unit, he looks to the public realm, in this case the
police and the legislature, for protection against Alex, although it was his
elision of public/private that caused the initial disruption. However, the
agencies of the state are shown to be inadequate against the power of the
other, the loose woman, specifically within a domestic context.[20] Throughout the text, Dan appeals to regulation (at the end of their weekend, he
confronts Alex with 'You knew the rules') but is unable to cope when the
game is continued outside those rules.[21] Dan is represented as bound inextricably within patriarchy, deriving his power from law and language –
he hopes to defuse the situation by talking with Alex and, when that fails,
by taking out an injunction. Therefore, although Beth holds her family,
and her own adult identity, together in fragile equilibrium, she can plunge
back into anarchic chaos and act outside both the law (even acting in self-
defence, she could be tried for manslaughter) and patriarchy (she super-
sedes Dan in ejecting the interloper) when she kills Alex. In exposing, but
drawing back from, his ability to kill, Dan demonstrates both his suscep-
tibility and his determination not to abdicate his obedience to the law he
upholds. He must delegate her death to his wife and by maintaining his
own position within the law, jeopardise his patriarchal authority.

Beth is represented as an entirely domestic being whose sexuality and
activity are entirely in the service of the father and the family. She is
located intrinsically within the private space – on both occasions when she
enters public spaces such as the party or the streets when searching for her
daughter, she is damaged. Beth's primary motivation is to strengthen and
unite her family. Like Aurora in *Terms of Endearment*, she is infantilised
and, in many ways, her innocence, her soft clothing and manner, mark her
as closer in representational terms to her daughter, Ellen, than to other

adult women. Both act as indexical markers to the sufferings of the family. When Ellen is stolen away, Beth is physically injured. Ellen is represented as an innocent victim, able to communicate when the adults can't. She answers the phone and lets the babysitter in during the opening scene, she asks when her Daddy is coming home after Beth has expelled him from the house. Ellen's emotions are the marker of familial health and unity, but she, like her father, must be protected.

In contrast to Beth's simplicity, Alex's character is diametrically split: in her androgynous name, her volatility from domesticity to wildness, her self-wounding and aggressive violence and her black/white clothing. She is highly mobile; as a working woman, she transgresses familial boundaries, moving between public and private spaces, city and country. This mobility marks her as excessively unstable and thus highly dangerous. From the first shot of her, rising from a sea of black dresses at the party, blonde hair blazing a radiance around her head, she is connoted as Other. Jimmy's comment, 'If looks could kill', describing her vehement rejection of his lecherous gaze, underlines Alex's assertiveness, her fascination and her danger. She challenges theoretical orthodoxies on women's inevitable specularisation. Although we first see Alex in a subjective shot from Dan's point of view, she holds and returns his gaze before disappearing into the crowd. Again, at the bar, when he sits beside her, it is she who first looks at him and compels him to look back. In contrast to Alex's defiant, enigmatic allure, Beth is familiar, practical and constraining. She calls Dan away from the party, she withholds sex, she confiscates Ellen's gum the next morning. Whereas Alex demands and asserts, Beth denies. In contrast to the Gallagher domestic scene, Alex's flat is a site of passion. Her physicality is underlined by her proximity to the meat market and the way in which she somatises her emotional states. The very framing of the sex scenes use crazy, tilted camera angles to signify the dangerous illicitness of Dan and Alex's relationship which form a skewed symmetry with their later fight, their coupling perilously close to violence, explicitly linking sex with death. Both episodes end with Alex bleeding – the first from a self-inflicted wound, the second from Dan's blows and her own knife-thrusts. She cannot win, her passion is somatised upon her body, disfiguring and, eventually, killing her.

In keeping with her schizoid life, Alex suffers two deaths – the beautiful Ophelia-like drowning and the shooting in which she has a hideous death-mask. Unstable and assertive, she explodes out of the family melodrama mode and pushes the film along the borderline between thriller and horror. In thriller mode, she is the woman who must be tamed but her coding as other and her duality mean that she must be destroyed. She pushes the text from the paranoia of the thriller (concerned with marking boundaries, regularity and containment) to the hysteria of the horror (concerned with the realm of the un-natural and the other, transgressing and stepping over boundaries). Thus she becomes the Monster, a fusion figure conflating oppositional categories, requiring the attention of horror's Final Girl – this time, the mother, Beth.[22] The narrative demands of both the horrific and melodramatic modes work in tension with this dominant structuring of the thriller. The narrative moment of suspense, paramount in the thriller, is specified by the content of melodrama – sexual and family politics. This combination of genres is partly the result of the film's ending which was altered, due to the film's reception at a preview; in the original ending Alex committed suicide to the strains of Madame Butterfly.[23] Such a resolution would have clearly resolved both the thriller and melodramatic trajectories and successfully contained the horrific impulses in the text. However, due to audience demand, the horrific resolution is worked through, producing excess in the realms of the thriller and the melodrama – which require only exclusion or inclusion (usually in the category of romantic love and heterosexual marriage). Such is the monstrousness of the representation of Alex, that nothing less than her destruction can restore equilibrium. As Alexander Walker wryly commented, the film proposed 'a big moral: don't screw around, particularly with women who are wired for a career but fired with having a man too'. Regina Rachelson warned in *The Guardian*, 'What *Fatal Attraction* is really about is that if you are an uppity career woman, you gotta be put down.'[24] The justification for such an excessive death is offered in Alex's perverse rendering of the family narrative in which she accuses Beth of usurping her in Dan's affections. It is secured in the closing shot of the Gallagher family photo which attempts to resolve and obscure the horrific events. Alex's false testimony is thereby contrasted with the visual evidence of the Gallagher family's apparent unity but it is also marked clearly as an alternative discourse within the text. We have, after all, already seen the visual evidence of their disunity.

Perhaps another reason for the choice of narrative resolution was the film's engagement with the discourses mobilised by the new folk-devil menace of AIDS. While in the UK at this time, HIV infection was still largely linked to homosexuality (the 'gay plague'), media representations were beginning to permit the possibility of heterosexual infection – specifically through casual, promiscuous or illicit sex. The film was frequently referred to as a metaphor for the disease, with Alex as 'carrier': the rewards, as the reviewers saw it, of casual sex.[25] Dan's brief affair with Alex leads directly to the material penetration of the family (unlike the 'rules' Dan invokes, AIDS establishes a two-way flow; for external penetration, there is the pay-off of internal penetration). This occurs literally in Alex's own pregnancy ('Part of you is growing inside me, you better get used to it'), but also in Alex's telephone calls and visits first to Dan's private–public space (his office) then to his home. Just as AIDS breaks down the body's immune system, so Alex attacks Dan's immune system (his family, which buttresses and services him for public life and production) to render him vulnerable. Alex's 'double death' signifies the almost certain incurability and immunity of the disease.

SUMMARY

It is possible to identify oppositional readings and contestations of the maternal representation in both these films; Beth's murder of Alex; the disputed ending; Alex's own contested character; Beth's rejection of Dan; the Aurora–Emma relationship and so on, but they are complex and elusive. Within the texts, such challenges are frequently articulated through generic volatility or textual contradictions. It is, however, in the failure of the father that the mother has the greatest potential for transformation. Such transformation was, in the eighties, tentative and frequently eclipsed by the paternal trials and tribulations and the demands of the child, but experiments *in absentia* (*Three Men and a Baby, Out of Africa, Kramer versus Kramer*) were beginning to stir alongside the reinforcement of normative conventions such as those which insisted that mothers could not be sexy, powerful or working. Where they try to be (*Look Who's Talking, Three Men and a Baby, Kramer versus Kramer, Honey, I Shrunk the Kids, Back to the Future, Terms of Endearment*) they are either punished or reincorporated into an incipient family. In addition, very few of these texts are narrated from a maternal, or even a female, viewpoint. Of those that are (*Terms of Endearment, Private Benjamin, Ghost, Out of Africa*) the woman (or mother, if present) is punished by loss. Yet, as we have seen, the transgressions and absence of the maternal figure have begun to unlock hegemonic discursive paradigms. Coupled with the social fragmentation depicted in these films and the increasing crisis over the paternal representation, spaces were beginning to appear for new representations of the maternal figure. Where the father failed, the mother gained a greater potential for redefining her own role, albeit in many instances from a very negative, mother-blaming start point. From outside, or at the margins of the text, mothers were afforded – or could seize – a greater capacity to contest dominant representations by the continuing failure of the fathers. However, the representational figure positioned to gain most from the father's fall was the child. It is to this figure that we next turn.

7 Look Who's Talking: Challenging Children and Parental Inversions

Into the dangerous world I leapt.
Helpless, naked, piping loud
Like a fiend hid in a cloud.
William Blake

'The baby was right.'
Eddy Valiant, *Who Framed Roger Rabbit*

If the fathers are failing and mothers are missing, what of the children?

As we have already noted, the figure of the child was highly privileged in the eighties. Across reproductive and familial discourses, the child was increasingly invested with oracular and legislative powers. Competitive research divided scientific communities over the great nature/nurture debate which gave valuable ammunition to various pro- and anti-familial agencies to invoke the interests of the child on issues ranging from their custody to immunisation. The child was represented as requiring protection from adults who were increasingly attempting to abort, abuse, neglect or corrupt it but it also possessed access to vital truths to which adults were no longer privy. Because of the highly privileged position of the child, adults required to lay claim to authoritative status were frequently represented within a familial setting. From Mrs Thatcher's famed origins as grocer's daughter to Madonna's notorious relations with her father, public figures established their credentials within a familial framework, frequently reconstituting themselves as children to access their association with wisdom, truth and innocence.

There are, therefore, two categories of actual child representations in these films: the adult 'child' represented within a familial structure, still working through the Oedipal scenarios of their own maturation while initiating that of the next generation (represented in around a third of the top box-office films of the decade) and the child-as-child, below the age of majority (represented in just under half of the top box-office films of the decade). Three films in particular, *The Jazz Singer, Coming to America* and *An Officer and a Gentleman*, show how the adult child functioned in the eighties, particularly in their deployment of the paternal seduction. I have chosen a broader range of films to investigate the representation of the child-as-child, particularly its redemptive qualities. There are enormous divergences in the treatment of gender; *Lethal Weapon 2* and *Three Men and a Baby* explore the contemporary conundrums of the daughter while *Look Who's Talking* and *The Golden Child* offer paradigmatic examples of represented sons. Alongside these actual representations, the metaphorical and absent children throw further light on the meanings and functions of the contemporary child. *Who Framed Roger Rabbit* provides a fascinating study of absence played through an innovative amalgamation of animation and realist techniques while *Ghostbusters* exemplifies a metaphorical representation of children rebelling against adults.

THE ABSENT CHILD

Most of these films represent a child as a key character in either a familial or familialised context. Given that the child, or the promise of one, is a precondition for an actual family, its absence is normally sublimated to the narrative goal of the Final Romance. The child's absence, therefore, does not motivate the narrative in such a significant way as the absent parent, although it is an assumed constituent of the resolution. Where an absent child haunts the margins of a familial scenario in films such as in *Out of Africa* or *Ghost*, it generally signifies incompleteness or frustration rather than any positive value. Whereas the absent parent triggered a quest to restore the broken family, the absence of the child is frequently displaced on to frustrated sexuality as in *Out of Africa, '10', Ghost* or *Superman IV*. Alternatively it may function as the subtext to an incipient romantic alliance in films such as *Who Framed Roger Rabbit*. This film provides an explicit example of such displacement, projecting the absent child on to its protagonist, Eddy, who cannot commit to his romance with the loyal Dolores. Eddy's brother was killed, he believes, by the animated Toons, represented as a utopian, anarchic, childish realm of lost innocence. In losing his brother, Eddy has lost his own utopian childhood and the childish side of himself. He is also alienated from the Toon world. Eddy is thus represented as blocked from fun, romance and a full life. In the guise of a murder investigation, the film follows a quest to reintegrate Eddy with his 'lost self', the absence of the child standing in for Eddy's dead brother and what is now missing in Eddy himself. He therefore cannot appreciate the Toons, find the real murderer or give himself fully to the woman who loves him. Once he discovers that it was not the Toons who murdered his brother he is able to find his childish, fun side again, solve the mystery and open the possibility of a utopian family through the Final Romance structure. Interestingly the only child represented is that referenced in the quotation opening this chapter. Baby Herman, an assertive, sexualised, wise Toon, knows the motive for the murder but is not listened to. This, as we will see, is the fate of many truthtelling children within these texts.

Eddy's brother was, however, an adult when he died. It is what was lost with him that is signified as childlike. In these films, children may be banished but their presence is never invoked as a child that once was, but is not now. In other words, the actual loss of a child is not the motivating factor in any of these popular narratives. It is as if this phenomenon was unrepresentable, too harrowing for the most popular texts to show in the eighties. Contemporary horror films, by contrast, explicitly concerned with transgressing boundaries, specifically violated the integrity of the child. The killer in *Halloween*, for example, started his crimes as a child and then continued by specifically threatening children and teenagers. The popular *Nightmare on Elm Street* series not only represents the death of children, but its anti-hero is driven by the desire to destroy them. As so often happens, the eruptions of the horror genre began to seep into mainstream releases by the early nineties as children became less innocent. To take just two examples, the heroine of John Boorman's *Beyond Rangoon* is driven by the murder of her husband and child and in *Shattered*, the heroine has to come to terms with the death of her baby in a plane accident while she held it. In the eighties, though, this actual loss was still unrepresentable in mainstream genres. Thus, although *The Golden Child* figures the search for a kidnapped child as its primary narrative driver, the child is ever-present within the text, featuring constantly through cross-cutting as a index of achievement for the hero and literally marking narrative time. In the eighties, the child, as investment for the future, had to be protected and could not be tolerated as an absence-as-was, only an absence-that-could-yet-be. In that respect it was always a possibility, always inviolate and impregnable. Children may be jeopardised in these films, but they are never killed. As an absence the child therefore disturbs, rather than drives the narrative, inflecting the representational and discursive field rather than directing the narrative trajectory. The narrative potency of the child becomes clearer as we examine those children who are present within the text, whether as children or as adult-children.

THE CHILD AS CHILD

Redeemer Children

Those children who are represented as primary characters in these films signify purity and innocence within a romantic conception of childhood. They are objects of exchange between adults, trophies within various conflicts, but trophies which are also invested with the power to redeem and reconstitute the family scenario. As redeemers, they act as catalysts for dystopian or utopian closures, often within a sexualised moral universe, as in *Lethal Weapon 2* or *Three Men and a Baby*, bartered between highly charged emotional and social positions. The child aims to transform a dystopian family to a utopian, fixed one. Their narrative object is the restoration of a family unit which has been penetrated or broken up. However, the very representation of a prior rupture of the family means that the utopia cannot be guaranteed and, in some instances, such as *E.T.*, closure cannot be achieved at all. As redeemer, the child evokes a stable generational future, a promise that the family can be universal and timeless. This is often secured by invoking a metaphoric, familialised unity, as at the end of *Rocky IV* when the child's name is linked to the ending of the Cold War or in *Superman IV* when a child triggers the entire narrative by his request to Superman to save the planet from nuclear arms proliferation. The contemporary modernist-utopian pressure for each generation to be wealthier, more leisured and happier than the last also permeates these films. In *Rocky IV*, Jim is his father's auto-enactment, the embodiment of his desire for the future: 'I fight so you don't have to fight.' This paternal sacrifice masks a vested interest. Rocky wishes paradoxically that Jim will succeed by not being like his father, but also that he himself can live again through his son. The child is the guardian as well as the condition for a utopian family, a family unit on which the father has staked so much. It is the child, therefore, to whom the moral power balance shifts when the father fails, not the mother. Thus Jim is explicitly positioned as the guarantor of resolution – the final appeal that everything will be all right. When the Russian premier and Politburo rise to applaud Rocky's victory over Drago, Rocky confides to the camera: 'I just want to say to my kid, Merry Christmas, Jim', summoning not only the approval of his son but the 'family time' of Christmas in perpetuity. Yet this stability is undermined by its dependence on the one family member who is guaranteed to mature and change and who is narratively impotent.

Children enjoy a specific moral authenticity and privileged access to certain forms of knowledge. However, they do not enjoy autonomous narrative power; their ability to restore the family is only operable under the licence and control of adults. Thus, although Shorty can psychically loose Indiana Jones from the spell of the other, he requires Indiana to physically release both the proto-family and the other children from incarceration in the *Temple of Doom*. Billy Peltzer reveals the truth about his family's suburban neighbourhood through the medium of the mogwais in *Gremlins*, but requires the intervention of the curio-shop proprietor to finally restore the family. Similarly, the eponymous Annie can reveal the truth of Grace and 'Daddy' Warbucks's affection for each other but she relies on Grace's resources and Warbucks's wealth to release her from the cruelties of the orphanage. In *Honey, I Shrunk the Kids*, Wayne's children demonstrate the fissures in their family but it is Wayne who must finally restore them to their normal size, releasing them from the physical endangerment he himself created. It is the constant paradox of the childhood paradigm that children speak the truth while only adults can act on it and adults – most frequently fathers – are the figures who place them in danger. Indiana led Shorty into the Temple of Doom; Billy's father gave him the mogwai; Annie's guardian exposed her to Lily and Rooster; Wayne's machine shrank his children. Fathers jeopardise children by activity, mothers do so by neglect or absence. Because the father has ultimate power over familial closures, the child cannot guarantee a utopian outcome, only influence it. The primary function of the child is to register the moral and emotional claims of competing adults across psychic and social terrains. In these contests, the child is frequently registered as a victim, although a victim with the power of truthful speech. The child indexes the moral centre of highly gendered power struggles, particularly the competing claims for 'true' parenthood staked in films such as *Kramer versus Kramer, Look Who's Talking, Fatal Attraction* or *Back to the Future* and even the international and interpersonal conflicts dramatised in the *Rocky* films. In all these films, children perform a dual role, both subject to, and subject of, larger social and family dynamics in which they mark the locus of truth.[1]

The redeemer-children embody an ideal, a romantic innocence, despite their streetwise talk and precociousness. Not only do children operate as moral and emotional barometers, they also comment on the narrative. *Honey, I Shrunk the Kids* is punctuated by multiple levels of commentary from the Szalinski and Thompson children on their own, and each others', families. Apparent dysfunctionalities (Wayne's scientific obsessions, Diane's job, Russell's machismo and Amy's disinterest) are smoothed out during the children's microscopic Oedipal journey through the back-garden to the house. They restore their own intra-generational hierarchies and sexual relationships in parallel with those of their parents, proving the value of

Wayne's work, modifying Russell's machismo and bringing Diane back into the home. The children act as indicators to their parents' metamorphoses – Amy grows more docile just as her mother decides to give up her job; Nick and Wayne become less dreamy and more purposeful in their scientific endeavours, finally pressing the shrinking machine into the service of the family to 'grow' the celebratory turkey; Big Russell and Ron become less aggressive and more courageous; Little Russell is transformed from peeping-tom wimp to leader–lover. The dysfunctional families are restored by the microscopic, parallel performance of the required transformation which is enacted through a truthtelling chorus of children. The children are both commentators on, and catalysts of change – truthtellers and performers within the Oedipal drama. By the same token, the redeemer-child anneals social difference and inequality. In *Indiana Jones and the Temple of Doom*, the rescued children are emblematic of a utopian family structure in which racial difference is subjugated under the rubric of an exotic other, signified in the final sequence. Willie is literally 'whipped in' by Indiana, melting in his arms, until Shorty, the heroic 'son' douses them in water – a predictable response to what is, in effect, a Primal Scene. The village children flood around them, pulling them apart in the final sequence and signifying that the Final Romance is doomed. Although Shorty rescues Indiana from his brainwashing by the Thugees, he cannot redeem Indiana's promiscuity and father-fixation. He is the heroic rescuer, liberating Indie from the spell of the Other but he cannot finally deliver him to a stable family unit. This would require a stronger differentiation from the father – a feat achieved in *The Golden Child* in which the child has a similar function to that of Shorty (effacing racial difference and achieving heterosexual bonding) but is able to bring about a romantic resolution.

As we have seen, the child's function as redeemer is frequently blocked. This is particularly true when the child is female or where the familial breakdown is due to pressures outside the family scene. Sons are far more powerful than daughters. They negotiate the symbolic realm and their own objectification and commodification within it, with greater ease and success. Daughters are more simply abandoned or victimised. Sons can actively construct new families for themselves – most literally in *Look Who's Talking* and *Back to the Future*. Daughters must rely on adult – usually female – intervention and support (in *Annie*, *Tootsie*, *Three Men and a Baby*, *Beetlejuice*, *Terms of Endearment* or *Fatal Attraction*, for example) which is one reason why maternal treachery or neglect is so insupportable. This paradigm of patriarchy prefigures the son's paternal power and allays male anxiety at not fully possessing the reproductive function. However, this paradigm is contested by powerful mother–daughter bonds. The daughter accesses affiliative rather than autonomous power to solve problems by forming strong, usually female, alliances.

Redeemer Daughters: *Lethal Weapon 2* and *Three Men and a Baby*

Lethal Weapon 2 cannot close on a complete family. Like *The Untouchables* or *Beverly Hills Cop*, the film is ruptured by the pull of the professional family, but also, more importantly, of the homoerotic buddy-bonding. Significantly too, the children in these films are female. Murtaugh 'trades in' his family for the final bonding with Riggs, a relationship which competes with his allegiance to the familialised regime of the police force. The sexualisation of his daughter, her literal translation into sexual commodity, epitomises the familial politics in play. Rianne is accepted by her father as adult and sexual, and thereby incorporated into the economy of male exchange through the police 'family', rather than Murtaugh's own. This exchange is intriguing. By starring in a condom ad, Rianne commodifies herself, literally putting herself 'on the market'. She is represented as a legitimate object of desire, the safe-sex message of the condom advert in which she stars consolidating her position within a heterosexual economy. She thus becomes 'available' to potential suitors and her father must give her up. She is actively selling the antidote to a fear which might once have bound her to him; the fear of pregnancy or, contemporarily, AIDS.

Murtaugh's reaction to the ad is perhaps predictable – he strenuously denies it, just as he has her new boyfriend moments before. It is Riggs who negotiates Murtaugh's reaction with his daughter, ensuring Rianne's sexual maturation and confirming her availability. The police family both confirms Rianne's availability and presents her back to her father. In giving him the 'rubber tree', the rowdy, jeering policemen ironically play back Murtaugh's own desire to him, consolidating his ownership and legitimating his desire while he releases her, by his reluctant laughter, to the objectification of his colleagues. He regains his position within the police family by giving up his daughter, but also by turning his possession into desire. This paternal threat to the daughter is then enacted through the penetration of Murtaugh's home by Rudd's henchmen, a crime Murtaugh has himself instigated through his own illegal penetration of the criminal 'family'. Our final image of Rianne is when she releases Murtaugh after they have left. The bonds between father and family are literally severed by Murtaugh's decision to continue to investigate Rudd, long after the police 'family' has withdrawn its support. Murtaugh thereby negotiates his daughter's entry to the symbolic, rendering her available to other men, while retaining control over her after she has, ironically, released him. However, he then allows his family to be endangered and the domestic space to be penetrated through his transgressive desire for Riggs. In this sexual negotiation, his family are the victims, evicted and endangered by the Riggs–Murtaugh bonding. The family harmony represented at the beginning of the film and sustained by the close mother and daughter tie is disrupted and invisible by the end.

In *Three Men and a Baby*, the child is not only commodified but fetishised. Abandoned baby Mary is constantly articulated in the narrative as a substitute or replacement for other forms of illicit pleasure, notably heroin. The parallel plots of two 'wrong deliveries' (the drugs and the baby) are intertwined and misrecognised until they become both verbally and iconographically indistinguishable. Jack disguises the heroin as a pregnancy, then hides the drugs in Mary's nappy. The men routinely talk about 'shit', confusing the baby's faeces (which they find disturbing) with the heroin, most notably in a farcical conversation with the investigating policeman. The film thus displaces its anxieties over the unnatural crime of maternal abandonment on to the criminality of drugtaking; the infraction of the symbolic law to the infraction of criminal laws. These latter transgressions can be handled by the conventional detective device of stepping outside the law in order to solve the crime. However, the former infraction is less perfectly healed. The abandoning mother is brought back into the narrative, but her appearance cannot gloss her crime or the way in which her primary function has been usurped by the men. Nor can it obscure the overt sexualisation of the infant. The baby has been fetishised as illicit object of pleasure and desire (heroin/baby) and the men have, after their initial distaste and incompetence, assumed the nurturing functions of the good mother. The sexuality which saturated the opening sequence of the film in the representation of the flatmates' promiscuity is transferred to the baby and their growing intimacy with each other. Mary's relationship to the three men is increasingly eroticised. In the obsessive nurturing of the infant girl, her body is repeatedly displayed and fondled. The men become preoccupied with her genitalia and bodily functions, neglecting both work and other relationships. This daughter can only redeem the fathers through complicit paedophilia or – as happens – by a hasty alliance with the mother at the close of the film. In this film, only the men can guarantee a utopian family. However, such guarantees are flawed by their homoerotic intimacy and their inability to form permanent, loving relationships with mature women.

Daughters on their own are powerless: Mary only gains the potential for narrative agency with the return of her mother. Similarly, Lydia, the

daughter in *Beetlejuice*, is quicker than the rest of her horrendous family
to see the truth of Adam and Barbara's ghostly existence, but is unable to
manage their responses to it. Her own alliance with Betelgeuse in a desperate bid to save the Maitlands from exorcism is doomed by her gender
– she must marry him to get him to cooperate. All daughters need help.
Emma must ally with Aurora (*Terms of Endearment*), Annie with Grace
(*Annie*) and Julie with Michael/Dorothy (*Tootsie*) to retrain the fathers and
redeem the families. Although they are privileged, they have no control or
authority in the narrative. Like Cassandra, they are doomed to express the
truth (articulated most frequently across their bodies rather than spoken)
but not to be heard or hearkened to. Even their names connote feminine
archetypes of passivity and powerlessness.

Redeemer Sons: *Look Who's Talking* and *The Golden Child*

The most privileged redeemer son is Mikey in *Look Who's Talking*. Two
structuring devices, the voice-over and the opening sequence, give him
authorial control over the narrative just as his conception initiates it. This
is an 'educational' movie in which Mikey and James together teach Molly
how to become a good mother by learning what makes a good father. The
pedagogical character of the narrative is indicated by the frequent
taxonomies of the perfect father. Molly's own definition is supplanted by
that of James who then steps into the paternal role. Just prior to Mikey's
conception in the opening scene, Molly lists Albert's (Mikey's 'real' father) qualities as a lover and father and rehearses the qualities she's looking for to her best friend Rosa. Later, Molly's mother lists the reasons she
married Molly's father, topped by James summarising the perfect characteristic to Mikey, 'I think being a good father is keeping the mother happy
so she doesn't drive the kids crazy' which Molly overhears on the baby
intercom and apparently internalises. In this sequence, James has 'become'
a baby too, privileged by his association with Mikey, the ultimate truth-
bearer. Mom listens to their baby conversation and 'knows' it to be true,
by virtue of its source. There is no further attempt to define the ideal father
after this. Within this discursive frame, it is the child who is overtly
privileged. Both father and mother are subservient to his needs, although
the mother is most subordinate of all, subject to the father's blandishments
and 'kept happy' like a perfect breeding machine.

The film addresses head-on the problem of paternity. Since the real
tension in the film is between social and biological determinants of paternity, the characters' reactions to Molly's (false) assertion that she was
artificially inseminated is a crucial indicator to social condemnation of a

mother's control over her own fertility. In severing the biological function, James enters the film already coded as a socially defined father. The film solves this not-father dilemma by allocating authorial control to Mikey who then validates James within the paternal role. The child has the power to confirm the father and it is the paternal role which is most important within this paradigm. The narrative is explicitly a trajectory of finding the good father and coaching the mother to accept him, a search in which the interests of the child are paramount, the desires of the mother sublimated and in which the father acts as tutor. The moment of resolution occurs with Mikey's first spoken word: 'Daddy'. Molly's relationship to the child is assumed and need not be spoken, James's must be struggled for. While this gives a certain amount of power to mothers, it is a power which is under the direction of the child. Molly must 'lose control' in order to find the father for Mikey: an injunction which is made explicit when James first teaches her to fly ('I'm so nervous. I feel out of control') and then makes love to her, to the strains of 'Daddy's Home'. Her final rebellion, as she rejects James by reclaiming control ('I can't get swept up in emotion and sex and stuff') is revealed as her own wilful ignorance and self-interest when it is finally obliterated by Mikey's closing statement, 'I'm glad I got you two together. I want James to be the daddy.' Mikey's voice-over commentary consistently distances the spectator from Molly's point-of-view narration. She is undermined by the knowledge the spectator is given of Mikey's real state of mind, notably his desire for James, the feelings she ascribes to him and the feelings she denies in herself. Mikey and James constantly compare notes on Molly, an exchange in which she becomes an object of scientific interest rather than desire. She is also constantly penetrated – the spectator has almost unlimited access to her – through Mikey's voice-over, through Molly's own words, through her fallopian tubes and via James's final insemination. Every decision she makes independently turns out to be wrong and she has to be guided by men. The messages proffered by the narrative are that women, especially mothers, are unreliable, that biological paternity is not the guarantee of good fatherhood; that female control over reproduction is not a viable or desirable option; that rigorous objective selection of a partner does not work; and that romantic love and choice are the correct bases for parenthood. However, the most intriguing aspect of Mikey's control over the narrative is his function as pander. He reproduces the primal scene in arranging his mother's relationship to James, thereby becoming father to his own parents. This reproductive loop is, as noted earlier, rehearsed across several of these films (*Back to the Future, Total Recall, E.T.*) establishing a discourse in which the reproductive desire of the son is to be one's own father, to be the ultimate creator, not only of future generations, but of oneself. Thus the anxieties of paternity are rooted in biology, but the solutions are constructed as social and psychic.

The Golden Child also elides the father–son roles within moral and narrational universes which are internally conflicted and frequently paradoxical. Constructed with an eye to a family audience, its primary genre is closest to that of fantasy while combining elements of the gumshoe thriller, comedy and horror. An exoticised racial dimension is further complicated by the casting of the black, wisecracking popular star, Eddie Murphy, as the hero. It is a complex film which articulates clearly the dilemmas of the represented child in this period. A magical Tibetan child is kidnapped by demonic forces, led by Sardo Numspa; and Chandler, an American who investigates the disappearance of children, is identified as the 'chosen one' to rescue him. Constructed by stark oppositions, the narrative nevertheless constantly reverses and conflates them. The eponymous child is excessively privileged, constantly bathed in golden light, endowed with magical properties and spiritual purity: he is seraphic and serene. He is moreover, an object of both worship and desire. His positioning is secured in the opening sequence of the film which depicts his childish delight at the puppet show and whimsical choice of jewellery but also his enormous power when the monks bow down before him as he heals a wounded bird. Diametrically opposed to his beneficial powers are the evil forces of Numspa who burst in, ruthlessly slaughter the monks and capture him. However, he is represented as infinitely superior, despite his entrapment; none of the demon's henchmen can touch him or they will be immediately converted. The iconography and significations of the child (gentle, passive, beneficent, wise, soft) all locate him in direct opposition to Numspa, who is aggressive, active, evil, cunning and hard.

Similarly opposed are the realms of Tibet and Los Angeles. The film is saturated in mythical geographic signifiers, the pre-credit and credit sequences establishing the film's topography. Tibet is represented as a cold, primitive, anarchic world which nevertheless literally has a heart of gold and access to powerful spiritual understanding. In Los Angeles, this 'heart of gold' (as represented by Chandler) is drowned out by competing egos and commercial attractions as he is drowned out by the chat-show host eager to talk about more sexy and self-gratifying subjects than missing teenagers. In a reprise of the *Beverly Hills Cop* montages, we first see Chandler delightedly gazing at a series of American, and specifically Hollywood, icons which mirror the Golden Child's earlier delight at his surroundings. The film constructs an impossible diegesis in this sequence, the condensed cutting and oblique camera angles purporting to be Chandler's point of view as he walks through the LA streets; sights which are desired but unachievable. Chandler thus both looks at, and delights in, the glitzy spectacle of Hollywood, but is signified as an outsider looking in. Chandler's race and morality bar him from full social membership. Despite his streetwise patter and immersion in city life, he remains untouched and uncontaminated. Pure of heart, he is the 'chosen one', who is constructed as physically and emotionally close to children – to being a child.

This opening sequence is also an ironic pastiche of one of the film's central problematics: the conflation of competing and contradictory genres coalescing around Murphy's own star persona. The generic tropes of fantasy (the magical gifts; the simple good/evil dichotomy; the oracle, the bestiary and fantastic devices) sit uneasily with those of *noir* and horror (Chandler, the gumshoe investigator; the complex moral patterns of urban street crime; the biker sequence; the grisly photos of the dead teenager; the bowl of blood; the nightmare dream sequences and particularly of Kee as fetish object) and, most damaging of all, the comic, even farcical, vein that runs throughout. At its centre is Chandler–Murphy, the proto-father who is also proto-child. One the one hand, he is pure of heart, a rescuer of children. On the other, he is streetwise, black (neither Tibetan nor WASP) and not above deceit. His role of investigator recalls the star's earlier successes as rebellious 'son', most notably within the crime thriller genre, consolidated by the parodies of his *Beverly Hills Cop* persona – an investigator who finds lost children, his incompetence in the action scenes (he constantly has to be rescued by Kee), the transfer of his professional affiliations from men to a woman, his dependence upon spiritual mechanisms for information and his final affirmation in a nuclear familial, rather than a professionally bonded, unit. Nothing in the text is as it seems. There is a preponderance of masks and screens and an elision of sleeping/waking sequences reminiscent of those in a horror film. Beggars transform into foulmouthed high priests, the virginal Kee into a leather-clad seducer, the smooth-talking Numspa into a scaly, winged demon, the librarian oracle into a dragon. Chandler's persona constantly veers between ironic parody and heartfelt sentiment, unlikely and unreliable, despite his final success.

It is the child who is reliable, privileged and pure. He is, however, only able to redeem his 'father' because Chandler himself has a pristine heart. This child is shown outside the domestic setting, a child who has to be constantly protected from a rude and ruthless world, a child that cannot come into contact with the ultimate impurity – a woman's blood, ancient symbol of transgression and taboo. Women are entirely marginalised within the film, despite the central presence of Kee Nang. Although Chandler is searching for a missing girl at the film's opening, it is not her murder that motivates the narrative, it is the threat to the son. Similarly, although Kee Nang is the prime mover in forcing Chandler to rescue the Child and constantly rescues him from danger, finally 'dying' herself while trying to save him, it is Chandler who is the chosen one and only he who can seize the Ashanti dagger and save the Child. No resolution is possible until the victim turns hero and Chandler resurrects Kee Nang. A woman's blood is the corrupting influence and a woman can become a wife only after being recreated by the father. Women are purely agents for the development of men rather than being developed or able to achieve resolution themselves but they are also potentially deadly and corrupting.

In this film too, then, the emphasis is on the social father, the father who can only claim the child after proving that he is pure and worthy enough to do so. This is an archetypal rite of passage movie, except the reversal here is that the child is always-already in existence, a magical entity who awaits the hero like a trophy and is, at the same time, the mechanism for enabling the Final Romance. Thus the child becomes father to the romance between Chandler and Kee Nang, a romance in which he is constructed as perfect son, the third corner of a nuclear triangle. The narrative combines the quest theme of the father with his desire to fix the family forever in time and space. The concerns of the narrative are definitively those of the father, the construction and fixture of the nuclear family, yet the solution is the son who paradoxically incarnates the defining anxiety of the father. This Golden Child will never age and is, therefore, most explicitly going to outlive and outperform the father. However, not only is his longevity a problem, but he lived *before* his father and was the cause in bringing the new familial unit into being. Again, we have the incestuous loop of generation which both ensures the circularity and maintenance of the family unit yet undermines its very existence.

The film's resolution is achieved through incorporating this anxiety into an archetypal scene of utopian Americana. The Golden Child, despite his immortality, is now dressed in a baseball cap and jeans, running through long grass. Behind him, bathed in sunshine, stroll the perfect couple, Kee and Chandler. The solution is posited as a utopian fusion of Tibet and America in which Americans are constructed as possessing power without knowledge and the other as possessing knowledge without power. As Kee's father puts it, 'Those magnificent Americans. So much power and so little understanding of what to do with it.' The knowledge is a spiritual knowledge – a knowledge possessed by children but lost to adults. The resolution to the dystopian urban nightmare is represented as a simpler, more 'Tibetan' style life – a life more akin to that of the child. As Chandler says on the chat show: 'All you have to do is care about children.'

The Redemptive Paradox

Although the children in these films are standard-bearers for the future, the standard they bear is a retrogressive one. They bear the imprint of the patriarchal impulse to fix the nuclear family in its public representation of private power relations as permanent and immutable. Here lies the unresolvable contradiction. The child is the hope for the future, the hope that things will be different from the way they are now ('I fight so you don't have to fight') but it is also constructed within a discursive field in which the always-already nuclear family is the ideal. The desire for difference is thus short-circuited by the holds of the past. The representation of the child is produced by the same discursive field which transcribed the rupture of the family which the child strives to anneal. In locating truth, the child also locates untruth.

Pushing the child-obsession even further, the foetus is invested with absolute powers. The foetus is privileged through its ability to represent in the most intensive, stripped-down form, a 'natural' discourse of morality and desire. In accessing the unborn, untainted by environmental influences (a preoccupation explored in *Trading Places*), films can claim to articulate an uncontaminated and unmediated truth – the truth of the innocent; a pure utopia. Thus, magically, the 'natural' desires 'spoken' by Mikey in *Look Who's Talking* come true. Molly sees that the 'true' (social) father for Mikey is James and renounces the 'false' (biological) father along with her own autonomous status, conflating romantic love with true fatherhood. As Mikey confirms, 'I'm glad I got you two together.' In *Back to the Future*, Marty is able to reconstruct his parents at a point in time before he was even conceived – the emblematic foetus-as-concept. Marty can be the perfect father through being the perfect son. The narrative is driven by the desire to create oneself, to be better than the previous generation. When his teacher brusquely asserts that, 'No McFly ever amounted to anything in the history of Hill Valley' Marty confidently responds, 'Well, history is gonna change.' Marty can make the future in his own image, manipulate the generative process and even be his own father. He recreates his family through the mechanism of the photograph which he laboriously reconstructs through his heroic feats. The threat of incest (to be his own father, he must copulate with his mother) is overcome by making Marty the broker for his parents' marriage. His mother's attraction to her son is transferred to the father through the operation of taboo. She is physically unable to kiss him in their transgressive romance. Although Marty, who 'knows' the truth she is excluded from, tries to prevent such transgression, it is his mother's instinctive aversion which preserves the taboo.

It is his father's failure which triggers Marty's quest to do better – to do anything you want, even recreate your own origins. But it is the son who becomes the cause in everything, even his own name. Doc's inspirational words themselves are revealed to have been originally spoken by Marty, before they are repeated back to him by his girlfriend, 'You can accomplish anything if you put your mind to it.' Yet, despite his ability to recreate his parental family, Marty is less successful at creating his own. The film closes on Marty's desperate race into the future to resolve the problems of his own offspring. Undermining his apparent omnipotence, the child is represented as repeating the mistakes of the past in creating the family of the future.

In these films, children are represented as having unique access, and therefore insight, to utopian realities, utopias which construct happy nuclear families. However, their own immaturity and the pressure to recreate the past means that they cannot create or guarantee them.

THE ADULT CHILD

In many of these films, the central characters enact the role of a child. They are the potential parents of the next generation yet have not resolved their relationship with their own parents. Some form of familial resolution is the primary narrative goal. The adult child is not represented as redeemer or as victim in quite the same way as the young child. They have been corrupted by an adult world but have not yet achieved a perfect entry to it. The vast majority of the adult-child narratives are constructed around the relationship with the father and most adult-children are sons. These are rite-of-passage movies, where maturation and a romantic alliance has been blocked by the failure of the father and incomplete separation. The father–child relationship is constructed as antagonistic, but it carries an erotic charge. In focusing, however antipathetically, on the father, the child is unable to successfully enter any other mature form of relationship. All passion is reserved for the father. The attempt to win back affection, therefore, is frequently represented as a seduction rather than persuasion.

The motor behind the majority of these films is the desire to redeem the alienated or disgraced father.[2] While the child-as-child was itself the trophy of parental unity and familial utopia, the adult-child must seek other trophies with which to seduce the father and prove himself worthy of paternal affection. In dystopian films, these trophies are usually the prizes of commercial or professional success, but in utopian films they may be the adult-child's own offspring, as in *The Jazz Singer*. In films such as

Pretty Woman, the *Indiana Jones* series or *Top Gun*, the adult-child sublimates his affections in the private realm to the pursuit of prizes in the public realm. Thus, Indiana Jones continues to bring trophies of his exploits to propitiate various surrogate fathers in his overarching quest to find and redeem the real one. But his attempts are closer to a seduction than a redemption. These attempts are directed at wooing and reclaiming the father, an enterprise in which women are merely surrogate love objects, markers of success in the paternal seduction rather than desired in themselves.

Paternal Seductions: *The Jazz Singer, Coming to America* and *An Officer and a Gentleman*

In *The Jazz Singer*, Jess must seduce his father, Cantor Rabinowitch, into accepting both his gentile single-mother girlfriend and his new career as a singer. The father–son axis is the pivot of the narrative, relegating Jess's career and new girlfriend to second place. In this film women are merely end-markers of the spiritual and emotional space between Jess and his father. At one pole is Ruth, the abandoned wife, clearly identified with the Jewish community. At the other Molly, the epitome of the American Dream. A series of oppositions are constructed: Jewishness/secularism, spiritualism/materialism, community/individualism, sacrifice/hedonism, public/private. *The Jazz Singer* essentially opposes the tightly regulated community of the father to the aspirant individualism of the son; the realm of the immigrant other to the native American Dream. In this film, both father and son must travel, physically and emotionally, to achieve reconciliation. Jess is in introverted, alienated flight from old and new worlds, until recalled by the birth of his child to be confirmed in his new family. The Cantor, though, travels further, between families and closer to accepting his son's new life. Both men are reconciled around the birth of Jess's son. The romance between father and son is played out between these poles as they dance through an inverted Oedipal narrative: the father 'kills' his son, declaring him dead when he deserts his wife and community. Jess finally converts his father by the creation of a new family – Jess, Molly, Cantor and baby – within the new community of show business. Here the dilemma of transience in the family unit is handled at one remove. By siting Jess's original family in the Jewish community, its transformation is positioned as desirable rather than dystopian. The family breakdown and regrouping is offered as a transformation from the abnormal to the normal. The film thus harnesses racial difference in the service of familial ideology, appealing to the meta-utopia of the American Dream as capable of erasing all forms of difference, inequality and contradiction. The film can thus accommodate the abandonment of Ruth and, temporarily, Molly, in the greater goal of father-son reconciliation and cultural unity.

Coming to America is also concerned with reconciling father and son around the ideals of (American) nationhood. Again, two realms are opposed, Africa and America. Along this axis familial values are arranged. In this case American values are those of family, romantic love, monogamy, affection, entrepreneurialism, privacy, discretion and friendship. By contrast, African society is represented as espousing dynasty, arranged marriage, adultery/polygamy, duty, feudalism, lack of privacy, excess and service. Rejecting his father's choice of bride and, implicitly his value structure, Prince Akeem insists on 'finding himself' in America, where he indeed finds his 'natural' identity and his bride. In the process, Akeem must seduce *two* fathers to achieve his object of creating a new family within the dynastic line. These are his own, King Jaffa Jeffer, who insists on an African bride and the traditions of casually exploitative adultery and McDowell, the father of his American girlfriend, Patrice, who insists on a rich husband for his daughter. However, the differences are more generational than national. McDowell is closer to African values than American ones. He is interested in a rich husband for his daughter, happily 'arranging' it as best he can. He runs his fast-food restaurant on a feudal basis and quickly pays obeisance to the visiting King. He is thus seduced by Akeem's attentions far more easily than Jeffer.

Akeem enlists the help of a close manservant, Semmi, and his own mother to seduce his father. The dynamics of the text operate in the father-son, buddy–buddy relationships rather than the heterosexual romance, which is the object rather than the subject of the film. The dynamics of Akeem and Semmi's relationship gradually change gear as both shift from the African value paradigm to the American one. Having always been confidantes, their intimacy changes as Akeem gradually transfers his attention to his new girlfriend. Semmi adopts the conventional buddy role, supporting his friend's efforts and creating spaces and modes of privacy that were unavailable in Africa. While Semmi easily adopts American values and thus has value conferred on him, Akeem's father, King Jaffa Jeffer, is irreparably tainted by Africa. It is he who arranged Akeem's marriage and dismisses the possibility of romantic love. He is linked to the past rather than the future, justifying his decisions by reference to precedent. In contrast to American individualism, Jeffer rules by feudal collectivism. He asserts polygamy as natural and presides over a palace in which private space is also public, in which servants have access to every area, including the royal bodies. Even in America, the King asserts his

Africanness, signified in the exotic retinue he brings with him to America and the excessive wealth he casually displays. Prince Akeem must win him over by the individualistic endeavour he imports from America – a quest which reverses the journey of *Heart of Darkness*, from civilisation to primitivism, to pose a mythically cathartic union of American and African blackness. The reconciliation is represented as an injection of American individualism, romanticism and enterprise to prevent decay and introversion in the African dynasty. In looking backwards and inwards, the African dynasty risks stagnation. Without the importation of American values, the dynasty's next generation would emigrate. Yet Akeem alone is not sufficiently powerful to seduce his father and must enlist the help of his mother, deploying her role as mother to future generations in securing the next one. Despite his natural affinity with America, however, Akeem settles within the same excessive frame he so insistently rejected at the start of the film. As in *The Jazz Singer*, the son can only recreate the past within the present, transforming the 'abnormal' African cultural tradition to a 'normal' American one.

The mechanism of other as Oedipal catalyst is continued in *An Officer and a Gentleman*, which proposes a father who has failed to facilitate the son's passage to adulthood, forcing him to create a surrogate who finally propels him into the symbolic and emotional maturity of graduation and a heterosexual relationship by defeating him in a brutal fight. Zack Mayo attempts to suppress his dissolute father, Byron, who has disintegrated after his wife's suicide, by outperforming him, leaving home to become an officer recruit in the navy. At first Zack strives to seduce his natural father by proving his entrepreneurial worth, launching a successful business servicing his fellow recruits' kit. As his father recedes into the background, he begins firstly to assimilate the values of fellow recruit Sid, and then of Sergeant Foley. Foley, who is persistently referred to as the recruits' 'Mom and Dad', is black and disciplined, marking his absolute difference from Zack's natural father. This otherness allows Zack to identify with, and separate from, him in a classic Oedipal trajectory. Yet he persistently denies Foley's surrogate role and his own maturation. Suspicious of heterosexual entanglement, he displaces his affections on to Sid, forming an intense and intimate friendship. He only achieves manhood through the sacrifice of Sid who commits suicide over his girlfriend's deceit, confirming Zack's suspicions about women. On his graduation, he confronts, and loses to, Foley in gruelling kung fu combat. This defeat allows him to accede to the girl he has been wooing throughout the film, but had earlier rejected when she grew too close. He is forced to admit the primacy of the father (albeit a surrogate), rather than trying to efface him or displace his passion into a buddy relationship. As Steve Jenkins noted, 'Zack embraces the dead body of his fellow trainee (who, he admits, reminds him of his dead mother) before a castrating kick to the genitals from Foley sets him on the correct oedipal path.'[3] Zack's relationships are all highly charged, sublimated attempts to woo the surrogate father (Foley) and supplant his buddy (Sid) in a bid to efface his mother's absence and to propitiate Byron. The trophies of his success in the paternal seduction are his graduation, the adoption of all-American values and, finally, his heterosexual liaison. This Final Romance is essential to defuse the explosive charges laid by his passionate relationships with Foley and Sid.

These are male dramas in which a modernist hope for a utopian future is vested in children and passed through the male line. Adult daughters are less easily incorporated in this paradigm. In *Out of Africa*, Karen's future strength and salvation is located in the maternal home she ran away from, yet she must lose her lovers and her fertility to find it. The eponymous heroine of *Private Benjamin* struggles throughout the film to propitiate fathers (both real and metaphorical) and achieve a romance of equality but finally has to turn her back and walk away. Until the final shot, she has always been bailed out by men; in the last sequence she rescues herself, but in the process, rejects all the affiliative structures offered by the narrative, truly becoming *Private* Benjamin. Julie, too, is alone at the end of *Tootsie*. She has been betrayed by lovers and friends. The propitiation of her father by the delivery of Dorothy/Michael to him as potential lover backfires with Michael's deceit. Despite Michael's final protestations, the closure is unstable and unpredictable. Julie's experience of constant betrayal and her struggles to please her father result in failure. By contrast, Julie's own daughter gains value by permitting Michael/Dorothy unfettered access to Julie through the babysitting device. While Julie seeks a different type of family set-up, Julie's baby articulates the 'truth' of her mother's desire for Michael and the nuclear family.

The truth which these adult-children bear is that of the father as potentiality – the father as that-which-can-be-redeemed and that potentiality in themselves. These narratives rehearse a utopian possibility which can never be achieved, precisely because it must enact failure in order to be triggered. Adult children are thus strung between two poles: a redemptive future and a dystopian past. As the product of failure, they strive to replace it with success but in linking success to a reconciliation with failure, the utopian family (and their own potential within that) is always-already flawed. Thus Zack is marked by the disintegration of his father and his subjection to the other, just as Akeem returns to his problematic dynastic heritage. These children truly bear the sins of their fathers and carry those sins into the future, perpetually recreating a dystopian past.

THE METAPHORICAL CHILDREN

Metaphorical families also privilege their children but, in the films in which they appear, the relationship is more conflictual. Children still carry the same privileges, their innocence, insight to truth and redemptive qualities, but are less likely to be reconciled to their parents or to the prevailing social order. These films represent dystopian 'parents' or parental structures, which the children frequently have to reject in order to claim autonomy. Perhaps these conflicts have to be enacted on a metaphorical canvas because they are unrepresentable in actual family terms. What is unrepresentable is the dystopian alienation represented in familialised organisations. Whereas adult children may feel rejected or seek to separate themselves from their parental home, they still aim to revive its values and moral centre. Where these are perverted or alien, they seek to reinstate the ideals of American culture. Metaphorical children struggle to assert any values or moral code in an increasingly fragmented environment. Thus *Lethal Weapon 2* and *Beverly Hills Cop* represent their heroes searching for a lost moral centre in a familialised police force which insists on bureaucracy at the expense of justice within an anarchic, criminal social milieu. Frustrated, they forge intense bonds with other men which both replicate and dislodge a lost familial structure. Metaphorical children frequently reject their 'families' outright, as in *Total Recall, Good Morning, Vietnam, Star Trek – the Movie, Ghostbusters* and *Rambo: First Blood Part II.* Others stay within them, but never really fully adopt their regulations or mores, such as *Beverly Hills Cop, Sudden Impact*, the *Police Academy* series or *Naked Gun.*

In common with many of these films, *Ghostbusters* rehearses an intense male–male bonding in which metachildren strive to create a new worldview. However, it offers a representation of the metachild which dares to show alternative possibilities, rather than a fully dystopian breakdown. As one of the biggest grossing films of the decade, its familial structures are particularly significant and its extra-textual dimensions also raised some of the issues around the child-as-spectator. Both the film's marketing and its plot opposed adult and child realms, while appealing to both. The film was designed and marketed as a blockbuster with a huge range of tie-in merchandising.[4] The men most closely involved in the development of the film, the director, screenwriter and its three stars, came from the American 'alternative' comic tradition, specifically the National Lampoon stage shows and the *Saturday Night Live* TV series.[5] Ivan Reitman had previously directed such anarchic and parodic comedies as *National Lampoon's Animal House, Meatballs, Stripes* and *Heavy Metal.* The film was thus signalled as a zany comedy which was nonetheless deeply rooted in American culture and on whose institutions it depended for its material. The film's own 'product-ness' was frequently commented on by reviewers who appeared to overlook the heavily constructed nature and profit motive of all films – and the necessarily market-oriented packaging of commercial films. The film was frequently damned purely on the grounds of its success and its cost. As the *New Statesman* put it, 'Here we are talking of product, impure and unsimple.'[6]

There were interesting contradictions in the marketing and distribution of the film, aside from those which denied or affirmed its nature as product. These concern the audience and the status of the comedy. The film and its merchandising appeared to expect a young audience, yet much of the language used by the Ghostbusters would normally not be used in a PG certificated film. In addition, these were comics whose credibility directly depended on their alienation from the mainstream, creating alternative 'adult' entertainment. Yet they were producing a highly commercial, mainstream product, paralleled in the text's own plot. In apparently opposing marginal and mainstream cultures, the film-as-product in fact underscored and reinforced the boundaries around which they were organised. Thus the 'adult' language is absorbed into the textuality of the film, marking the characters who use it as transgressive yet binding the spectator into the regularity of language in the very act of recognising the transgression. The actors – who were very clearly conflated with their characters through the publicising of their comic background – could therefore both be different *and* work within the confines of the mainstream. Both these contradictions were noted by reviewers. Philip French commented that the film was 'populated for the most part by lecherous, foul-mouthed cynics, apparently aimed at adults and awarded a PG certificate' and Michael Wood remarked, 'In fact, I'm not sure the movie's success doesn't in a way imitate its plot . . . an amusing endorsement of those [American] types and attitudes, for example?'[7] This simple operation clarifies the dependence of subversive comedy on the institutions which it seeks to subvert, a genre which cannot, by its very nature, propose alternative realities, but only parody existing ones, what French called 'anarchic conformity'. Comedy's investment is in the preservation of the *status quo*, the maintenance of stasis against the disruptions of anarchy.[8] Other genres – such as sci-fi and horror – operate a very different and, potentially, more subversive opposition through their ability to show alternative worlds. Comedy ultimately depends on subverting (usually by straight inversion or disorder) the regularities of the existing one. The swearwords thus become the very mechanisms for suturing the child-spectator into the symbolic realm.

The plot is simple: a team of academic parapsychologists are expelled from their university for their failure to produce scientific research. They establish themselves as a commercial team of 'Ghostbusters' and rid the city of a particularly nasty scourge of Ancient Egyptian deities threatening to bring about an apocalyptic end to the world-as-we-know-it. The actual family is noticeably absent from the representational field. The one exception to this is the phone-call which Dana receives from her mother. She is quickly dismissed as Dana is preparing for a date with Dr Peter Venkman. The term of mother, in this instance, clearly represents a nuisance and is quickly evacuated from the narrative. *In absentia*, however, the family structures the affiliative group of Ghostbusters. They are signified as children without – and, very deliberately, repelling – parents.

In the absence of the actual family, the film opposes familialised worlds of patriarchs and subversive children. The spectator is positioned in the latter camp through the narrational agency of the Ghostbusters team. Although they start the film within the familialised, public adult realm, actually purporting to engage in the serious work of educating young adults themselves, they are quickly expelled. Their work is immediately undermined by Venkman's unscientific biasing of his psychic tests to attempt the seduction of a young, attractive student. The formation of the Ghostbusters business initially appears to be a sign of their growing maturity as they debate the nature of the public versus private sectors and Ray is encouraged to remortgage his house. However, the move proves to be from a public, adult world of science to a private, amorphous and amoral world of commerce which is signified as child-like. Venkman hands out chocolate bars to signify approval and they turn the establishment of their ghostbusting business into an elaborate game. While the supernatural is proposed as their primary enemy, the real problem for the Ghostbusters team is the adult realm and, specifically, women. The adult sphere is represented through state institutions such as the police and the Environmental Protection Agency and depicted as interfering, petty, bureaucratic and rulebound while the Ghostbusters' child-world is entrepreneurial, anarchic and fun. The primary drive of the narrative is to liquidate adult and supernatural threats. Both are dispelled by the techniques of childhood. The EPA are repelled, in the form of Walter Peck, first by an explosion, then by public declaration (the mayor's office recalling a headmaster's study) then by envelopment in marshmallow. The Paranormal Destroyer (personified by Goza) is destroyed by the activation of a taboo (crossing the beams) which effectively causes her to implode ('reversing the particles') to an imaginary/childhood realm, creating her as if she had never been – a favourite device of childhood storytelling.

Women, however, are doubly problematic – both threat and victim, the one often a reciprocal move of the other. They either bring disorder (such as the female ghost in the library or Goza herself) or are exploited

(Venkman's female student, Janine). Dana is both threat and victim. Desiring her, Venkman risks entering the adult world of (hetero)sexuality but he must also compete for her body with the supernatural forces which possess it. The project of the film is to bring them under control within a newly constituted child–adult realm. Dana succumbs to Peter's seductions, Janine is incorporated into the Ghostbusters team, the librarian to a restored world and, finally, in a universalising gesture, the women in the crowd to a proper adulation of the Ghostbusters. Thus incorporated women can be marginalised and dismissed. In the final sequence, for example, Dana is dismissed to the car by Venkman just as, earlier, she cut her mother off the phone.

The film's narration and marketing created a synergy which provided a rich and complex resource for its audiences. The pressure in the narrative is to keep the Ghostbusters together and restore them to a position of approval in the public eye. At the close of the film, Venkman appears to have entered the realm of maturity. He reclaims and kisses Dana, but their future together is problematised both by her previous possession by the alien, and by Venkman's allegiance to the team.[9] The three men leave together as the crowd wave Ghostbuster T-shirts at them, imploding intra- and extra-textual strategies to signify their unity. Thus the Ghostbuster team are ambivalently positioned at the close of the film, approved by the adult world, but not of it, in a position (in Venkman's and Egon's cases) to complete oedipalisation by heterosexual romance and union, yet either oblivious to, or ambiguous about it. The Ghostbusters are represented as a group of children without adults – but a representation offered from the child's point of view. This begins to explain the film's attraction for a 'family' audience, as it is the children who are privileged through the representation of adults who have assumed their characteristics and consciousness and who win against the adult, symbolic world. Yet this victory is one of adjustment rather than revolution. These metachildren do not want to supplant the established social order, only modify it. That the disruption is provided by a supernatural force which has judged humanity wanting, reinforces their stake in saving the world-as-it-is, warts and all. The metachildren who attempt more radical overthrow, such as Rambo, cannot be incorporated, only alienated.

SUMMARY

During the eighties, the biggest familial investment was made in the child. Most popular films were consequently unable to represent the actual child as absent. While parental figures might divorce or die, the child's demise or defection was too traumatic for mainstream films to address. The absent child therefore haunted the narrative as potential, underwriting the Final Romance, rather than structuring the narrative as an absent parent might. This potential was fulfilled in the representation of the child-as-child. Represented in a romantic paradigm of innocence and prophecy, the child functioned as familial redeemer, indexing the family's moral centre but lacking narrative agency, its redemptive ability frequently being blocked by intrusions from the public sphere and by the failings of the father. Daughters enjoyed even less narrative agency than sons, who had greater power to recreate the family. However, sons repeated the mistakes of their fathers, whereas daughters held out the hope of creating a different social and familial order. The child representation was also present in the adult heroes of the most popular films, still struggling to resolve familial problematics in order to separate from their parental ties and establish new families. These narratives generally revolved around a father–son axis in which the son attempted to seduce the father into accepting a new (or recuperated) familial order by offering various gifts and trophies of personal success. However, by focusing on the parental generation, the adult children were also doomed to re-enact the past in the future and risk repeating the failures of the parents, particularly the father. Metaphorical children, by contrast, were gifted with properties similar to those of the actual child, but they struggled to overthrow or subvert the social order, within or through their familialised organisation, a feat they could achieve only if they were seeking to adjust, rather than destroy it. Where they attempted more radical change, or where social structures were more fragmented or dysfunctional, metachildren were alienated rather than incorporated. However, metachildren did at least explore the possibilities of social change, even if the outcomes of that change could not be fully represented. Metaphorical films actively debated the opposition of public and private spheres, scrutinising what would happen if the family, and society, could change.

The child therefore occupies a paradoxical and contradictory status within these narratives. Representing access to emotional and moral truth, the child is the father's best hope of stabilising the family unit, and his own power base within it, in perpetuity, yet the child's essentially transient status undermines any possibility of permanence. As the child occupies such a privileged position in relation to truth, it is also a position that the adults, most notably the fathers, want to usurp. Thus the adult-child is a pivotal feature of many of these films and generates some of the chief paradoxes. The desire to control reproduction, to insert the male capacity to generate and therefore ensure total power over the future lies behind the father/son conflations in many of these films. As we have seen, paternal failures and anxieties are the strongest narrative drivers and the usurpation of the child's role, effacing that of the mother's, is frequently posited as the solution. This solution itself renders the narrative unstable, for the father cannot become the child without collapsing vital psychic, social and cultural boundaries. The narrative drive of the adult-child is backward-looking; propitiating or seducing the father and seeking to take his place in history. The child-as-child's narrative momentum is emphatically forward-looking, introducing a tension of desire and nostalgia within these texts. Adult-children want what-has-been to be transformed while children look forward to a future which will be radically different from the past. In their desire to be children and also to be their own fathers, these adult men expose the sterility of their desire and fundamentally undermine the power dynamics they seek to shore up.

8 Family Dramas:
The Family in *E.T.* –
The Extra-Terrestrial

> Fine, we'll just put a smile on our faces and try to get through the
> evening. That's all I want to do.
>
> Mother overheard by surveillance team in *E.T.*

I had not seen *E.T.* when the first graffiti began appearing on railway
bridges and hoardings but I knew what prompted them. As if to assert the
film's mythical, omnipresent status, the film's catchphrase and central
dilemma, 'ET phone home' was scrawled across urban spaces in the latter
half of 1982.[1] Indeed, the graffiti appeared before the film did.[2] *E.T.* was
the biggest grosser of the decade and therefore deserves a closer look. It
is also a film primarily concerned with familial relationships, directly in-
terrogating contemporary preoccupations with the power balances between
father and son, but a film which cannot achieve resolution. It therefore
rehearses the core contemporary familial paradigms which took a firm
social and cultural hold on the decade.

E.T. AND THE EXTRA-TEXTUAL

Aside from its phenomenal box-office success, the film was significant for
the scale of pre-release publicity which it generated. Between the film's
mid-May release in the States and its pre-Christmas release in the UK, it
was steadily built into a box-office phenomenon, heralded by a rash of
press articles boasting of its success and the effect it was having on the
American public. The tabloid press ran competitions featuring *E.T.* merchandise as prizes, a fan club was created and an 'E.T. Adoption Kit'
produced. *The Star* printed a five-day storyboard of the film in the first
week of its release and the Daily *Mirror*, too, had an *E.T.* week.[3] Most
impressive of all, however, was the campaign to suppress illegal video
recordings of unreleased movies in the UK, which was allegedly triggered
by the 'flood' of illicit *E.T.* videos in circulation ahead of its theatrical
premiere. Stories of the capture and trial of video 'pirates' abounded in the
trade and national press resonating with the dynamics of the film's internal

narrative and creating an extra-diegetic narrative about the film itself in which potential audiences were created as actors.[4] One element in this was the relentless speculation as to whether audiences would pay to see *E.T.* once they had seen the video – a question which could only be resolved with the release of the film and which, of course, in turn became its own self-fulfilling prophecy. Agents in this narrative were morally polarised between the film's producers and distributors, merely trying to earn their living, and the evil pirates, trying to profit without labour at others' expense. Potential audiences were effectively invited within this narrative to identify with one side or another and to prove their allegiance in the only way possible – at the box-office.[5]

The film's distributors, UIP, estimated that the film generated over $30m of free media coverage – six times the official marketing spend of $6m. Prefiguring *Ghostbusters*, this was carefully orchestrated. The film was the latest release in the glowing filmography of the decade's most successful director, Steven Spielberg, one of the so-called New Hollywood school of directors. *E.T.* was filmed in close secrecy under the working title *A Boys' Life* while Spielberg was simultaneously co-producing *Poltergeist*, a film for which there was a great deal more production publicity.[6] The budget for *E.T.* was modest ($10m) and it came in on time, generating little speculation or gossip. Once it was released in America, there were regular press releases about its box-office performance, but the distributors refused to give out photographs or narrative information in the UK. Further fuelling the fantasy, 'rags to riches' story of commercial innocence being promoted around the director and his cast, a major merchandising licence was granted to a small retailer, Eric Snow, who had just three outlets in Bath and one in London. *E.T.* was the first film in history to gross $300m in the first six months of its release. The week before opening in London, *E.T.* was released in Japan, France, Australia, South Africa and New Zealand. By the end of 1982, it was released world-wide and was breaking international box-office records. The film grossed over £1.5m at the UK box-office in the first week of its release, topping the list of the top twenty films at the box office in 1983, ahead of such prestigious Hollywood rivals as *Return of the Jedi, Tootsie* and *An Officer and a Gentleman* and overtaking the major successes of homegrown products *Octopussy, Gandhi* and *Superman III*.[7] At the height of the decline in cinema audiences, one critic observed that '*E.T.* thus comes to a beleaguered industry like a gift from the gods' and indeed it certainly seemed that the film's internal narrative found echoes in the material world – this time in the film industry itself.[8] The phenomenon was sustained by careful management. Following a marketing pattern established by Disney, *E.T.* was pulled from public viewing just one year after its release, having grossed over $400m.[9]

E.T.'s production history is a paradigmatic example of the patterns of Hollywood production in the 1980s. The film was not a pure package (it had no star names) but was sold to Universal on the strength of its director. In stark contrast to the old studio days, Spielberg was not under contract to Universal (*Poltergeist* was being produced with SLM Entertainment and was to be distributed by MGM) and was represented by the Creative Artist Agency. It was thus a classic example of 'independent' output which was in reality financed by the major studios. Spielberg commanded a phenomenal amount of power. He and George Lucas were the most bankable directors in Hollywood in 1982 and Spielberg's name alone was guaranteed to turn concept into financial reality. The plot had originally started life as a story about what young boys got up to after school and took shape in its final form while Spielberg was filming *Raiders of the Lost Ark* in Morocco.[10] It was by virtue of this tremendous power that Spielberg was not only able to add to the critical and popular narratives surrounding the text by claiming authorial control over it, but also to cast himself as a character within them. Right from the outset, Spielberg claimed a special relationship with the film, suggesting that '*E.T.* is closer to my heart than any film I've ever done' and winsomely confessing that 'I think I've reached the stage in my life where I'd like to have children.'[11] This close, familialised association between director and text was speculated on by many popular reviewers. Paul Connew in the *Daily Mirror*, a popular tabloid which featured the film heavily before, and immediately after, its release, suggested that 'Even Spielberg, who gave the world *Jaws, Close Encounters of the Third Kind* and *Raiders of the Lost Ark* – has more than just a financial soft spot for *E.T.*'. He went on to speculate that there existed a father-son relationship between the director and his 'star', ET. Echoing the ambiguous role played by the diegetic ET, Spielberg was constructed as both father and son in relation to 'his' text.[12]

The significant investment in both intensifying the realist aesthetic of the film and implicating the powerful director in an emotional relationship with it, effaced Spielberg's financial interest in its success (and the labour of the others who worked on it) and created a massive market not only for the film but also its associated merchandise.[13] It also provided extremely effective marketing material in familiarising potential audiences with the thematic and narrative concerns of the text as well as prompting a flurry of reviews in which the authors constructed themselves as children, aligning themselves with a very specific, high-profile reading of the text.[14] The realist project indulged in by the majority of reviewers remarked in

Chapter 6 was in this case guaranteed by the emotional reality accorded
to the film's director and by the fantasy of being, or becoming, a child.[15]
Even those reviewers who dismissed the film for its sentimentality and
infantilisation of the spectator, did so on the grounds precisely defined by
the 'Spielberg' discourse.[16] The work of the pre-release publicity was to
inscribe spectators into the text as 'children' (a concept never fully defined, but in a reciprocal move, defined in the position constructed for the
spectator in the film) and to promote a particular reading of the text. This
reading is perhaps best summarised in the words of Michael Sragow who
proposed that children are, 'in suburbia, an embattled majority, dependent
on often absent parents for food, money and transportation. *E.T.* inspires
them to rise above their circumstances and take fate into their own hands.'[17]
In this discourse, children are privileged, redemptive creatures, their parents negligent and selfish – a discourse which, as we have seen, circulated
throughout the contemporary canon.[18]

While it is easy to continue the litany of *E.T.* records (its prominence
is, after all, built upon them), the important line of investigation is not so
much the nature of the success but the reason behind it. What was it about
the film which generated such huge audiences and the massive wave of
critical and media discourse and, more germane to our enquiry here, what
did it have to say about the family in the early part of the decade? *E.T.*
enjoyed a mythical status before anyone occupied a cinema seat to see it
in the UK. What was the hold exercised on the public imagination?

E.T. AND ITS NARRATIVES

Spielberg has been quoted as summarising the plot of *E.T.* as follows:
'Boy meets creature, boy loses creature, creature saves boy, boy saves
creature' – a theme which clearly chimes with the discourses of redemptive children identified in other popular contemporary films.[19] Having landed
on earth to collect botanical specimens, a spaceship of aliens is forced to
abandon one of its number when unexpectedly disturbed by a group of
scientists. The alien escapes capture to be befriended by Elliott, a young
boy with whom he develops a symbiotic relationship. Elliott, his elder
brother and younger sister hide the alien, now named ET, from the adults
in the film and try to unite him with his spaceship. However, ET begins
to sicken and is captured before they fully succeed. ET dies in the hands
of his captors, only to be resurrected by Elliott's declaration of love and
belief. He is finally rescued by the children and delivered safely back to
his spaceship.

Despite the apparent simplicity of narrative construction, there are several narrative lines vying for attention – all of which distribute their narrative energy across and around the figure of the family and all of which are motivated by loss and abandonment, demanding either the intervention of a redeemer-child or substitution of the father. At one level, this is the story of Elliott's family – a human family inscribing its development and dynamic into the narrative. At the opening of the film, the disruption has already taken place. Elliott's father, Mary's husband, has abandoned the apparently happy nuclear family for his girlfriend, Sally. The momentum at this level is thus towards the healing and restitution of Elliott's family. As the disruption is figured by the absence of the father, narrative closure demands the return of the father or the installation of a surrogate. At a second level, it is the absence of an entire family, rather than a single member of it, which causes the disruption. The equilibrium established at the opening of the film is the cohesiveness, sense of purpose and completeness of the alien family. This equilibrium is disturbed by the forced abandonment of ET – a result of the same tragic flaw (his curiosity) which later leads to other downfalls and obstacles. The narrative drive at this level of the plot is to reincorporate ET with his family. The narrative tension, and the source of the narrative's many contradictions and inconsistencies, lies in the solution to the former level being sought through the resolution of the latter. The film locates its narrative tension in the competing pressures of two opposing narrative discourses. The overriding narrative drive is to restitution and reincorporation: of a father-figure to Elliott's family, of a husband for Mary and of ET to his family. Yet Elliott and his siblings, Mike and Gertie, attempt to wrestle ET into a surrogate-father role, endeavouring to inscribe him into their family gap which directly conflicts with the urge to reinstate him within his own family. The tragedy of separation, of loss and of abandonment is played out through the figure of ET. Each character projects their own suffering on to the alien and increases the obstacles which face him by endeavouring to persuade him to abandon his family too.

There are five key perspectival narratives reverberating across these two levels. The two which dominate are those of Elliott and of the aliens, individuated to ET. The remaining narratives are those of the children's mother, Mary (separated from the other adults), the adult men (individuated in the figure of Keys) and Elliott's brother and sister (who oscillate between the narratives of Mary, Elliott and Mike's friends). ET's is the most complete narrative cycle. His abandonment leads to his encounter and identification with Elliott and his subsequent semi-incorporation through his acquisition of gender, language and culture. His mischievous drunkenness exposes his real desire to return home and he begins the laborious process of communication and his first abandonment of Elliott in the forest. The second moment of abandonment comes after his capture when he releases Elliott moments before dying. Although resurrected and rescued by Elliott in the final scenes, he must abandon him for the third and final time in the last scene in órder to be reunited with his own family. Elliott's identification with ET intensifies throughout the first half of the film, reaching the point where he uses the first-person plural pronoun to describe their joint agency. This identification climaxes in their mutual deterioration and ET's subsequent death. ET revivifies, apparently in defiance of medical intervention, in response to Elliott's declaration of love and belief.

In ET's narrative cycle, both the obstacle and the assistant to narrative closure is Elliott himself. Both figure ambiguously in the narrative of the other. Yet ET's narrative leads successfully from abandonment to reincorporation. Elliott's narrative resists such closure. The loss of his father leads directly into his self-identification as an outsider (he is first shown standing behind the kitchen counter, a physical barrier between himself and Mike's friends) who actively opposes the regeneration of the family group.[20] As an outsider, he seeks another like himself; it is he who searches for ET and the clue to the mysterious noises and footprints in the night. Once he has found ET, his close, affective identification with the alien enables him to use their telepathic liaison as a vehicle for intervening in his external environment. Although he assists ET to construct the radar set and communicate with his home, he ultimately abandons him by falling asleep in the forest. This failure to save ET leads to their separation, first physically, then psychically and finally to ET's death. Although Elliott is able to resurrect, rescue and release ET, he has not resolved the issue of loss with which his narrative began, only intensified it. The family to which Elliott must return is still fractured by the loss of the father and by his own alienating behaviour. There is no guarantee of transformation, except through Elliott's acceptance of a surrogate father – the likely candidates being Mike (whose authority Elliott has continually rejected) or Keys (the scientist who stands with Mary in the final scene and who shares Elliott's desire for ET). The diegetic trajectory of Elliott's narrative moves from Elliott's separation from his family to his merger with, and eventual separation from, ET. The final shot of the film is of Elliott standing alone in the glade, looking wistfully after the spaceship.

By contrast, the men's cycle is almost complete. The rhythm of their narrative moves from hunting to penetration to the acquisition of knowledge. The first phase of this pattern is figured in the hunt for ET which delivers the knowledge of his whereabouts through firstly a technological, and then physical, invasion and search of Elliott's home. The hunt then switches to those associated with him in order to amass further information. The chase of Mike is immediately followed by the invasion and capture of the house and by the technological penetration of ET himself. This odyssey produces knowledge about ET's appearance (through the interrogation of Mary and Gertie), his psychic, intellectual and affective traits (through the interrogation of Mike) and his physiology (through scientific examination). The extent of this knowledge is signified in the triumphant discovery of one of the scientist-doctors that 'He has DNA.' Yet although they gain knowledge, it is only partial – they do not have ET and they do not have access to his family or his origins. Only the children are privy to that. The nature, diegetic objectives and exact occupation of the men is never disclosed, universalising them as the adult threat of invasive science. Although they appear in civilian clothes at the start of the film, they possess a medico-scientific-legal authority in their easy assimilation of medical and space paraphernalia, discourse and clothing and by the cooperation of their police entourage. They are led by the figure of Keys, named after his metonymic association with the bunch of keys hanging at his groin, a classic symbol of authority and possession.

The men possess the power of movement in the film but are only shown outside until they invade Elliott's home. Assuming dominance in the domestic scene, they move assuredly between outside and inside, only entering the latter to expel the threat of the other. The only interior scene prior to this is in the mobile black van where one man systematically bugs family conversations, monitoring their health and immunity from invasion. Their faces are not revealed until the moment of ET's death, when, symbolically, they begin to remove their masks. Keys displays his face just prior to this in a shot characterised by its visual excess. As he enters the birth/death chamber, his face is framed in closeup, lit from inside his space mask like a halo. The meanings generated by this device are contradictory. The faceless, amorphous hunters are now individuated, particularly in the highly sympathetic figure of Keys with whom Elliott deigns to talk and even to hold hands. He is clearly privileged, to the extent of sharing Elliott's position as disciple ('He came to me, too. I've been wishing for this since I was ten years old'). Yet he is one of the invasive hunters; his statement of mutuality may also be read as a challenge and a portent. Elliott's discourse and attitude to ET has become increasingly possessive and Keys inserts a counterclaim to ownership. He also signifies what Elliott may become – the authoritative patriarch with access to science and knowledge himself. Across the film, most narrative weight is given to the male activity of hunting and pursuit. The first half of the film is characterised

by the narrative thrust of the hunt; the second segment (around a third of
the film's running time) is characterised by penetration and invasion and
the final segment reverts to escape and pursuit. There is an obvious power
accorded to the final segment by virtue of its positioning within the text,
yet this cannot detract from the overwhelming period of time devoted to
the hunt and invasion. The men are thus signified as the active subjects of
desire, aggressively pursuing and possessing their objective. The fact that
ET eludes their final capture suggests that it is containment or elimination
which is their ultimate goal.

The maternal narrative is one of constant loss, deprivation and a perverse sexualisation. It is a narrative which is, however, constantly represented as originating in Mary's failure as a woman and, more importantly,
as a mother. Her children arbitrarily call her either by her first name or by
the role term of 'Mom', an oscillation which suggests a casual and ambiguous relationship with her. The loss of her husband appears to lead to
a perverse sexual availability as she is routinely sexualised and rejected
through the film. She is represented as alienated from her youngest son,
despite her efforts to integrate and care for him and this ostracism leads
directly to her deception over ET by all her children. Her exclusion is
constructed as a deliberate form of self-deception in the farcical scenes in
which she fails to discover ET and subsequently by her sexual objectification
as, dressed in a provocative Hallowe'en outfit, she becomes the object of
ET's admiring gaze. As before, this sexualisation leads to further abandonment and deception as the children set out to assist ET to communicate
with the aliens and Elliott fails to return home. The impression of culpability is increased when she leaves the house to search for them, thereby
abandoning the house to the investigations of the men. When she is finally
introduced to ET, her first reaction is one of disbelief (constructed as a
cardinal sin in the movie) and her first impulse is to deprive her children
by wresting them away from ET. Their screams accompany Mary's flight
directly into the arms of the invading men. This ambivalent positioning is
indicated at significant moments throughout the film. During ET's death-
scene the narrative plays with her acceptance/rejection by Elliott, inter-
mittently drawing mother and son together and then separating them through
a series of reverse-angle shots. With the resurrection of ET, the deception
and abandonment begins again as Elliott and Mike steal ET away, merely
leaving a note for their mother. The final scene suggests a closer alliance
between Mary and the men than we have hitherto witnessed, and the
suggestion, in her proximity to Keys, of her alliance with the male adults
rather than the children. Mary is ostracised from all groups in the text, yet
she is the nurturer and provider for each. In all the family dramas outlined

above, she is characterised as passive and as a victim. She is continually deserted or deceived.

Mary's status within the film is indexed by her appearance, which ranges from staid and sensible working clothes to the glamorous costume on Hallowe'en. Each time she moves to the latter end of this spectrum she is punished. By the final scenes, when the men have penetrated and invaded her house, she is unobtrusively but attractively dressed in skirt and sweater, contained and submissive, the object rather than the subject of desire. Her words, too, are simply suppressed or ignored and she is proved to be an unreliable source of information. From her first appearance, she is represented as gullible and simple. She is deceived over the pizza, patronised for not understanding the boys' game and crudely harassed by one of Mike's friends.[21] The boys' response to her question as to who is winning is answered by 'It's like life, you don't win at life.' The reply is both contemptuous and exclusive. It is clear that a mother has no access to, or knowledge of 'Life'. The boys, by virtue of their maleness, have possession of reality and interpret it to her. When she commands them to stay indoors when Elliott reports an intruder, they ignore her. She has no authority and is merely represented as a servicing, servile figure. Unable to interpret the world for herself, she must have it interpreted for her, gaining access to the symbolic only through male permission. Gertie cannot show her ET for she too is marked apart as female, her words untrustworthy and subordinated to the predominant task of servicing the boys. Only Mike can eventually lead Mary to look on ET and her belief is reified into knowledge by the validating apparatus of the adult males. The men in the final chase typify her paradoxical position. They use her information and knowledge (the note passed to Mary by Gertie) to discover that ET is resurrected and escaped but they ignore her pleas for moderation, not to use the guns they carry as a matter of course.

By contrast, the absence of Elliott's father structures the narrative and defines the other characters through his representation as an active, authoritative figure. Mary is the first to invoke his presence when she suggests that Elliott telephone to tell him about the strange intruder. The inference is that he can handle situations which she is unable to, in this case Elliott's irrational belief in the 'goblin'. He will be able to restore order and introduce authority – even at a distance – where Mary cannot. However, Elliott is immediately able to use the suggestion to punish her by his rudeness and rejection. The reason for the punishment is unclear. It may be that Elliott holds his mother responsible for his father's absence, it may be that she is barred from speaking his name or it may be Elliott's resistance to being controlled and reincorporated within the family group. The father's presence is evoked again when Elliott and Mike reminisce about the past and Elliott asserts a possessive authority over the validity of their memories, disputing with Mike over his brand of aftershave. The third invocation occurs when Mary threatens a stern patriarchal figure who will bring discipline and authority to her wayward children who are not back when they have promised to be and have again forsaken her. The final reference is made during her interrogation by the policeman. He implies that Elliott's disappearance might be laid at her door by asking if there has been any family row which might have precipitated Elliott's flight. Mary is compelled to reply that her husband has recently left them and, on her implicit confession of guilt, Elliott is restored to her. Thus, despite the constant acknowledgement that the father deserted the family, it is Mary's guilt which is signified and her constant failure which is represented. The absent father is the lawgiver, the authoritative figure who has the power to restore order and bring discipline to the family. His absence has triggered the chain of disruptive events which bring ET to the household for which, we are left to infer, Mary is in some way to blame.

Elliott's siblings operate in a narrative similar to that of their brother once he has wrested them from the path of familial transformation by the introduction of ET and they share the goal and activity of reuniting ET with his family. At the beginning of the film, they are attempting to insert themselves into a new family form, compensating for the loss of their father. Mike constantly abjures Elliott to 'grow up' and he is clearly represented as having assumed the paternal mantle. He hands over this authority with the penetration of ET into the family group, deferring to Elliott's sovereignty and repeating the renunciatory oath which Elliott made him swear before he would reveal ET to him: 'You have absolute power.' At the beginning of the film, Mike has entered the realm of patriarchy and is assuming the role of father. By accepting the authority of Elliott, he regresses, signified by his foetal sleep in the closet, which ET had made his home, during ET's death-scene. Gertie, on the other hand, is far closer to the romantic paradigm of child-as-child. She is an innocent abroad, a truth-bearer by virtue of her age and corresponding lack of corruption but, by virtue of her gender, doomed to be ignored. It is Gertie who penetrates to the heart of the problematic of ET's location within the symbolic order by asking about his sex and, by doing so, forces Elliott to commit himself to an answer. It is Gertie who offers the model for ET's language-learning as she parrots her brothers' words and it is Gertie who teaches ET to speak. She is the emotional and moral barometer of her family, signifying dismay at Elliott's treatment of his mother, pointing out the damage Mike has inflicted on her mother's car and insisting on telling Keys the truth of her brothers' escape with ET, despite even her mother's protestations. She articulates thoughts that others suppress, such as her disgusted reaction to ET's body and eating habits, but is ignored or derided. Her words must be backed by empirical evidence for anyone to believe them – she must show Elliott that ET can talk and must hand her mother the note explaining her brother's rescue. She is thus positioned closest to ET and to her mother in her representation as female and Other. However, because of her age, she is tolerated within the sibling group and used to run messages and provide commentary.

GENDER AND LOSS

The human family's loss occurs before the film opens. It is the aliens' loss, ET's abandonment, which opens the film and motivates the narrative of the plot. The adult male group, individuated in the figure of Keys, is experiencing a different form of loss at this point; the absence of Knowledge, of empirical evidence that aliens exist and of access to a form of language whereby they can be described and contained. A very specific and highly gendered form of difference is thus established from the film's opening moments. Male adults experience epistemological and intellectual forms of loss – a symbolic absence manifested in the desire to expose and circumscribe the alien, the Other. The loss and absence experienced by female, child and alien characters is positioned purely in the affective, relational realm. It is a family loss – a physical separation and rejection, caused by the withdrawal of one or more members and it is experienced as abandonment. Reactions to these losses are also represented very differently. The adult male response is aggressively active, hunting down the object which will fill the epistemological gap. It is the drive to wholeness, to protect a threatened intellectual integrity and to restore the illusion of a complete and comprehensive domain of knowledge. The response of the woman and children is adaptation, even transformation, of the old family form into a new one which will be different, but whole. While they are represented as passive victims of the father's abandonment, the general thrust of the family's affective energy is towards reestablishing themselves as a group. Elliott is the obstacle to this propulsion, constantly referring backwards in time, recalling the family's wholeness to contrast an earlier health and happiness with their current status. It is Elliott who taunts Mary with his father's desertion to Mexico with a new girlfriend and Elliott who finds his father's shirt and prompts a stream of reminiscences when he powerfully asserts his authority over the authenticity of his memories. He is simultaneously the guardian and guarantor of his father's presence. While Mike seeks to step into the father's role, Elliott deliberately and repeatedly subverts his efforts, recalling his biological father's absence and assuming significant forms of power and authority within the family group. ET, by contrast, exhibits a set of very contradictory responses to his familial loss, which, as we will see, are consistent with his role and function within the film as a whole. On the one hand, he undergoes a humanised transformation in his attempts to appropriate language and a cultural history and in his bonding with Elliott, on the other, he actively seeks reconciliation with his own family, constructing his radar machine, signalling his whereabouts and refusing to stay with Elliott.

FAMILY DRAMAS

The film's family dramas can be read across the text in three specific and distinct interpretations. The first is a patriarchal drama in which the family, particularly, the role of the mother, is positioned as fractured, requiring the insertion of a new father. The second is one in which the symbolic order has become a realm of conflict, requiring resolution. The family is still problematic, but the solution lies within its own control. The third drama is one in which the symbolic order has totally broken down and a state of psychosis has resulted.[22]

In the first of these dramas, the absence of Elliott's father has caused the family to become undisciplined, out of control. The mother has failed to keep the father and is now failing to keep the family together. Mike and his friends infantilise and disregard her and Elliott has become alienated. This fragmentation allows the penetration of the alien, which leads to further disruption, signified by the increasing separation of the children and their deception of the adults. Contiguous with this breakdown is the inappropriate sexualisation of the mother. Mary is the perverse object of sexual harassment by the teenage boy and dresses up (apparently for her children's benefit) on Halloween in a sexually provocative costume, exciting the attention of E(Elliot)T. Resolution is achieved by the intervention of the adults, who kill the alien. Despite the final rebellion of the children, the alien is expelled and the family contained. In this narrative paradigm, the final signifier of resolution must be sought in the final sequence, in which Keys and Mary are framed together, witnessing the ritual expulsion of the alien. This narrative is not, however, able to contain the ambiguous functioning of ET himself, who slides between identification with the adult males and identification with the children. It is also disrupted by the final segment of the text which focuses on the leavetaking between ET and Elliott. The closing shots of the film – the vapour-trail 'rainbow' left by the spaceship and the last closeup of Elliott's ambiguous expression as he gazes after the machine are unable to guarantee closure in the form of Keys as replacement father.

A second family drama proposes that the absence of the biological father requires the construction of an ideal, surrogate patriarch. This takes two forms – the first is the idealisation of the absent father and the rejection of all inferential substitutes such as Mike or Keys. The second is the construction of ET as ideal father. In this scenario, ET invokes patriarchal law and discipline in the form of paternal allegiance, consistent goals and unified subjectivity within the children. Through his intervention, the children act more purposefully and create an 'alternative' family. Gertie assumes a nurturing role, bringing food and presents, clothing ET and teaching him language. Mike becomes far less dominant, granting power and authority to ET/Elliott and acting on their wishes and instructions. Elliott begins to merge his identity with that of the ideal father. Through this identification, he begins to desire not only other girls, but also, more problematically, his mother. A struggle for separation/union then ensues between Elliott and the ideal father, ending with physical separation but a continuing identification through ET's final benediction. The resolution here is represented as residing within the family – specifically within the figure of Elliott. Through his assimilation of the ideal father, he can take his place within the family, either as its head or as one of the members of a different family form.

The third family drama can be traced in Elliott's failure to enter and negotiate successfully the symbolic realm. With the withdrawal of his father, Elliott retreats from patriarchy. In this drama, the psychic energy of the narrative hovers between hysterical and schizophrenic states. While the narrative exhibits the hysterical symptoms of Elliott's repressed desire for his father through their displacement into the figure of the alien and the corresponding aetiolation of Elliott's own body, ET's arrival also specifies a schizophrenic desire to return to a pre-Oedipal state of fusion.[23] The schizophrenic has retreated from the symbolic realm and the corresponding ability to mark boundaries. Language and temporality are evacuated. ET arrives without recognisable gender or language, the differences between Elliott and himself are blurred and become more so with their affective integration. He has no history and no clear point of origin. The children's attempt to locate him within the framework of their knowledge fail dismally.[24] Yet despite his obvious difference, he is marked as similar through his anthropomorphic expressions and articulations, correspondence of body parts, physiology and genetic makeup, his orientations, feelings and desires. Thus ET functions simultaneously as hysterical projection (of Elliott's desire for his father) and schizophrenic introjection (Elliott's disregard for authority, symbiosis with another, lack of temporal awareness, increasingly 'irrational' behaviour). The tension between these psychotic states is represented in ET himself. Simultaneously surrogate father and ur-child, he displays a functional volatility which constantly disrupts and threatens to subvert the narrative drive and paradoxically motivates the power of its closure. The resolution of the hysterical narrative is that of the patriarchal drama – Elliott must suppress the hysterical symptoms through articulating his desire for the absent father and accepting a surrogate. To achieve closure to the schizophrenic narrative, Elliott must separate from the maternal state of fusion and identify with the paternal principle of the symbolic. The problem for these narratives is that ET has come to function in both roles – as ideal father and as maternal principle of fusion – the mother–child. ET slips between operating as patriarch and as symbol of the ahistorical, parthenogenic maternal principle. He elides categoric oppositions: men's clothes/women's clothes; sexual attraction to mother/child-like fusion with mother; injunction to Gertie/own bad behaviour and drunkenness; healing/weakening of Elliott; authority/total dependence.

The film cannot achieve closure in any of these dramas. Although a potential resolution to the first and third dramas may be signified by the presence of Keys in the final scene, Elliott has clearly denied his mother again while separating from ET. Both ET and Elliott acted autonomously in stating their terms on parting ('Stay.' 'Come.') but the final image of their relationship is one of complete psychic union, either in the form of symbolic injunction or of ultimate fusion. ET rests his phallic forefinger on Elliott's forehead, 'I'll be right here.' It is Elliott's head, not his heart, that is pointed to and a psychic rather than affective union that is indicated. While the earlier integration is described by Mike as being one of 'feelings', ET's resurrection has initiated a union which incorporates all psychic activity. In this parting shot, ET signifies either that Elliott's psychosis is complete – the boundaries will be broken forever – or that patriarchy has been reinstated. The text does not privilege either reading.

The central boundary which is transgressed is ET's oscillation in familial role and function between father and child. The intensity of his presence in the narrative constantly alternates with that of Elliott's natural father. As ET withdraws when he begins to build his radar set, the natural father 'enters' in the form of Mike and Elliott's reminiscences. Elliott's first encounter with ET occurs immediately after the scene in which he has articulated his pain at his father's absence and his inability to communicate with him ('I can't – he's in Mexico with Sally'). Inarticulacy reverberates throughout the narrative. Elliott is rendered speechless by ET's first appearance as are Gertie, Mike and Mom when they meet him. ET thereby plunges the family members back into a pre-Oedipal realm of fusion and speechlessness while simultaneously acting as a catalyst for the intensification of technological and scientific discourses. This disturbance of the symbolic order is, of course, associated with the fractured communication between Elliott and his 'natural' father. E.T. thus straddles symbolic and pre-symbolic realms. As patriarch, ET is constructed as a figure of authority, particularly in relation to the containment and regulation of the female characters, punishing Mary through becoming a catalyst for her exclusion and deception. As a result of his manifestation, she is ridiculed and isolated, excluded from her children and other adults. Similarly, he enjoins Gertie to 'Be good', an ironic combination of a single letter learned from a TV reading lesson and Gertie's praise for his learning of it. As with so much of Gertie's speech, these words are taken from her and reflected back in a different context and with very different connotations. Later, in a parody of the failing father, ET gets drunk and throws beer cans at the television, abusing the home as site of leisure and consumption. He wears the absent father's clothes and uses his tools to make a radar set. As healer and restorer, he is able to master and handle technology and the only character who is empowered to achieve resolution and unity.

However, ET also functions as a child. He is clearly most closely aligned with the group of children and shares childhood traits – irresponsibility, curiosity, a total dependence. Discovered without clothes or gender, he is assigned both. As a child, he is constructed in the romantic innocent tradition signified by Gertie rather than the more worldly-wise modernist conception represented by Mike and Elliott. His ambiguity is signified in his positionality. ET is not only extra-terrestrial – he is extra-contextual. His name is generic, just as Elliott's family is made to stand for all families; he is made to stand for all Extra-Terrestrials. Although individuated he is accorded no personalisation except that allowed to him by the children. We do not know whether he is child or adult or the nature of his 'real' gender. The only diegetic speculation about the alien's origins and social organisation is offered by Mike (the proto-father at the opening of the film) and this is quickly lost. To underpin this ambiguity and obscurity, ET is frequently represented as hooded, cloaked or cowled. He makes his temporary home in the closet which connects Elliott's and Gertie's bedroom, a conventional repository of secrets and of repressed or discarded objects – the unconscious of the house. From this position, he can act as voyeur, drawing Elliott into this form of scopophilia as they listen to Mary reading the story of Peter Pan to Gertie. He is both an intruder into, and observer of, the household, a similar figure to Pan himself at the close of the Barrie narrative. He makes a repulsive figure, his scaly grey skin deteriorating to chalk white as he falls ill, his flattened, extended head, elongated fingers, truncated legs and gnarled feet. Like the adult men in the film, ET is withheld from the spectator's gaze, metonymically represented by shots of isolated parts of his body, and the parts of his body which are foregrounded are closest to those of a human. The most prominent feature is the phallic wand of his finger. This digit is, by turn, gardening tool, a signifier of intimacy and friendship, a device for healing and restoration and a tool for penetration and exploration. Also privileged is ET's face, particularly his eyes and expressive forehead and his diaphanous chest with its pulsating red heart. He is, ironically, a miracle-producing figure who is himself a production of special effects technology, both repelling and attracting spectatorial attention and pleasure.

These contradictory functions are played out through different forms of psychic drama. Within these, ET functions both as Phallic principle and as the pre-Oedipal child/mother. ET possesses the phallic, healing finger while castration is simultaneously signified by his truncated legs and curious, waddling gait. In one sense, the narrative of E.T. can be read as the classic Oedipal drama in which Elliott struggles to enter the symbolic realm and to separate from his mother. The failure of the Oedipal scene is signified by the absence of the father and Elliott's suspension between pre-Oedipal and symbolic realms. Through the creation of a *doppelganger* (the figure of ET) he attempts to achieve maturation and separation from the family but the identification with ET produces confused responses. Although he romances a female schoolmate, it is through ET's agency. The liaison is heavily coded as fantastic and impossible by cross-cutting with the televised images of *The Quiet Man*, by the stylised choreography and the girl's height, signifying that Elliott still has some growing to do before he can consummate the union.[25] The sequence ends with the authoritative figure of the schoolteacher, controller of this aspect of the symbolic realm, snatching Elliott away. The fact that he had defied the Law of the father in this scene only emphasises Elliott's own exclusion rather than securing his position within it. He is not John Wayne. It is also through his identification with ET that Elliott is heavily implicated in the desire for his own mother when ET voyeuristically admires her on Halloween, symbolically masquerading as Elliott himself under his cowl. Elliott flirts with an attachment to his mother, desire for his father and identification with ET – all three conflicting and psychically differentiated positions which point up Elliott's own ambiguity within the text. Elliott's inappropriate impulse to create himself as an authority within the family is signified by his

continual insistence that he has 'the power' and by his claim to the ownership of ET. It is also possible to detect the trajectory of a family romance
in which ET is made to stand for the fantasy of an ideal parent to substitute for the absence and shortcomings of the real one. In this scenario, ET
is again constructed as the father on to whom Elliott may project his desires.

Constantly in tension with these dramas, is the construction of ET as
pre-Oedipal maternal principle – the bringer of chaos and subjective implosion. ET cannot succeed as father-substitute because he also enacts the
role of female principle. He cannot speak except in the language of the
Other. As a disruption to Law and to Language, ET must be contained.
The two narrative choices exercised in managing disruptive women –
expulsion or death – are also those available for containing ET. He is
similarly excluded, doomed to exemplify the acquisition of language by
the Other in his parroting of key words which those in possession of the
symbolic order choose to prioritise for him. He, at least, by virtue of the
gender assigned to him, can command attention. The boys listen to him
and do not deceive him. When he points at objects, they name them. As
spectators, we know he is not deceived in the naming, yet ET is in a
position of total trust, total dependence. He has no control, except what the
boys choose to grant him. Even his miraculous powers can only be used
on those objects which they allow him access to. It is possible to read this
acquisition of language as a variation on the Oedipal/mirror phase. ET's
gender is a linguistic rather than a biological construction: ET 'is' male
because this is the symbolic position that Elliott has accorded to him. Yet,
despite having apparently gained some form of access to the symbolic
order, by virtue of his gender and his limited speech, his choice is to return
to precisely the unknown space from which he must separate to achieve
male adulthood. For patriarchy, the only access to space is through penetration, not withdrawal or return. ET's journey is opposed to that of
earthly spacemen precisely because it is a journey from, and back to, the
unknown, rather than a journey into it. It is a realm which men cannot
know, by definition, thus it is excluded from the domain which can be
comprehended and articulated by the symbolic. There is no language to
describe it and neither ET nor Elliott try, beyond the very rudimentary
representations of the planetary system. Yet even these must be linked to
man's current scope of knowledge and prove inadequate. Elliott can only
show ET what is known – the solar system and the globe. ET can only
point to the unknown, pointing out of the window into the night sky. Even
ET's own representation of home, the spinning food items, cannot be
maintained on earth and the symbols drop from mid-air on to the floor at
the intrusion of patriarchy. ET has no power to signify his origins. In
deciding to return to them, he signals his decision to abandon the Oedipal

trajectory to return to a pre-Oedipal or extra-Oedipal realm. In human terms, ET fails to develop and grow. He also fails as a principal player in the family drama unfolding in the rest of the narration. Elliott's tragedy is that he can, or will not follow him but, by association, has now excluded himself from the symbolic.

It is also possible to detect the operations of a primal-scene fantasy in which Elliott observes and explores his own origins through the apparent parthenogenesis of E.T. and the subsequent death–rebirth sequence. Elliott's desire for his father is displaced on to the desire to witness his own origins – the moment of his conception – and thus vicariously to rediscover his father. The moment of ET's death is also coded as a moment of birth. Gowned and masked figures surround the operating table on which he lies within a sterile, tented cubicle.[26] Moments after releasing Elliott (the first rebirth) and just before his own 'death', ET is framed from his feet in a conventional 'birthing' shot, doctor standing by his head, shouting instructions. The house has itself become a monstrous womb, entirely sheeted in plastic and linked to the outside world by a long umbilical cord. Not only is it figured as a place of reproduction, but as a site over which men have total control, a control which is exercised through the medium of technology. Everywhere equipment bleeps, VDUs flicker and monitors scan. Outside a cordon of men control access to the house/womb resonating with contemporary debates over reproductive technologies and the respective rights of father, mother and medical professionals to exercise control over women's bodies. The house has been represented throughout as a female domain but control has been exercised over it by constant surveillance and self-regulation. This is now refined to house as womb, and the mother's role diminished to the function of her reproductive organs. Whereas biological reproduction is inextricably linked with women, who are contaminated and diminished by its physicality, technological reproduction is linked with men, who are thereby enhanced. However, Elliott 'reproduces' ET while also able to assist ET in building the radar machine. The dismissiveness normally associated with biological reproduction, here manifested in Mary's ostracism, is conversely celebrated in the resurrection of ET and Elliott's own regeneration in his interpenetration with ET. None of these family dramas, however, can reconstitute the family or stabilise the volatile positions of ET or Elliott.

E.T.'S SPIRITUAL HOME

ET is also the child–father of Christianity, a link which Spielberg himself made in an interview with David Lewison: 'They [theatres and cinemas] are – together with the church – one of the only ways in which people are physically able to share laughter and tears and all the emotions with one another.' ET is both beatified son and the forgiving father. The eight-day narrative structure is organised around the ur-events of the Christian gospels, initiated by the annunciation where Elliott is given the first signs of ET's arrival. The nativity is attended by Elliott who gazes on ET's metonymic appearance at the open door of the garden shed – a construction bathed in non-diegetic ethereal light for the early part of the film. At the epiphany, ET's alien nature is revealed to Mike and Gertie and is repeated when ET reveals himself to Mike's friends. ET is crucified on the cross of medicine, science and reason, sacrificed to man's thirst for empirical knowledge and denial of faith and is revived by Elliott's declaration of love and belief at his resurrection. Finally ET completes his ascension by rejoining his spaceship. Such a reading is endorsed by the naming of the mother as Mary and the emblem associated with Keys, aligning him with St Peter at the gates of heaven.

Hugh Ruppersberg has read ET as an 'alien messiah' coming to redeem mankind through love and suffering yet his arrival is an accident and his departure technologically assisted.[27] It is actually Elliott who revives ET through a declaration of love and complicated by the close identification of ET and Elliott (signified in their names – ET is a compression, a cypher of Elliott). It is also difficult to identify the outcome of the beatific mission. ET can be interpreted as an intruder, disrupting the family's attempts to find a new, transformed form. In a parallel move to the men's activity, he comes as an invader, penetrating first the earth's atmosphere, then the family, then Elliott's own subjective integrity. In addition, he is the cause of the mother's rejection and deception. In this reading, too, ET plays an ambiguous role. Perhaps the most interesting outcome of this interpretation, is an understanding of the special effects which ET initiates. Unlike the conventional science-fiction effect which makes the extraordinary ordinary, ET makes the ordinary extraordinary. In this respect, they are closer to miracles than to the special effects of the genre.

E.T.'S GENERIC HOME

How does *E.T.* deploy its generic discourses? Although the generic impulse lies within science fiction, both director and critics commonly described the movie as a 'love story' and there are important continuities and discontinuities with the configurations of science fiction. For example, in contrast to science fiction and endorsing Spielberg's own categorisation, there is an unusually heavy emphasis on character- and relationship-development and the establishment of particular romantic emblems. *E.T.* shares many characteristics of the melodrama in its foregrounding of familial desire. In addition, while the proliferation of chase sequences are typical of many science-fiction movies, they generally feature the alien as pursuer and the humans as pursued. This film reverses conventional hierarchies, constructing the rarer representation of the Other as vulnerable but beatific, a perfect but fragile being, establishing resonances with the contemporary representations of the child.

As opposed to horror, which inserts the extraordinary into an ordinary world, science-fiction creates the extraordinary as ordinary. While *E.T.* appears less concerned with special effects, parading them as miraculous transformations, the use of such effects, are nonetheless, a primary feature – not the least of which is the construction of the film's star.[28] *E.T.* is constructed through oppositions between science and technology (associated with the adult males and inherently bad) and nature (associated with the family and inherently good). Thus the alien's moral and social acceptability rests upon his allegiance to the affective rather than the cognitive realm, an interesting reversal of the conventional gender alignments of these paradigms. Our responses to ET will thus bear a generic pressure for evaluation. In opposition to the 'naturalness' of the children runs the technological discourse of the adults. Technology itself is physically articulated in *E.T.* – the continual bleeping of the instruments actually drowns out the men's speech as they hunt ET in the early scenes. Later, the commentary on ET's state of health is validated through scientific equipment. Speech is mediated through sterile masks, helmets or walkie-talkies. Even the spellchecker talks. The discourse of technology – from the television to the bugging device – is everywhere; all of it seeking to reveal essential, hidden realities but failing to articulate the real truth of affective belief held by the children and expressed in Elliott's revivifying declaration to the dead ET. The clothing of technology (the suits and overalls) also serves to eradicate sexual difference, another key indicator of truth since one of the first acts in talking about ET was to assign 'him' gender.

Science fiction conventionally foregrounds the naturalisation (and thus, the circumscription) of the Other. Its core project is to eradicate or contain difference which, unlike difference in most other genres, (melodrama, say, or the western or *film noir*), is not explicitly sexual, but a difference of origin, of lineage. Thus in science fiction, although frequently absent from representational forms, the family (in this instance, the genus) is everything and the nurture/nature dichotomy paramount. Central to the narrative drive is the compulsion to distinguish 'them' from 'us' and, like a bowdlerised wildlife documentary, to display the rituals, instincts and habits which characterise difference. Most important of these, of course, are mating habits and lines of descent. Roy in *Bladerunner*, Ash in *Alien*, even the eponymous Terminator, must have their genesis meticulously and scientifically outlined before they can be adequately positioned in the narrative – and it is frequently the problem of this positioning which structures the narrative. Unlike these characters, ET is clearly Other and it is his similarity, rather than his difference, which is investigated and displayed in the text. Central to this construction of similarity and difference are the different epistemologies which are developed with their own codes and conventions. Science fiction is concerned less with what-is, than what-could-be. On the one hand, there is the authoritative, scientific knowledge possessed and delivered by the adult males – the medico-scientists – and regulated by the police. On the other, there is the belief which is possessed by the children. ET has access to each of these domains of knowledge – as does Keys, the sole individuated adult male. However, it is the epistemology predicated on belief which is privileged in the text and which resurrects ET. Elliott is constructed as authoritative in the text because he is able to turn belief into empirical evidence (he finds ET and he is able to resurrect him) and is therefore able to achieve mastery over the others. He also claims authority by virtue of, and in contrast to, his mother's oscillation between *naiveté* and oblivion. Elliott thus becomes a guarantor of truth within the narrative, reifying a diverse mix of science and fantasy. His discourse reflects the operation of science fiction itself: a fantastic narrative and *mise-en-scène* made credible through the application of science to its norms, codes and conventions. Through these conventions, however, run some narrative disruptions and tensions which pull the text towards other generic propulsions.

Fantasy in contemporary science-fiction forms is specifically located in the interstice between psychic and scientific activity, the field of virtual reality where the mechanisms and representations of desire are expressed through the workings of technology. Mike and his friends play Dungeons and Dragons, a game structured on the fantasy literary epics of authors as diverse as Malory and Tolkien, but whose imagery, rules and dimensions are more closely correlated with the cybernetic space of contemporary computer games.[29] It is in this context that one of his friends proudly boasts to Mike, 'Don't worry, I can resurrect' when his character is killed. The theme is reiterated in the enactment of *Star Wars* which Elliott performs for ET as he trains him in the brand-names and icons of contemporary American popular culture and again in Mike's first piece of news as he bursts into Elliott's room to announce a record-breaking feat in computer-games mastery. ET departs in a spaceship which is not only a fantastic object in itself (round, shiny, with an eye for an entrance which leaves rainbows in its wake) but a technological construction. The technology of science/fantasy erupts into the text but there also is a continual slippage between material and representational forms. This is structured into the film through the almost arbitrary distribution of fantastic and realistic visual codes, the continual use of non-diegetic music and occasional extension of diegetic sound to bridge non-contiguous shots. The lighting throughout *E.T.* is also frequently inconsistent and apparently non-diegetic. White light and bright colours are associated with the adults in the film while ET and Elliott seem happiest in the dusk. Elliott often shuts light out, closing blinds and operating in chiaroscuro or near dark. Much of the important activity takes place in a strange ethereal light, apparently motivated by sunsets or sunrises but where adjacent shots appear to be taken at night in almost total darkness. ET and the adult men are routinely shot in silhouette, hiding against or in front of, strong sources of light. Elliott is often obscured in a half-light, but rarely silhouetted. ET is, of course, able to emit his own sources of light – white light from his finger which signifies power and healing and red light from his chest, signifying strong emotion. Thus the lighting not only problematises the formal boundaries of generic codes but also reinforced ET's ambiguous linkages to the key character groups.

These slippages are also ontological ones. Elliott conflates the real and symbolic realms in his training of ET, not merely by drawing on intertextual references such as the Tarzan-derived introduction and posture (You no talk? Me, human. Boy. Elliott.') and the litany of film characters' names as he introduces his toys but the elision of each representational signifier with its material referent. Elliott calls the toys 'little men', he talks of the ceramic, oversized peanut-shaped money-box as if it were an edible food and introduces a toy car by stating 'This is a car, this is what we get around in.' Perhaps the clearest example of this tendency is Elliott's summation of the entire food chain in which a synthetic, constructed representation is elided with its material referent and metonymically forced to stand for an entire scientific discourse. Elliott dips a toy shark into his goldfish bowl as he lectures ET, 'Look, the fish eat the fish food and the shark eats the fish, but nobody eats the shark.' To complicate the model further, both goldfish and fish food are also manufactured objects and the shark is a knowing wink in the direction of the cognoscenti who will recognise a further intertextual reference to Spielberg's earlier work on *Jaws* – another shark whose entire *raison d'être* was to gorge – in that case on people. These Chinese boxes of signification also signify the biological concept of the food chain. Thus not only does this sequence point forwards to the unnaturalness of the frog-dissection in the classroom and the danger of extracting knowledge from nature through distorting the natural chain of predation but it apparently contradicts itself by compounding the error.[30] Elliott is himself attempting to transfer knowledge by conflating symbols with material objects – and by terrifying the fish. This conflation is signified by the metaphor of pain. The Elliott and Mike reassure first Gertie and then their mother that ET will not harm them just as teacher reassures the class that the frogs will feel no pain. The symbolic pressure of ET into service for the production of knowledge, the conflation of represented and actual objects and the dissection of the frogs as a learning tool all produce a distortion of the 'natural' and cause pain, despite reassurances to the contrary. Elliott uses the shark again later in the same scene as he confronts his angry mother over the state of his room. He has already insisted on his authority in the oaths he has compelled Mike to swear. Now he holds the toy shark, symbolising the top rung of the food chain, to signify his authority over his mother and his power to deceive her. 'This is reality', says Elliott, when one of Mike's friends asks why ET can't 'beam up'. The irony is, of course, that it isn't. While the text invests heavily in the display of contemporary signifiers (the building-site suburbs, the constant brand-name references, and so on) to locate it within a realist, contemporary milieu, the dominant realist aesthetic of the film is disturbed and, in places fractured, by the text's own signification of its status as representational, fictional form and of its relation to other textual forms.

SUMMARY

What is really at issue here is the mega-success of this movie. What pleasures did spectators and audiences draw from such an open narrative? *E.T.* marks a crisis in familial representation already identified in other films of the decade. This crisis is figured by the failed or absent father and the drive to create surrogate families in which the child is privileged. However, as I have attempted to show, not only does the fantasy aesthetic of science fiction cut across this grain, but there are a number of oppositional and conflicting readings to be made around the family. While the absent father motivates and structures the narrative, he is an ambivalent figure and his surrogates equally ambiguous. The nostalgia for the family's earlier wholeness is problematised by the illicit family discourses overheard by the eavesdropper in which every family is represented as dissonant. The desired model appears as flawed. Within the text, adult males can be read as anonymous but also as uncomprehended, simply left outside the film's field of concern. Elliott can be read as rejecting or ignoring the psychic demands of patriarchy and thus occluding the catalysts for its resolution. The narrative struggles between the proposition of an alternative family form (the alien family; Elliott's fractured, but mending, family) which is Other and uncomprehendable, and the reconstruction of what is lost, which is represented as unsatisfactory and impossible. We are confronted with two representations of the father – one is ideal but absent, the other absent and idealised-present only in the form of desire. Thus, while the text can be seen to play with discursive materials outside itself (and vice versa), no simple correlation or discursive position can be identified.

The central problematic of *E.T.* is centred on the nature of the alien himself. He is the screen on which all the characters project their fantasies. Denied access to the symbolic realm himself, he is the ultimate shapeshifter, a fantastic creature who transgresses boundaries because he cannot recognise or define them. He is the chaotic pre-Oedipal principle, nameless and formless, who is only given name and form by others.[31] ET is thus the manifest embodiment of the other characters' desires. As such, he enables the figure of the father to be displayed and interrogated. As the object of desire and of narrative resolution, the natural father is a flawed and ambiguous figure. His presence/absence both brands him as culpable but also as ultimately controlling and authoritative. He commands the narrative and the characters' attention by his absence. His absence both triggers – and is the solution to – Elliott's psychosis. By withholding his presence, he prevents Elliott's reincorporation into the symbolic order and renders ET's valediction as an ambiguous one. If ET is indeed a projection of Elliott's ideal father, then his inscription to patriarchy is guaranteed by ET's introjection as controlling super-ego. If, however, ET is, as I have suggested, a projection of the chaotic maternal principle, then Elliott can be assumed to be fated to operate as an eternal Peter Pan, a schizophrenic who will not enter patriarchy. *E.T.* is a confused, and often contradictory film, slipping between paradoxical scenarios of manifesting and containing difference, between different functions and levels within the sign and between differing psychic levels and activities. Its conclusion is deeply ambivalent. Having signified the loss of the father as the primary motivation of the narrative, it is finally unable to contain or to resolve that loss, displacing closure on to the removal of the substitute father/disruptive child, on to the final excess of special effects and the potential for Keys as replacement husband/father. As endings point back to beginnings and slip all the links in the chain back into line, the readings become a jostling, volatile cacophony.

Mike's friend asserts, 'You can't just join any universe in the middle.' Perhaps the pleasure for the spectator lies in being offered a choice of universes to join, perhaps it lies in the reassurance of being reinscribed into the familiarity of patriarchy or perhaps in the consonance of extra- and intra-textual narratives. The text in itself cannot set a seal on the dilemma of the discourses with which it intersects and which it itself invokes.

9 Conclusions and Futures – Stasis and Change

THE EIGHTIES: CONCLUSIONS

The demographics of the contemporary social family emphasise its continuing volatility and fragility and the enduring robustness of alternative forms. While some imbalances of power were corrected, others were created or reinforced. Representations of the family throughout this period were engaged with these shifts of power and composition. Close textual analysis suggests that these representations reverberated with a key political moment when social anxieties were projected on to a rhetorical familial entity in order to secure a discourse of permanence during a time of social crisis and that this transformation was rehearsed throughout the discursive fields of popular Hollywood cinema. Yet the eighties movie was actually unable to represent this, its ostensible desire – the fully-achieved ideal of the nuclear family. The nuclear family, although idealised, was represented within dystopian paradigms in which it was rarely achieved or achievable. In many films, it was not even represented as desirable. The sensibilities of the most popular movies framed contemporary mythologies for explaining social crisis, yet they were shot through with the social discourses of contemporary actuality and desire. This conjunction of ideology, desire and actuality resulted in torn, fractured narratives and a cultural discourse that was inadequate to the complexities of lived experience but continually measured against it. Worse still, for the traditionally patriarchal, phallic dominant narratives of Hollywood, the failures in the texts were almost universally introduced by the fathers, who remained the centre and subject of the narrative, yet only by becoming its hermeneutic, the problem to be resolved, jeopardising the very families they were trying to restore. Coping with increasingly complex diegetic worlds, these fathers were faced with difficult choices and, all too often, they chose wrongly. They could no longer 'have it all'.

To attempt some stabilisation in a social and cultural realm that was fragmenting and diversifying, the greatest narrative investment was made in the figure of the child. The child became the moral index of the dominant discursive field, able to redeem, but also to speak the truth of the diegesis. However, the child as the very embodiment of change and growth, represented antipathetical qualities to the patriarch and tension grew between the increasing failure of the father and the privileging of the child. Victory for each was mutually exclusive: either the father must win, or the child. Central to this paternal problematic was the trope of rescue and redemption, usually through a journey or quest which both asserted the primacy of the family-as-goal but also asserted its fundamental weakness, which was, in perfect circularity, the father himself. The journey motif also denoted paternal agency. Only the father could secure narrative resolution but his activity was blocked by his own failure. Thus the father was active but frustrated in the role of redeemer while the child was represented in the role of redeemer but denied narrative agency. These family dramas were built on shifting sands of power and maturity.

Whereas fathers were problematic and children were privileged, mothers disappeared. Although at one level, this was deeply regressive, such shifts also opened the field to alternative readings in which mothers, as absent terms, frequently offered alternative positions to a familism which was demonstrably faulty. It has become fashionable to look for any gains in female representation as highly progressive. However, one should not overlook how far these have had to come and how far they have yet to go. As Modleski has pointed out, 'however much male subjectivity may currently be "in crisis" . . . we need to consider the extent to which male power is actually consolidated through cycles of crisis and resolutions, whereby men ultimately deal with the threat of female power by incorporating it'.[1] It is certainly the case that, while fathers could not sustain a utopian familial trajectory, they were not voluntarily relinquishing narrative space or agency to mothers or daughters. On the contrary, patriarchs actively usurped representational spaces and functions that had traditionally belonged to the mother. Preferred readings are still deeply regressive and spectators have to be predisposed to, or work hard for, oppositional interpretations.

The family is a vital, dynamic factor in social organisation. But it is not the only one, nor is it the only mechanism for managing and organising social and cultural reproduction. By celebrating the nuclear family as the single form for reproducing not only other human beings, but also cultural values and social status, familial ideology does grave disservice to the multiplicity of relationships and lifestyles that human beings have developed. In cultural terms, the disservice was recognised in the eighties purely as an absence, as a space which could rarely be filled and in which alternatives were rarely successful. This book has moved some way towards defining that space and identifying the problems inherent in positing the nuclear family as both the source and resolution to narrative disruption. In assuming the proposition of the nuclear family as ideal, it is clear that it became unrealisable in this period, if it ever was. That recognition is itself productive. It opens the possibility of finding alternative forms of social and reproductive organisation which can be just as central to cultural mythologising but which need not conform to a universalised ideal. Instead these might explore, rather than contain, contemporary cultural desires and anxieties as we approach the next millennium. As the world becomes a faster, more information-rich environment, we need social structures which enable us to embrace change rather than suppress it. The hegemonic strategy of promoting the family as the vehicle of social stasis, a refuge of unchanging composition, only represses the anxiety: it does not remove it. Reality is a realm of infinite change and variability, impossible to fully comprehend or describe. To pretend that the family is going to halt or dispel its volatility and complexity is naive – a naiveté driven by a patriarchal desire to protect existing power bases and epistemologies.

The Hollywood movie is both symptom and cause in this process. Neither simply reflecting nor determining social dynamics, it circulates in the process of creating and expressing social desires and anxieties, a resource for audience imaginations and desires. On the one hand, texts proffer readings in which the family is desired object; on the other, they represent alternatives, however unsuccessful. Most importantly, these narratives demonstrate the folly of making simple generalisations about the mechanics and outcomes of interpretative activity. They display the possibility of fracture, of fragmentation and of difference. In opening up the play of desire and reality for the individual spectator, they licence us to imagine other possibilities in which the nuclear family need not be a limitation or the only option and in which change might be welcomed rather than feared.

THE NINETIES: FUTURES

This book has only scratched the surface, not only of the theoretical scope necessary to analyse the complexities of familial representations, but also the body of film susceptible to that analysis. Most germane to further investigation would be, I suggest, a broader historical context. Analysing contemporary films has rendered the dominant contemporary narrational and rhetorical forms available to us but it would need comparative analysis to understand how these might differ from, or be similar to, family representations in, say, the fifties. At the end of this book, though, I want to look forward and to sketch what I see as both continuing and innovative trends in the nineties although we are still too close to the period to do more than suggest further lines of research.

Social Concern and the Family

From a brief overview of the first half of the nineties, it is clear that the issue of the family has not gone away. Nor has much progress been made in distinguishing the rhetoric from its material counterpart; reproductive organisation has remained the fulcrum for public morality and the object of increasing legislation. Indeed, anxiety over the nature and role of the family has increased, highlighted by an increasing focus on social and personal values. In clear contrast to the popular perception of eighties values, a recent national survey into social attitudes identified that the primary criteria shaping popular respect for social institutions were intrinsic rather than extrinsic and concerned the nature of the relationship between individual and institution. The most important were identified as personal interaction, the transparency of the basis on which relationships rested and the absence of a commercial agenda. The family was the institution which benefited most from these factors, significantly increasing its influence and respect in society over all other named forms of social organisation. By contrast, the Royal Family, the epitome of eighties family values, was widely denigrated, freighted by intense scrutiny and the burden of its own representation.[2] Dragged into the public domain, the fragility of the private sphere quickly fragmented.

Despite its prominence, the family was not represented as healthy. Persisting in the family-as-problem research paradigm, a report published by the influential Joseph Rowntree Foundation at the start of the 1990s attracted widespread media interest. With its basic assumption that 'the family is, to adopt a widely-used metaphor, a building block of society', the report sustained the moral panic over the family, by asking: 'should we be surprised if statistics like some of those just cited [notably the rising numbers of single mothers and high levels of divorce] give rise to fears that the whole edifice is starting to crumble?'[3] The report drew on research predicting familial trends into the millennium, anticipating continuing change along the demographic pattern established in the eighties. These predictions were couched in a perspective of 'social concern', and closed a report in which change was synonymous with crisis.[4] Thus moral panics over fragmenting or alternative social forms continued to reverberate through public discourse with the family as the lens through which all social breakdowns were viewed and to which they were attributed. As a result, politicians continued to invoke the family with persistent regularity. While political divisions became less sharply defined in both Britain and the United States as all political parties restaked their claims to the centre ground, the political differences that existed were played out around the family once again.[5] The discursive formation most at issue was figured as 'community'. The property of both left and right, it was the definition, responsibilities and rights of this community which were struggled for. While on paper, at least, it appeared to be a more progressive standpoint than merely collapsing all social institutions to the level of the family and its male breadwinner, it was still conjured through the familiar rhetoric of family values. As Tony Blair, the new leader of the Labour Party put it, 'I have no doubt that the breakdown in law and order is intimately linked to the breakdown of a strong sense of community. And the break-up of community, in turn, is to a crucial degree consequent upon the breakdown of family life', a sentiment which is not so far from the hard-right position stated by John Redwood, pretender to the Tory leadership, that 'the natural state should be the two-adult family caring for their children' and the Conservative Party's, albeit discredited, 1994 'Back to Basics' campaign which was founded on the bedrock of familism.[6]

In America, too, family values increased their purchase. Religion and politics, always closely affiliated, found common ground, and magnetic electorate appeal, in the family. In May 1995, the powerful Ralph Reed, executive director of the Christian Coalition, announced his 'Contract with the American Family'. Proclaiming itself the 'McDonalds of American politics', the Coalition boasted serious influence in determining the Republican Presidential candidate for the 1996 election. Shadowing Newt Gingrich's 'Contract with America' which wrested popular support from the Democrats in 1995, Reed's Contract prescribed a list of demands which subsequently formed the basis for Republican activity and lobbying on Capitol Hill, robustly associating the nuclear family with hard-right Republican policies. In the same vein, the Reverend Wildmon, founder of the militant American Family Association, successfully targeted multinational corporations in his bid to 'protect the family', bonding family values with an extremist reactionary agenda in a form of familist terrorism. In 1990, for example, AFA members boycotted K-Mart, causing a dramatic fall in sales, for including 'pornography' on their shelves. The AFA had the mass media, particularly Hollywood, in its sights and, by 1995, boasted two million members, the backing of eight senators and the endorsement of over half the new republican members of the House of Representatives during their election campaigns.[7]

Changes: Killer Children and Wicked Mothers

Within the community-as-family paradigm, there were some pivotal shifts in familial representations. Characterised as a more caring period than the hard-edged, selfish entrepreneurial eighties, the 'nurturing nineties' opened the family up to even deeper levels of contradiction. While public values softened, attitudes towards the family and the responsibilities of its members hardened. These cultural shifts were inscribed in representations of the child. Having enjoyed unprecedented rights and privileges inscribed in law on both sides of the Atlantic, the child now suffered a cultural backlash. The most prominent example of this was the attention devoted to the Jamie Bulger case. The story of the Liverpool toddler, abducted, tortured and murdered by two older boys, reverberated in both Britain and the United States and spawned a rash of 'evil child' stories. In this case, the new and paradoxical role of child as both perpetrator and victim was clearly delineated. Significantly for the case's cultural implications, the judge sentencing the boys blamed a specific video, *Child's Play 3*, for their crime and the case was used to justify further restrictive legislation on video.[8] Following the trends of the eighties, the child was again fore-grounded as a rationale for social regulation but there were very different inflections to this. A naive reflexive position on the relationship between the media and reality was employed to construct the child simultaneously as passive victim but also as potential psychopath. The implication was that any child, exposed to certain visual material, was capable of vicious criminal acts. This implication not only opened to the way to some of the tightest restrictions governing access to videotaped entertainment in the world but also permitted a more complex and paradoxical representation of the child itself.

Questions were raised more frequently over children's culpability. No longer could they inhabit the realm of simple victim but were corruptible, even instrumental in their own abuse. Dominant anxieties over the security and integrity of the child moved to threats from outside the home, rather than the intra-family abuse of the eighties. Despite quantitative evidence that child murders were no more prevalent in the nineties than they ever were since records began, this period saw epidemics of parental panic over the safety of their offspring, catalysed by ever more sensational media reports and professional initiatives. In the first half of the nineties, the focus was on babysnatching and paedophilia rings and there was a spate of stories concerning the seizing of small children by people impersonating social workers and snatching new-born babies from hospitals. In every case, the implication, if not the direct accusation, was that mothers were negligent in handing their children over to complete strangers, despite the subordination of the mother's voice and agency to that of professionals in every other realm. Mothers were exhorted to physically tie their children to them while out shopping and to question anyone who wanted to talk to or approach their offspring. At the same time it was revealed that children's health was suffering from being driven everywhere and not being allowed to walk or play unaccompanied. Mother-blaming was therefore firmly back in the spotlight and it particularly focused on single mothers. In Britain, this culminated in a public witch-hunt in 1994–95 in which politicians of both sides fought for the moral high ground over the figure of the evil mother. Despite demographic evidence that the majority of mothers had been abandoned or widowed, single mothers were universally demonised as wilfully choosing to have children outside wedlock for personal gain. This positioned the mother securely as the perpetrator of family breakup.

Two examples of social welfare reorganisations serve to illustrate the political constructions of, and responses to, this selfish-mother paradigm. In the United States, Senator Whitburn of Massachusetts engineered the eradication of welfare benefit for single mothers and replaced it with 'Transitional Assistance'. This was behaviour-based welfare which depended upon the mothers' conformity to prescribed norms and expectations in order to retain the cheques and a place in a home or hostel. Any deviation was rewarded with punishments ranging from house imprisonment to expulsion from the home or hostel and removal of the child(ren) into care. Men were no longer entitled to any benefit and everyone was forced to work in whatever capacity they could for their entitlement. Thus the mother was not only represented as entirely at the service of her child, but specific criteria were developed to circumscribe her role and responsibilities. Failure to conform to this prescription forfeited her social identity as mother and a claim was placed on her child by the state. This model was heavily publicised throughout America and Britain and considered by all parties as a blueprint for future social policies. Meanwhile, in Britain, the Child Support Agency compelled fathers to pay for the upbringing of their child, even if they chose not, or were unable, to live with them. Mothers were forced to reveal the names of fathers they might no longer be in contact with, or had abused them, thus risking their own safety to ensure the material welfare of their child. Thus the 1991 Child Support Act criminalised fathers and victimised mothers. Responsibility was the watchword, but it was a responsibility bought even more heavily at the expense of female identity and the subordination of women to their responsibilities for their child. Men could 'buy out' of the family, but mothers were always in thrall to it.

And what of the films of the nineties? What did they make of the family? In the first half of the nineties Hollywood displayed both a reaction to, and a petrification of the trends of the eighties. To some extent, the focus shifted from the child to the relationship between adult men and women, the proto-parents, which perhaps signified an age of greater maturity and social concern. However, this was not the conventional classic Hollywood plot mechanism of the Final Romance. These movies were less interested in generative potential than in exploring the dynamics of power *as inflected by* procreation. The disturbance over generative capacity, for so long explored in horror films where the return of the repressed stemmed primarily from anxieties over origins and gender difference, moved firmly into the mainstream. Fathers struggled to control the domestic space by pirating reproduction itself, but the dynamics of that space frequently proved uncontrollable and permitted contesting representations of both mother and child. The overview in this chapter can only offer a snapshot of the possibilities available in familial representations of the nineties, but a swift glance at the respective representations of families and family members in a few of the more successful box-office draws of the first half of the decade can lead us to some tentative conclusions.

A Family for the Nineties: *The Addams Family*

Analysis of one explicitly family-oriented film indicates some key trends in the decade. Characterised by a perverse decadence, *The Addams Family* drew on its comic-book and television antecedents to celebrate an inverted form of family organisation, a family explicitly contrasted with its social environment. Constructed within their own domestic space, a gated, forbidding fortress, the Addamses forcibly expel any intrusions from the 'normal', human world yet send their children to school and participate in significant social occasions. While the film concerns itself with the separation of private and public spheres, it primarily addresses itself to the boundaries of the family itself; specifically, the establishment of a dynasty and the criteria for membership.

Although organised around the core nuclear family of mother, father and two children, the plot centres on Gomez's quest to restore his estranged brother, Fester, within the family bosom which nurtures a broad constituency. One of the longest sequences is a gathering of the clan at a ball and the ancestral heritage is constantly emphasised in the repeated visits to the family graveyard, the family heirlooms and ancestral portraits. The narrative hermeneutic is Fester's identity. He is inserted as impostor, but subsequently revealed to be Gomez's natural brother, a revelation founded on his conformity to Addams family values. Although Fester's incorporation is tested by his inability to recall shared family memories, his acceptance is assured once he proves he can dance the celebratory mamushka. The film explores and subverts the family romance. Rather than wanting to attach himself to more glamorous families, Fester actually wants to penetrate or, if his identity is authentic, return to the Addams family bosom. Gomez thereby restores his family through the recovery of his lost brother who is a literal manifestation of Gomez's desire for dynastic integrity and intactness. The father's reproductive power is thereby doubly proven by actual and metaphorical paternity.

The maternal role is significantly developed from that of the eighties, licensing both sexuality and narrative agency. The family matriarch, Mortitia, is calm and authoritative in her governance of the household, coolly asserting her will to which all members unstintingly bend, in contrast to the anarchic, childish japes of her husband. It is Mortitia who saves the family when they are ejected into the 'real world'. While Gomez sinks into a televisually induced stupor in a trailer park, the kids try to earn money and Mortitia returns to the family home to confront Fester. Privileged above all other relationships, and the bedrock of the family itself, is the intensely erotic interaction between mother and father, an eroticism which receives both confirmation and absolution in her pregnancy at the end. However this latter cannot efface the luminous images of their seductive intimacies at the opening of the film ('You were unhinged last night. Do it again.') or their embraces during the school play itself. Contrasted with Mortitia is the similarly controlling mother of the Fester-impostor, who inserts Fester into the Addams family by a manipulative emotional blackmail. Mortitia's authority is leavened and confirmed by her sexuality while Abigail Gamm's is undermined by her emotional, almost sexual demands upon her son. While Mortitia's love is a given, constantly iterated in her actions, Abigail's is a form of currency, demanded and gifted in the form of words. Angered by Fester's wholesale integration into the Addams family, Abigail sarcastically declares, 'I'm just your mother. You only owe me your entire existence on this planet. Please by all means, sing, dance, date', forcing him to placate her by passionately declaring his love for her. Abigail is punished and ejected while Mortitia is confirmed in the family line by her pregnancy.

The paradox latent in this epitome of familial rectitude (it has a powerful moral centre, is separated from the social sphere and has clearly defined boundaries) lies in its self-proclaimed deviance. The interpretations of this are ambiguous. Either the Addams family is only deviant because its environment has become perverse, representing normality in a world which has become abnormal (in this construction, they represent a nostalgic return to their fifties antecedents, a familial throwback to the golden era of familial perfection which is no longer present in their contemporary social world of stuffy teachers, dysfunctional families and TV dinners) or, alternatively, the film proposes that the values represented by the Addams family are themselves deviant and that society, glimpsed in all its variety from the upscale Charity Ball to the sordid trailer park, is the normative ideal. What fractures both these interpretations is Mortitia's own sexuality, inadequately neutralised by her pregnancy, which penetrates every element of the text and requires uncharacteristic domestic activity, knitting, to attempt its liquidation. Thus the opposing maternal representations are both linked by their eroticisation; one is damned through the sexualisation of her relationship to her son, the other is renewed, but also problematised, through her highly sexualised relationship to her husband. The film closes on the whole family digging in the graveyard, resurrecting their forebears on Halloween, the ultimate extended family. As Mortitia murmurs while knitting babyclothes, 'What more could we ask?'

The sequel, *Addams Family Values*, acknowledges and evades these difficulties by transferring its attention from the parents to their children, particularly Wednesday (an adult–child) and Fester (a child–adult). Exploring the mature, blunt, subversion of the former against the infantile, sentimental convention of the latter, the film opens up a different dynamic which is equally hard to resolve. Fester's infatuation with the murderous nanny is easily and artlessly displaced to her replacement when she fails to murder him for his wealth and is herself killed. Wednesday meanwhile, knowingly exposes her summer camp's hypocrisies and its tyrannical directors. The values in this text seem to be an unsentimental, tell-it-like-it-is maturity in which those who cannot look out for themselves should be protected and those who can have a duty to protect others and to speak the truth. The truth-telling child is again foregrounded but it is a female child, and these values of care and interdependency are a world away from the New Right family values of the eighties.

Representations of each one of the family terms appeared to be undergoing subtle but significant changes by the nineties. While the bulk of realist narratives remained centred on the male hero, the mother was moving further into the spotlight. Two films in particular, *Junior* and *Terminator 2* showed how paternal anxieties were focused even more intensely on the reproductive function. Ironically, this allowed the mother some freedom to escape it and redefine her role, as films as diverse as *When a Man Loves a Woman, Terminator 2, Alien*[3] and *Mrs Doubtfire* all testify. Finally *Jurassic Park*, the biggest box-office success to date, demonstrated just how problematic child-representation had become and how fascinated audiences were by its dilemmas.

The Nineties Father: Romance and Parthenogenesis

The trope of personal redemption through fatherhood which characterised eighties films such as *Kramer versus Kramer* and *Three Men and a Baby* still resonated in nineties Hollywood in movies like *Junior, Jack and Sarah* and *Sleepless in Seattle*. However, this time paternity was the route to the utopian Final Romance. Not only could fatherhood save the masculine soul, it could also lead him to the perfect mate. In both *Sleepless in Seattle* and *Jack and Sarah*, the death of the mother foisted parenthood on to the father. Not for these fathers the incompetences of the earlier films. These New Men rocketed straight to the perfect parenting depicted in the final half of *Kramer versus Kramer* and *Three Men and a Baby*. For them, the dilemma was not how to look after the child (this came 'naturally') but how to find the perfect mother – and wife. The emphasis was firmly back on romance and the father looked for a mate who was romantically perfect but on whom the seal of approval was set by the child, often in defiance of male desire. Paternity was thus not dependent on, and could even precede or replace, a permanent romantic relationship.

Junior went a stage further, proposing that not just the nurturing but the reproductive function itself could be usurped by the male, a function that also enabled him to select the appropriate mate for himself and mother to the baby. Science and nature are opposed through the male scientist's self-impregnation as he struggles to master both. He cannot, however, control the raging hormones which soften his spirit and render him susceptible to the romantic entanglements he has hitherto evaded. The film both reinforces and undermines biologically determined constructions of gender and reproduction, its Final Romance providing an uneasy resolution to the questions raised. Since the film ends on the birthscene there is little indication as to which of the new 'parents' the nurturing and childcare role will fall – to the male 'mother' or the female 'father'.

Paternal representations thus incorporated the mother without necessarily assuming her responsibilities, or her representational burdens. *Terminator 2* explores a similar theme, in which the perfect father-substitute is a cyborg who was actually constructed by his 'son'. Although reprising the time loops and 'mindfucks' of *Total Recall*, this film creates a utopian version in which the father destroys himself in order that the son might live. The father not only commands the affection of his adoptive son but commits the ultimate act of unselfishness, an act usually associated with the maternal sacrifice paradigm.[9] In these films, the father had not fully resolved the problems of the eighties, but by incorporating maternal functions and placing the emphasis on utopian romantic paradigms, he was shoving his way further into traditionally female spaces. However, in opening up representations of the father and assuming maternal functions, more space was paradoxically created for competing constructions of motherhood.

The Nineties Mother: Out of the Closet?

For the first time, bad mothers could be redeemed rather than inevitably punished. In *When a Man Loves a Woman*, Alice Green, played by the normally wholesome Meg Ryan, is actually seen to strike her child on screen – and get away with it. Admittedly, she has a cast-iron alibi in her alcoholism, but she is redeemable – and redeemed – by the end of the film. In this popular mainstream movie, the burden of redemption has moved from the child to the mother's new circle of friends and, to a lesser extent, her long-suffering husband. While this can be seen as reinforcing traditional patriarchal forms of power and the passive-victim paradigm of motherhood, it also permits a trajectory of change and development for the mother – a phenomenon rarely seen in popular eighties films. Alice is defined in other terms than simply her motherhood, an intelligent, assertive, working woman, who is seen as actively sexual in the opening and subsequent scenes. Alice is not confined to the domestic scene either at the beginning or the end of the film, nor is her husband solely responsible for, or rewarded by, her fight back to health. When he won't change with her, despite all his previous support, she leaves, recognising that it is the pattern of their relationship which will reconstruct the conditions for her alcoholism and which must change for her health. The film acknowledges the problematic nature of marriage for women and the burdens it exacts upon them. While these are still expressed through the woman's body, a conventional form of displaying female dis-ease within patriarchy, rather than articulated within the narrative itself, they are more explicitly acknowledged than ever before. Alice actually leaves her husband in a positive, self-affirming way and their reconciliation is enacted within the circle of her friends, rather than in a private space which he has constructed and over which he is the guardian. The final scene is a celebration of mutual affection and respect, rather than the contract of protector and protected.[10] Despite Michael's assertion that 'I won't let you leave this family, I won't let you destroy yourself', it is not within his gift to prevent or to assure it and it is Alice herself, with the support of her friends, who ensures her own survival and offers Michael a part in it.

The representation of the independent, active mother gained further circulation in another hugely popular film, *Mrs Doubtfire*. Rhyming with

Tootsie some ten years before, it points up interesting parallels and differences. Daniel Hilliard has to become more like a mother to be permitted near his children after his divorce. Disguising himself as a nanny, he penetrates the family space and gradually assumes a position within it. Despite Daniel being the epicentre of the film through his development from irresponsible, neglectful father to committed, responsible matriarch, the real mother acquits herself well and remains the guardian and regulator of the domestic environment. Allowed passion and sexuality, her relationship with ex-boyfriend Stu is allowed to develop, despite Daniel's best efforts to break it up. Nor does the narrative permit the final ambivalent compromise at the end of *Tootsie*. Daniel will be allowed greater access to his children, but there is no cosy marital reunion and the conditions under which he sees his children will be those set by the mother. His response on the TV programme he is given in his Mrs Doubtfire persona is to proclaim that it will represent 'all sorts of different families', an acknowledgement which is worlds away from a compulsive drive to a nuclear familial resolution.

Terminator 2 pushes the maternal sacrifice paradigm to its limits. Sarah Connor, John's mother, physically reconstructs herself, the display and performance of her muscularity perfectly mirroring that of the Terminator and undercutting any conventional construction of motherhood. The narrative explores some of the deepest paradoxes of motherhood – such as the expectation that the mother will override her 'natural', nurturing passivity to defend her offspring as depicted in *Fatal Attraction*. In this case, the expectation required that Sarah should forgo a feminine shape and actually lose her son in order to shield him. By protecting him from the threat from a future only she has knowledge of, Sarah is characterised as psychotic by a patriarchal medical community which will not permit women access to epistemologies from which men have been excluded. Thus Sarah has privileged knowledge to the consequences of the scientific discovery which cybernetics genius Miles Dyson is only fumbling towards and which renders the science itself obsolete. While she cannot, or refuses to, assume the masculine characteristics necessary to kill Dyson, she is able to command sufficient faith in her revelations to inspire him to destroy his research himself. Confounding both the maternal sacrifice paradigm and classic ideals of femininity, Sarah Connor represents a new type of single mother and, as a byproduct, Linda Hamilton who played her, became a lesbian icon. However, the strong narrative focus on the spiritual values of the hero threatens to obscure the genderbending of both father and mother and the opportunities both are afforded for transgressing conventional parental paradigms.

'Don't be afraid. I'm part of the family. You've been in my life so long I can't remember anything else', mutters Ripley, as she stalks the Xenomorph through the convict camp of Fiorina 161, in a film which is significantly different from its prequels and signifies the increasing ambiguity of the maternal representation. Constructed as archetypal single mother in *Aliens*, Ripley experiences the destruction of her adoptive family in the opening sequence of *Alien*[3] and becomes, instead, inheritor of the alien matriarchy she tried to destroy. Stalking the mother while its progeny gestates inside her, Ripley is constructed in a complex matrix of mother/ not-mother; human/not-human dimensions, further complicated by her struggles with the only other humans represented: the penal colony and the Company. This matrix is constructed through gendered distinctions built into the narrative from the beginning when Ripley is confined to her quarters so as not to upset the all-male prisoners. Sharing the hardbody mould with Sarah in *Terminator 2*, Ripley's own sexual difference is rendered invisible by the shaven head and militaristic clothing she adopts. The threat of her sexuality is enhanced by its effacement, just as the threat of the alien is heightened by its invisibility. The implication is that the real danger comes from what cannot be seen. Ripley is not identifiably different, yet she is female and a Xenomorph is growing inside her. In another parallel with Sarah Connor, Ripley has to sacrifice herself to save the universe, but this time redemption depends upon simultaneously destroying the 'child' at her breast rather than protecting it. The nature of the universe she is saving is also far more ambivalent. Neither identified with the prisoners of the colony, from whom she is specifically segregated, nor the rapacious, duplicitous, masculine Company which exploits and betrays her, she is far closer, as the opening quote suggests, to a female-identified matriarchy, defined by a strong moral core and a desire to nurture and protect those it adopts. While she is not permitted to fully embrace a matriarchal structure, the ending leaves sufficient ambiguity to indicate where Ripley's desire might tend and to suggest alternative familial prototypes.

The Nineties Child: Frogs and Snails and Puppy Dogs' Tails

Child representations in the nineties were far more complicated than the eighties Romantic-redeemer manifestation. Other forms of representation became possible. There was even a series of films called *Problem Child*. Children also started to grow up, particularly in sequels with a family at their centre, posing the problem of transformation and change arousing parental, particularly paternal, anxiety. While *Ghostbusters II* tried to erase the fragile 'family' established at the close of *Ghostbusters*, other films acknowledged familial development and tried to deal with it in different ways. In *Three Men and a Little Lady*, for example, the highly sexualised desire for the infant was displaced to her mother, Sylvia. In *Look Who's Talking Too*, the running joke of the talking foetus/baby was extended to the birth of a sibling and the development of their parents' relationship. By the release of *Look Who's Talking Now*, the focus had shifted from the talking infants who could no longer remain mute without being retarded, to talking dogs and the convoluted relationship of their parents. Thus the anxiety over the maturation of adulterated infants who are actually maturing, signifying their parents' mortality and change, was displaced onto anthropomorphised animals and deflected to the actuality of the parents' entanglements, although these films were still unwilling to engage with the family as process. Thus, as we have noted, the focus inevitably began to shift from the child to the parents who can be 'fixed' in stasis at the closure of the narrative by the implication of an undying, unchanging romantic liaison in contrast with the child who, by its very nature, cannot freeze time.

Narratives also deliberately placed the child in jeopardy, exploring some powerful childhood fears by exposing their young protagonists to risks that only the adult–children faced in the most popular eighties movies.[11] Many nineties box-office hits, such as *Home Alone, Jurassic Park, The Lion King, Batman Returns, Terminator 2* and even *Silence of the Lambs*, played explicitly with the common childhood fear of being abandoned. However, as we have seen, the child was no longer unproblematically virtuous and sometimes desertion, or even death, was represented as justifiable. In *The Good Son*, for example, Henry, played by popular child star of the late eighties and early nineties, Macaulay Caulkin, is actually killed, an event which caused some audiences to applaud. Not only did such audience reaction display ambivalence to an amazingly popular star, but also to the precocious, streetwise characters he portrayed and which were played against the duplicitous character of Henry. The film's director, Joseph Ruben, had already made an inverted family film in the eighties, *The Stepfather*, a horror movie in which he explored the perfidy of the father and the nature and consequences of the perfect nuclear family. Ruben bequeathed the apparently perfect stepfather's schizoid nature from the earlier film to the apparently perfect son, Henry. On learning his true character and, in an explicit rejection of 'natural', biological ties in favour of learned, affective bonds, his mother allowed him to die in order to save her adopted idealised son, Mark. As in *The Addams Family*, it was conformance to familial values, rather than the blood-tie itself which determined familial affiliations. This permitted the father to usurp reproductive functions and liberated the mother from them. Although the film pursued a Manichean construction of childhood – either perfect or irredeemably evil – some difference in the representational form had begun to make its way on to the screen. The child as innocent redeemer survived (in *The Lion King*, for example), but these representations became more problematic, were often not the central focus of narrative resolution and usually required additional adult support.

The most popular box-office hit of all time, *Jurassic Park*, explicitly rehearsed a paradigmatic scenario from the eighties: the desire of the patriarch to freeze temporal change in order to retain order and power through the vehicle of the child. Both sexuality and technology explode out of control, threatening patriarchal authority and the children's safety. Lex and Tim are endangered by their grandfather, John Hammond, who is prepared to sacrifice them both to prove his ability to control time through the creation of a prehistoric theme park. In a scenario similar to that of *Honey, I Shrunk the Kids*, the children are put at risk by a patriarch's attention to science and must make a journey to save themselves and him. The narrative is an inverse display of the domestic scene: the rampaging, loose monster–female regains control of her reproductive capability, overcoming her own castration at the hands of the male scientists. Drawing on the most prevalent of childhood nightmares and the signifiers of pre-Oedipal chaos, the mother threatens the child itself within an area designated as safe, the theme park. Both children escape, through their own ingenuity rather than the intervention of the adults, to finally defeat the monsters' attentions. The final resolution, however, is fundamentally flawed in its bid to recreate a family amid the chaos exposed by the wild implosions of sexuality, science and technology. The new father is both scientist and reformed child-hater – two characteristics which must undermine the spectator's faith in him as the new patriarch. The glimpses afforded of the loose female, wilfully changing sex in order to become the pre-Oedipal mother, inflects our view of Ellie who is also a scientist and therefore implicated in the same drive to control time and nature. The children have 'rescued' the adults but cannot guarantee their integrity. Both scientists are 'reformed' by the experience, but still able to go on practising the scientific interference with nature which the film so uncompromisingly condemns. The film (as, even more convincingly, did the bestselling book on which it was based) stresses the imperviousness of the dinosaurs to man-made interference and destruction, an imperviousness based on a matriarchal ability to mutate and evade scientific regulation and the controls of patriarchy. The film's resolution is further undermined, not only by this threat of invisible evasion and maternal chaos, but by the redeemer-son's use of technology – he saves them by restoring the very tools which threatened them, creating a perpetual cycle of regression.

While it is certainly possible to claim that the film held its undeniably powerful purchase on popular imagination through its display – and, at least partial, diffusion – of the contemporary moral demon, genetic engineering, there are more disturbing questions at issue. Why was a film which displayed so spectacularly the jeopardy of children, a jeopardy rehearsed in such sexualised and voyeuristic terms, so popular? Nature is sold through the intervention of science – the haggling over the reconstructed embryos, the exchange value of the ticket to the theme park – a transaction which the film absolutely condemns. But it is a transaction which is firmly rooted in familial terms, Hammond is selling the possibility of dinosaur generation and the theme park itself is an excessive display of what is possible in procreative organisation. Perhaps what is being destroyed here is the possibility of alternative forms of familial organisation, particularly matriarchal structures. However, it is also possible that the vehemence of their destruction indexes a growing probability of their realisation.

Appendix 1:
Family Paradigms

Actual Family	Metaphorical Family					
	Absent		Present		Foregrounded	
	Utopic	Dystopic	Utopic	Dystopic	Utopic	Dystopic
Utopic						
Dystopic		Out of Africa '10'* Ghost The Fox and the Hound Trading Places Superman IV		Condorman** Airplane** Raiders of the Lost Ark**	Pretty Woman** Top Gun** Who Framed Roger Rabbit** Star Trek** Ghostbusters**	Total Recall** Indiana Jones & the Temple of Doom** Good Morning, Vietnam Beverly Hills Cop Sudden Impact** The Naked Gun** Police Academy I–IV** Rambo II
Absent						

Metaphorical Family

Actual Family		Absent — Utopic	Absent — Dystopic	Present — Utopic	Present — Dystopic	Foregrounded — Utopic	Foregrounded — Dystopic
Present	Utopic						
	Dystopic			Rocky III* Rocky IV*			Staying Alive Lethal Weapon 2 The Untouchables* Beetlejuice* Any Which Way You Can** Beverly Hills Cop II
Foregrounded	Utopic		Three Men and a Baby** Coming To America**		Honey, I Shrunk the Kids** Look Who's Talking** Annie**		The Golden Child**
	Dystopic		Gremlins Arthur** Back to the Future* Terms of Endearment** The Blue Lagoon**		Indiana Jones & the Last Crusade E.T. Rain Man Fatal Attraction* Kramer versus Kramer		The Jazz Singer* Tootsie An Officer and a Gentleman** Return of the Jedi** Private Benjamin The Empire Strikes Back

* closes on Final Romance which was represented at the beginning (7 films)

** closes on Final Romance which was *not* represented at the beginning (29 films)

Appendix 2: Synopses of Selected Top Box-Office Hollywood Films, 1980–90

The films are organised by their box-office popularity within the year of their UK release. The date in the credits refers to their US release date. The production company is preceded by the distributor in the brackets. The main stars and central characters are shown below. A very brief elucidation of the paradigmatic assignment follows the narrative synopsis.

e.g. **Film Title** '
Director (Distributor/Production Company) US release date
Actor (Character)

1980

The Empire Strikes Back
Irvin Kershner (20th Century Fox/Lucasfilm for 20th Century Fox) 1980
Mark Hamill (Luke Skywalker)/Harrison Ford (Han Solo)/Carrie Fisher (Princess Leia Organa)/Billy Dee Williams (Lando Calrissian)
A further sequel in the *Star Wars* series. Darth Vadar, the evil Lord of the Imperial Starfleet, is intent on tracking down Luke Skywalker and his band of freedom-fighters. After escaping from the iceworld of Hoth where they were ambushed, Luke sets off to train as a Jedi, tutored by Yoda. Meanwhile, her spurned suitor, Solo, rescues Princess Leia from the Starfleet but unwittingly leads her into a trap set up by his old adversary, Lando Calrissian. On learning of their plight, Luke leaves his training to rescue them. During a fight with Vadar, Luke learns that his opponent is in reality his treacherous father. Solo has been frozen and taken hostage and Leia is left to rescue Luke from Vadar. Wishing to make amends for his own treachery, Lando sets off to look for Solo.
Foregrounded dystopian, foregrounded metadystopian.
The film represents a family broken by a treacherous father which is unresolvable in the text; no actual nuclear family is represented as a solution to the dystopian metaphorical family (the Starfleet/Freedom Fighters) in which the key meta-familial protagonists share the same textual space as the actual family; Vadar (father) Luke (son).

Kramer versus Kramer
Robert Benton (Columbia-EMI-Warner/Stanley Jaffe Productions) 1979
Meryl Streep (Joanna Kramer) Dustin Hoffman (Ted Kramer)
After being neglected by her husband, Ted, who is pursuing a high-flying advertising career, Joanna abandons him and her son to 'find herself' in California. Ted learns to care for his son but increasingly neglects his work and is forced to seek

a lower-paid, lower-status job. Having established her own very successful career, Joanna returns and sues for custody which she is awarded. Realising Ted's pain at losing the child, she relinquishes them both at the end of the film.

Foregrounded dystopian, present metadystopian.

The family is represented as broken as a result of parental neglect and there is no positive nuclear model offered as an alternative – Ted's eligible neighbour, the similarly abandoned Margaret Phelps, also being rejected. The metaphorical world of advertising is similarly dystopian – Ted's patriarchal boss, Jim, quickly jettisoning him as his protégé once he assumes his childcare responsibilities.

Star Trek-The Motion Picture

Robert Wise (CIC/Paramount) 1979

William Shatner (Admiral James T. Kirk)/Leonard Nimoy (Mr Spock)/DeForest Kelly (Dr Leonard 'Bones' McCoy)/James Doolan (Engineering Officer Montgomery 'Scotty' Scott)/Stephen Collins (Commander Willard Decker)

23rd Century. Kirk returns to *Starship Enterprise* to wrest control from the young, dynamic Decker in order to lead a mission to save the Earth from a mystery cloud. He jeopardises the mission by his age and lack of recent experience while Decker constantly proves himself the better commander. Their rivalry is resolved at the end of the film when, having discovered that the origin of the cloud was the ancient lost *Voyager VI* ship trying to discover its Creator, Decker and Ilea unite to create 'a new life form', liquidating the V'ger cloud and leaving the *Enterprise* to the original crew.

Absent dystopian, foregrounded meta-utopian.

Although the Enterprise *is now led by a failing father (Kirk) who continually falls short in his actions and decisions, a utopian alternative is represented through the union of Ilea and Decker. This is represented purely in metaphorical terms, however, the generative process being a new life form rather than a familial form of reproduction and the only closure on the actual family is the Final Romance. The familialisation of the Starship is consolidated by the generative nature of their opponent: the alien. However, the creative impulse of the space mission has been soured by the corruption of V'ger which has unwittingly turned on its own creator. In an inverse parable of the Oedipus narrative, the ship threatens its patriarchal makers, only to be liquidated by its sons. The time loop and generative dysfunction prefigure those of* Total Recall *and* Back to the Future.

Airplane!

Jim Abrahams, David Zucker & Jerry Zucker (Walt Disney/Walt Disney) 1980

Robert Hays (Ted Striker)/Julie Hagerty (Elaine Dickinson)/Dr Rumack (Leslie Nielsen)/Rex Kramer (Robert Stack)

Surreal comedy in which Ted, an ex-fighter pilot who lost his nerve after a disastrous mission in the Far East that he believes was his fault, chases air-hostess Elaine (his ex-lover) aboard a plane. When the cabin staff collapse from food poisoning, Ted has to take control aided and abetted by Dr Rumack, on the plane, and by his old commander, Rex Kramer, from the Control Tower. On learning from the doctor that he made the right decision on his mission, Ted saves the plane and is reunited with Elaine who is prepared to accept him now he has apparently matured.

Absent dystopian, present metadystopian.

None of the main characters' families are represented and the professional family of the flying world is so anarchic that it cannot represent a solution to the absence of the actual family. Even the Final Romance is undercut by its comic duplication in the form of the inflatable couple.

'10'

Blake Edwards (Columbia–EMI–Warner/Orion Pictures) 1979
Dudley Moore (George Webber)/Julie Andrews (Samantha 'Sam' Taylor)/Bo Derek (Jenny)
Composer George is 42 and unhappy at the prospect of middle age. Jealous of a swinger he spies on over the road, he abandons his girlfriend Sam and pursues Jenny, a newly-wed on her honeymoon, engaging in an orgy and coldhearted one-night stand *en route*. He is granted sex with the object of his desire when he saves her husband from drowning but, sickened by it, is impotent. Disappointed, he returns to Sam. The title refers to his penchant for rating girls he sees on Californian beaches and the original score he first awarded Jenny.

Absent dystopian, absent metadystopian.

No primary or metaphorical families are represented and the general familial sensibility (represented mainly through Jenny's unpleasant father and George's unrequited lust) is dystopian.

1981

Any Which Way You Can

Buddy Van Horn (Columbia–EMI–Warner/Warner Brothers) 1980
Clint Eastwood (Philo Beddoe)/Sondra Locke (Lynn Halsey-Taylor)/Geoffrey Lewis (Orville Boggs)/James Beekman (Jack Wilson)
Philo decides to give up prizefighting but is forced back into a final fight with Wilson when the Mob kidnap his girlfriend, Lynn, with whom he has just been reconciled. On learning of the terms under which he is to fight, Wilson and Philo join forces to rescue Lynn and cancel the contest. In their own private fight 'to see if they're even', Philo knocks Wilson down, despite a broken arm. Philo is accompanied throughout the film by his eccentric mother, Xenobia, and close buddy, Orville, and Clive, an orang-utan, who each slowly and reluctantly adapt to his relationship with Lynn. Alongside this subplot, his progress is dogged by the Black Widows, an incompetent gang of bikers whom he also wins over by his particular brand of laconic courage.

Present dystopian, foregrounded metadystopian.

Philo's relationship with Xenobia provides a background, dystopian timbre to the text – she is constantly meddling, dishonest and promiscuous, needing to be 'tamed'. The meta-family that Philo creates (the close bonding with Orville and Clive) and which is counterpointed by the brutal but incompetent Mob (a highly familialised criminal organisation) and the hopeless bikers, is inadequate to present a metaphorical alternative resolution to this dystopia.

Private Benjamin
Howard Zieff (Columbia–EMI–Warner/Warner Brothers) 1980
*Judy Benjamin (Goldie Hawn)/Eileen Brennan (Capt. Doreen Lewis)/Armand
Assente (Henri Tremont)/Robert Webber (Col. Clay Thornbush)*
Judy is persuaded to join the army when her second husband dies *in flagrante,*
having already been rescued from the first by her domineering father. When she
fails dismally at training camp, her father comes to bail her out but she confronts
him and re-enlists. This time she is outstandingly successful and is signed up for
the elite Thornbirds by Commander Thornbird himself who then tries to rape her.
She blackmails him into posting her to SHAPE where she is successful despite
opposition but leaves to marry the authoritarian Henri whom she abandons at the
altar.
  Foregrounded dystopian, foregrounded metadystopian.
  *An attempt at a female Oedipal movie which represents both actual (Judy's
own) and metaphorical (Army) families as deeply flawed, finally failing to incorporate Judy into any relationship at the end. Her growing assertiveness is
represented as incompatible with a successful patriarchal resolution.*

Raiders of the Lost Ark
Steven Spielberg (CIC/Lucasfilms for Paramount) 1981
*Harrison Ford (Indiana 'Indy' Jones)/Marcus Brody (Denholm Elliott)/Karen Allen
(Marion Ravenwood)/Paul Freeman (Belloq)*
Indiana Jones is persuaded by Army Intelligence to leave his post at the Museum
with mentor Brody in order to prevent the Nazis from finding the lost Ark of the
Covenant in Cairo which they are excavating with his old rival, Belloq. Jones stops
off in Nepal to collect an artefact from his ex-lover Marion, whose father (now
dead) was Jones's mentor until they quarrelled. Marion insists on accompanying
him to Cairo where, after a series of exploits, she is captured and Jones finds the
Ark. They escape with it by sea but are captured again by Belloq and the Nazis.
The Ark is opened on a small island *en route* to Hitler and everyone except Jones
and Marion is liquidated. The Army commandeers the Ark and stores it in a large
warehouse, to Brody and Jones's disgust.
  Absent dystopian, present metadystopian.
  *The actual family which Jones explicitly seeks to restore in the final film of the
trilogy is here only hinted at through the presence of Marion. Jones has created
an alternative metaphorical family of archaeologists but this is damaged by his
rift with Marion's father and by the opposition of highly dystopian familialised
forms (the ruthless Belloq – whose morals are too close to Jones's own to be
comfortable – and the Nazis). This proximity is signified by the implosion at the
end in which Nazis and archaeologists are literally collapsed into themselves
leaving the Ulyssean figure of Indie tied to his mast.*

The Jazz Singer
Richard Fleischer (Columbia–EMI–Warner/Warner Brothers) 1980
*Neil Diamond (Yussel Rabinovitch, 'Jess Robin')/Laurence Olivier (Cantor
Rabinowitch)/Lucie Arnaz (Molly Bell)/Catlin Adams (Revka [Ruth] Rabinovitch)*
Based on the Al Jolson story. Jess resists the entreaties of his father, Cantor
Rabinowitch, and wife Ruth, to pursue his vocation as a cantor within the Jewish
community, in order to go and seek his fortune as a commercial jazz singer. Aided

by Molly, he is successful, divorces Ruth and is disowned by his father. He runs
away but returns when he learns Molly has had his baby. He becomes reconciled
to his father by singing cantor again and showing him pictures of the baby. The
final sequence depicts Molly and father watching Jess's new show.

Foregrounded dystopian, foregrounded metadystopian.

*Both actual and metaphorical (showbiz/Jewish community) forms are repre-
sented as dystopian since neither is a full resolution to the inadequacies and
failings of the other. The Final Romance and new family (grandfather-Jess-
Molly-baby) is flawed by our knowledge of how Jess abandoned his first wife,
Ruth, to join the meta- family of American culture signified by the show-business
community.*

The Blue Lagoon

Randal Keiser (Columbia–EMI–Warner/Columbia) 1980
*Brooke Shields (Emmeline)/Christopher Atkins (Richard)/Leo McKern (Paddy
Button)*
Two children, Emmeline and Richard, sail on a Victorian schooner to San Fran-
cisco in the care of Richard's father. After a fire, they are cast adrift with Paddy,
the ship's cook. He teaches them basic survival skills when they land on an island
but dies after drinking too much rum. Finding a new site to live, they grow to
puberty. On discovering a bloody statue on which Richard discovers human sac-
rifices are performed, Emma believes it is God after it heals her when she is
poisoned. Following her recovery, Emma becomes pregnant and their baby, whom
they name Paddy, is born. They decide to sail back to their first home but, falling
sick from eating poisonous berries, they drift out to sea. They are picked up by
Richard's father.

Foregrounded dystopian, absent metadystopian.

*All familial forms are represented as failing, largely through neglect. Richard's
actual father cannot protect them, the meta-family of Paddy Senior-Emmeline-
Richard fails for the same reason and the only alternative, the metaphorical,
invisible Other, is engaged in human sacrifice, by its very nature, an anti-
generative practice. In turn, Emmeline and Richard cannot protect their own
baby, the baby whose name invokes the failed surrogate-parent.*

1982

Arthur

Steve Gordon (Columbia-EMI-Warner/Orion) 1980
*Dudley Moore (Arthur Bach)/John Gielgud (Hobson)/Liza Minnelli (Linda Marolla)/
Jill Eikenberry (Susan Johnson)*
Arthur is heir to a fortune and enjoys a spoiled, leisured life of promiscuity, self-
indulgence and infantile behaviour supervised by his disapproving butler, Hobson.
Arthur's father forces him into an engagement with socialite Susan but Arthur falls
in love with Linda whom he meets when she is shoplifting to support her father.
Abetted by Hobson, Linda crashes Arthur's engagement party, but Susan interrupts
their *tête-à-tête* to get Arthur to visit the ailing Hobson who subsequently dies
in hospital. Arthur dumps Susan at the altar after proposing to Linda, and
Arthur's grandmother bestows her fortune on them when learning how Arthur has
'matured'.

Foregrounded dystopian, absent metadystopian.
The building/rebuilding of the family is the subject of this narrative but it constantly falters – all three fathers (Arthur's, Linda's, Susan's) fail their children and the final rescue by the grandmother is represented as far from altruistic. The world of work is the metaphorical familial structuring here, but only in absentia *– as something Arthur does* not *want to engage in.*

The Fox and the Hound
Art Stevens/Ted Berman/Richard Rich (Walt Disney/Walt Disney) 1981
Animation. Voices: Mickey Rooney (Tod)/Kurt Russell (Copper)/Jack Albertson (Amos Slade)/Pearl Bailey (Big Mama)
Tod, the fox, is abandoned by his mother and adopted by Widow Tweed. Having struck up a friendship with Copper, the hound, Tod learns to hunt with Amos (Tweed's neighbour) and an older hound, Chief. When Chief is hurt during a chase of Tod, Tod is blamed and Widow Tweed releases him in a game reserve. There he is helped by Big Mama (a wise old owl) and Vixey. Amos continued to set traps for him but when Amos is caught by a bear and Copper is wounded, Tod rescues them and Cooper defends his old pal from Amos's wrath. Tod and Copper are reconciled.
Absent dystopian, absent metadystopian.
The narrative is motivated by Tod's abandonment and his search for a replacement 'metaphorical' family, uneasily strung between the human and anthropomorphised animal families. The resolution is not familial, or even a Final Romance, but a male–male bonding.

Condorman
Charles Jarrott (Walt Disney/Walt Disney) 1981
Michael Crawford (Woody Wilkins)/Oliver Reed (Krokov)/Barbara Carrera (Natalia)/James Hampton (Harry Oslo)
Woody Wilkins, a cartoonist, always tests out his eponymous character's exploits in real life before drawing them. He shares a Parisian flat with a CIA bureaucrat, Harry, who asks Woody to deliver diplomatic papers for him, taking the soubriquet 'Condorman'. A complex series of counterplots ensue in which Natalia, a KGB agent, defects with Woody, chased by her ex-boss, Krokov. They finally foil Krokov's pursuit, only to have Woody framed for a murder in Italy. Harry rescues them but by reading *Condorman* comics for clues, the KGB capture Natalia in Switzerland. Woody changes into Condorman and rescues Natalia. Reunited at a baseball match in Los Angeles, Harry reveals there is a new mission for Condorman.
Absent dystopian, present metadystopian.
The only familial structures present in the film are the CIA/KGB organisations in which the fathers are either absent or failed, the mothers missing and the children (in this case the sons, Natalia proving herself weak and vulnerable) are heroic. The more active and daring the man, the more successful he is – Harry is represented as a mere bureaucrat while Woody saves the day by becoming the superhero he created. As in Total Recall *and* Back to the Future, *Woody/Condorman is his own creator, father to his own father, son to his own son.*

Annie
John Huston (Columbia-EMI-Warner/Rastar for Columbia Pictures) 1981
Aileen Quinn (Little Orphan Annie)/Albert Finney (Oliver 'Daddy' Warbucks)/
Carol Burnett (Miss Hannigan)/Ann Reinking (Grace Farrell)
Set in New York during the Depression. Annie is taken into an orphanage supervised by the cruel matron, Miss Hannigan, after Annie's parents die in a fire. After
running away to find her parents, she smuggles in a dog, Sandy. She is subsequently selected by the tycoon Warbucks' secretary, Grace, as his protégée for a
week to help redeem his appalling reputation. When Sandy saves Warbucks from
a Bolshevik assassin, Grace is able to persuade Warbucks to adopt Annie. But after
Warbucks offers a reward for finding Annie's parents, whom she believes to be still
alive, Miss Hannigan's brother and girlfriend claim Annie using a locket supplied
by Miss Hannigan. The orphanage children rescue her and she is reunited with
Grace and Warbucks.
    Foregrounded utopian, present metadystopian.
    The narrative object is to establish a family setting for Annie, which is repre-
    sented as utopian and realised through the combination of Grace and Warbucks
    at the end. The background to this is a dystopian social fabric, most clearly
    realised in the familial structuring of the orphanage and the usurping 'family'
    of Lily and Rooster.

Rocky III
Sylvester Stallone (UIP/United Artists) 1982
Sylvester Stallone (Rocky Balboa)/Talia Shire (Adrian Balboa)/Burt Young (Paulie)/
Carl Weathers (Apollo Creed)
Taunted by his brutal rival, Clubber Lang, successful but ageing boxer Rocky
accepts Clubber's challenge to fight once more before retiring. Micky, his manager, walks out revealing that Rocky's last few fights were carefully selected to
save him from injury but relents to help him train. During the fight, Micky suffers
a fatal heart-attack and Rocky, unfit and ill-prepared, is humiliatingly defeated.
Apollo, the champion Rocky himself defeated, offers to help him train on the
condition that he surrenders his pampered lifestyle and for a favour he will reveal
after the return fight. Apollo puts him through a gruelling training regime in a poor
black neighbourhood and, fired by his wife's pep talk ('you're not really a loser')
Rocky goes on to beat Clubber and regain the title. Apollo reveals his favour – a
private fight, Apollo's skills against Rocky's determination.
    Present utopian, foregrounded meta-utopian.
    Rocky's actual family reinforces the metaphorical familialised boxing commun-
    ity to foreground a discourse of utopian realisation. In this interpretation, the
    family is a vehicle for righting individual wrongs and for restoring the rightful
    champions of the metafamily.

1983

E.T. – The Extra-Terrestrial
Steven Spielberg (UIP/Universal) 1982
Henry Thomas (Elliott)/Dee Wallace (Mary)/Robert MacNaughton (Michael)/Drew
Barrymore (Gertie)/Peter Coyote ('Keys')
Elliott discovers 'ET', an extra-terrestrial abandoned by his spaceship when

scientists surprise them. Elliott protects ET from the adults, including his recently divorced mother, Mary, but introduces 'him' to Michael and Gertie, his brother and sister. Elliott and ET become telepathically attached but ET slowly sickens and Elliott realises he must get him home. Captured by the scientists, ET 'dies' but Elliott resurrects him with a declaration of love. The children kidnap the revived ET from the scientists and return him to his spaceship.

Foregrounded dystopian, present metadystopian.
The drive of the narrative is to restore ET to his spaceship-family which directly conflicts with the drive to complete Elliott's fractured family. The substitution of father-son ET or proto-father Keys the scientist cannot be successfully achieved within the diegesis or even represented as achievable. Although the meta-family of ET's alien race may be construed as utopian, the only terrestrial counterpart – the scientific (adult male) community is represented as deeply dystopian.

Return of the Jedi
Richard Marquand (20th Century Fox/Lucasfilm) 1983
Mark Hamill (Luke Skywalker)/Harrison Ford (Han Solo)/Carrie Fisher (Princess Leia)/Billy Dee Williams (Lando Calrissian)
The last of the Star Wars series and follow-up to *The Empire Strikes Back*. Luke bargains for Solo's life with Jabba who holds him captive. Leia arrives disguised as a bounty-hunter and all are captured by Jabba until released by Lando Calrissian. Leia kills Jabba and Yoda confirms that not only is the evil Darth Luke's father but Leia is his twin sister with the potential power of a Jedi herself. All the rebels travel to Endor to defeat the Death Star and, urged on by Emperor Palpatium, Luke almost kills Darth in a duel but pulls back. In a final fight, Darth kills the Emperor but is himself fatally wounded. Calrissian blows up the Death Star and Leia and Han acknowledge their own romance before joining Luke.

Foregrounded dystopian, foregrounded metadystopian.
The Final Romance (Leia–Han) cannot efface the incestuous attraction explored throughout the series between Leia and Luke and the fact that the hero himself is left alone at the end. The treachery of the father hangs over the entire series and his simultaneous position as meta-father establishes both meta and actual families as dystopian. The only consistent characters in the films are the 'friendly' aliens, specifically Chewbacca, C-3PO and R2-D2, but their idiosyncrasies and, more importantly, their position as clearly Other within the text marks the human alternative as dystopian.

Tootsie
Sydney Pollack (Columbia–EMI–Warner/Delphi Productions) 1982
Dustin Hoffman (Michael Dorsey/Dorothy Michaels)/Jessica Lange (Julie Nichols)/ Teri Garr (Sandy)
Struggling actor Michael Dorsey disguises himself as a woman to land a part in a soap opera. He falls in love with Julie, a single mother and one of the leads, and juggles his growing attachment for her with his male persona and badly treated lover, Sandy. Shocked when Julie's father proposes to him, Michael reveals his deception live on TV and tries to pick up the pieces. He finally tries to reconcile himself with Julie but this is left inconclusive.

Foregrounded dystopian, foregrounded metadystopian.

Michael's promiscuous love life, his ambiguous gender and the nature of his profession all render the Final Romance highly unstable. The narrative drive veers between the twin propulsions of incorporating Michael/Dorothy within the meta-family of the soap opera and creating a proto-family with Julie. Julie's own family is also dystopian (mother dead, father fooled by Michael's gender transference).

An Officer and a Gentleman

Taylor Hackford (UIP/Lorimar) 1981

Richard Gere (Zack Mayo)/Debra Winger (Paula Pokrifki)/Louis Gossett Jnr (Sgt Foley)/David Keith (Sid Worley)/Lisa Blount (Lynette Pomeroy)

Zack enlists to train as a naval pilot and officer to escape from his drunken, whoring father. To endure the gruelling programme meted out by Sgt Foley, Zack and Sid romance two local girls, Paula and Lynette, and Zack exploits his entrepreneurial skills by hiring out polished equipment, for which he is severely punished by Foley. When Zack ends his affair with Paula to retain his independence, Lynette tells Sid she's pregnant. Meanwhile Zack becomes increasingly unselfish during the training, finally saving Sid in a flight exercise. Sid immediately quits to propose to Lynette but kills himself when he finds that she lied to him and intends to marry a pilot. When Foley beats him in a bitter Kung Fu fight, Zack decides to go through with his passing-out parade and then carries Paula off in triumph.

Foregrounded dystopian, foregrounded metadystopian.

The suicide of Zack's mother (mirrored in Sid's suicide) motivates the narrative. Zack cannot achieve oedipalisation with his failed father and absent mother and goes through a quest of self-sacrifice and buddy-bonding before constructing Foley as surrogate father, achieving manhood, professional status – and the girl. However the represented families (Zack's and Paula's) are unpleasant, discouraging environments and their Final Romance is still coloured by the earlier fractures within the narrative and by the undercurrent of homoerotic attraction between Sid and Zack. The meta-family of the navy is equally unsatisfactory, riven by conflict and rejection.

Staying Alive

Sylvester Stallone (UIP/Paramount) 1983

John Travolta (Tony Manero)/Cynthia Rhodes (Jackie)/Finola Hughes (Laura)

The hero of *Saturday Night Fever*, Tony has now abandoned his deprived childhood home to pursue his ambition of becoming a professional dancer. Becoming increasingly entangled with Laura, a successful but hard-bitten dancer, he repeatedly neglects his faithful girlfriend, Jackie. He is finally rejected by Laura whom he subsequently humiliates in a big dance number watched by the forgiving Jackie and his mother.

Present dystopian, foregrounded metadystopian.

The showbusiness world, fathered by invisible, tyrannical directors, is foregrounded as a brutal, alienating community for which Tony will sacrifice all – including a Final Romance – to enter. His own family (absent father, wise but passive mother) is represented as the environment he is struggling to leave, not to enter.

1984

Indiana Jones and the Temple of Doom
Steven Spielberg (UIP/Lucasfilms for Paramount) 1984
Harrison Ford (Indiana Jones)/Kate Capshaw (Willie)/Ke Huy Quan (Short Round)
Escaping from Japan with Willie, a nightclub dancer and Shorty, his streetwise
child assistant, Indiana Jones crash-lands in India where villagers beseech him to
find their stolen children. Jones sets off to find the village's magical stone and
release the children from the thrall of the Thugee cult but all three are captured and
Jones is brainwashed. Shorty revives him and they release the children, returning
them to the village.
   Absent dystopian, foregrounded metadystopian.
   The meta-family of Indie, Willie and Shorty are counterpoised against the
   familialised Thugees. Their resolution is fractured, however, by the resistance
   of Shorty to the Final Romance and the overt cynicism of Indie.

Police Academy
Hugh Wilson (Columbia–EMI–Warner/The Ladd Company for Warner Brothers)
1984
Steve Guttenberg (Carey Mahoney)/Kim Cattrall (Karen Thompson)/Bubba Smith
(Moses Hightower)/Andrew Rubin (George Martin)
After the mayor opens up the police recruitment policy, an eclectic group of new
recruits turn up for the next intake of the Police Academy. Led by Mahoney,
Hightower and Martin, the new recruits successively overcome the plots hatched
against them by Lt Harris and Sgt Callahan under the bumbling leadership of Cdt
Lessade. Finally, having quelled a riot, they graduate in the final parade.
   Absent dystopian, foregrounded metadystopian.
   The police 'family' is deeply divided over its new offspring, the father-figure
   (Lessade) seriously lacking in both authority and gravitas *and the pretenders,*
   Harris/Callahan signally failing to achieve their own ambitions of purging the
   new recruits. The brief actual family representations in the opening sequences
   all suggest that the family is the cause of the new recruits' eagerness to enlist
   rather than something they are looking to recreate.

Sudden Impact
Clint Eastwood (Columbia–EMI–Warner/Warner Brothers) 1983
Clint Eastwood (Harry Callahan)/Sondra Locke (Jennifer Spencer)/Pat Hingle
(Chief Jannings)
Callahan is sent to San Paulo on an enforced vacation to investigate a murder
where he immediately antagonises the local police chief, Jannings, by his unortho-
dox methods. He finds that the murder is connected to a rape which Jannings
covered up because it was committed by his son alongside the psychopathic Micky.
The killer is the rape victim, Jennifer, who is now seeking revenge. By this time,
Jennifer has also killed her lesbian friend, Ray, who led the rapists to her in
revenge for being spurned. Attracted to her, Callahan rescues Jennifer from Micky
and allows him to take the blame for the killings.
   Absent dystopian, foregrounded metadystopian.
   The police-fathers are represented as highly dystopian, either corrupt or incom-
   petent, blinded to the abilities of their wayward 'son', Callahan. Neither the

police nor the actual family are achievable or desirable and, by the end, the police ethics are indistinguishable from those of the criminals. Transgressively, Jennifer is actively rewarded for her vengeful behaviour, outside conventional patriarchal structures.

Terms of Endearment
James L. Brooks (UIP/Paramount) 1983
Shirley MacLaine (Aurora Greenway)/Jack Nicholson (Garratt Breedlove)/Debra Winger (Emma Horton)
After her father's death, when Emma was still a teenager, she was charged with looking after her neurotic mother, Aurora. Emma later marries Flap and moves away, to her mother's distress. Flap is constantly unfaithful while Emma bears two children and Aurora gradually develops a romance with her anarchic neighbour, Garratt. When Emma dies of cancer, Aurora takes on her children since Flap admits his inability to care for them.
Foregrounded dystopian, absent dystopian.
The good mother is punished for failing in her filial duty and for her brief affair, while the errant husband is free to create (and abandon) a new family. Neither Emma's own family, nor the one she creates, are represented as solutions to the narrative hermeneutic, which is to fulfill the father's absence and recreate a stable family unit. Although the film closes on a Final Romance (Aurora–Garratt) and a proto-family, this is destabilised by the punishment of the mother, by substitute mother Aurora's neuroses and by Garratt's previous infantilism and promiscuity.

Trading Places
John Landis (UIP/Paramount) 1983
Eddie Murphy (Billy Ray Valentine)/Dan Ackroyd (Louis Winthorpe III)
After being wrongfully arrested for mugging commodity broker Louis Winthorpe, Billy (a street hustler) becomes the subject of a bet between Winthorpe's employers, Randolph and Mortimer Duke, as to whether genetics or environment determines character and behaviour. Billy proves himself an able broker while Winthorpe is framed and humiliated as a thief. On learning of the bet, Billy and Winthorpe take revenge and bankrupt the Dukes.
Absent dystopian, absent metadystopian.
The film proposes that the metafamily is vital as an environment for maturation if the actual family has failed. However, the metafamily is itself tainted by the actions of the two brothers while there is no foregrounded nuclear family represented. The Dukes, related by marriage to Winthorpe, suggest a dystopian form of actual family.

1985

Ghostbusters
Ivan Reitman (Columbia–EMI–Warner/Columbia-Delphi) 1984
Bill Murray (Dr Peter Venkman)/Sigourney Weaver (Dana Barrett)/Dan Ackroyd (Dr Raymond Stantz)/Harold Ramis (Dr Egon Spengler)
After being sacked from the University for being a 'poor scientist' and losing his grant, Venkman, researcher of the paranormal, sets up a team of Ghostbusters with

his colleagues, Egon and Ray. They set about investigating the threat caused by a paranormal disturbance which centres on Dana whom Peter continually attempts to seduce. Finally, despite resistance from the City authorities, they liquidate the Destroyer, and are hailed as heroes.

Absent dystopian, foregrounded meta-utopian.

The meta-family of the Ghostbusters team is represented as a successful nucleated family unit, finally incorporating Dana as absent 'mother'.

Gremlins

Joe Dante (Columbia–EMI–Warner/Warner Brother for Amblin Entertainment) 1984

Zach Galligan (Billy Peltzer)/Phoebe Cates (Kate)/Hoyt Axton (Rand Peltzer)/ Frances Lee McCain (Lynn Peltzer)

Billy is given a mogwai (Gizmo) by his father. He disobeys the instructions given to him and it produces malignant offspring who set about trying to destroy the neighbourhood. Billy's mother liquidises some of them but they kill Mrs Deagle, a neighbour whom Billy detests. Billy rescues Kate, his girlfriend from their clutches and sets about destroying them, initially by blowing up a cinema, then, with Gizmo's assistance, exposing the mogwai's leader to sunlight. The proprietor of the curio shop who sold him to Mr Peltzer retrieves Gizmo from the family.

Foregrounded dystopian, absent metadystopian.

A powerful homily on the results of crossing children. Billy vicariously liquidates his detested neighbour through the malignant force introduced to the home by his father. Evil lurks constantly within the familial environment – the generous father introducing the threat of destruction to the home, the perfect mother using the domestic armoury as a weapon against it. The mogwais themselves assume the characteristics of the adults in the neighbourhood, representing ghastly caricatures of the local inhabitants and signalling the masquerade of the suburb, routinely exploited in contemporary horror films.

Rambo: First Blood Part II

George Pan Cosmatos (Columbia-EMI-Warner/Carloco for Anabasis) 1985

Sylvester Stallone (John Rambo)/Richard Crenna (Colonel Trautman)/Julie Nickson (Co Bao)/Charles Napier (Marshall Murdock)

Rambo is retrieved from a labour camp by Trautman and Murdoch and sent on a mission to prove there are no American prisoners of war still languishing in Vietnam. Betrayed by Vietnam Intelligence and by Murdoch, who was using the mission as a PR exercise in order to keep the reparation money, Rambo is captured and tortured. He is rescued by Co, a Vietnamese aide and now his lover, who is subsequently killed in an ambush. Furious, Rambo releases the prisoners he has discovered and returns to HQ to confront his treacherous commanders. He storms off into the jungle after destroying the command computer.

Absent dystopian, foregrounded metadystopian.

Rambo rebels against the treacherous 'fathers', protectors now of a motherland he feels alienated from. The nationhood represented in the film is one the hero cannot be part of and is no solution for the affiliative lack constructed by the narrative.

Beverly Hills Cop

Martin Brest (UIP/Paramount) 1984

Eddie Murphy (Axel Foley)/Judge Reinhold (Detective Billy Rosewood)/John Ashton (Sgt Taggart)/Ronny Cox (Lieutenant Bogomil)

Axel Foley, unorthodox cop, abandons the case he is working on in Detroit to avenge the death of his buddy, Mikey, who has just been released from jail. He travels to Los Angeles where he first humiliates, then forms an uneasy relationship with, the local police. Taggart and Billy finally ally with him, against the orders of their superiors, to expose the guilt of Maitland, a leading businessman. In a final gunfight, they kill the entire criminal gang and force Lt Bogomil to support their actions. Billy returns to Detroit, tailed by his two new buddies.

Absent dystopian, foregrounded metadystopian.

The police 'family', with its authoritarian fathers who 'don't understand' their anarchic, but well-intentioned son, Axel Foley, is not presented as a solution to the absent nuclear family. Instead the main drive of the narrative is to create a perverse nuclear 'sub-family' of Axel–Taggart–Billy – a homoerotic bonding triggered by the brutal severance of Axel's relationship with the criminal Mikey. The relationship is further inflected by Axel's own criminality and his racial difference, issues never fully resolved or contained within the text.

Police Academy 2: Their First Assignment

Jerry Paris (Columbia–EMI–Warner/Ladd Brothers for Warner Brothers) 1985

Steve Guttenberg (Carey Mahoney)/Bubba Smith (Hightower)/Howard Hesseman (Capt. Pete Lassard)/Art Metrano (Lt. Mauser)

Given thirty days to stem the current crimewave, Capt. Lassard takes on six rookie recruits, the main characters of *Police Academy*. Lt Mauser disrupts their efforts, intent on seizing his boss's job. Finally, after Lassard is forced to stand down, Mahoney infiltrates the main gang, led by Zed, and the recruits defeat them. Lassard is reinstated and two of the rookies (Tackleberry and Kirkland) are married.

Absent dystopian, foregrounded meta-dystopian.

As in the original film, the meta-family is still disrupted by warring fathers who strive to prevent the new generation from achieving their potential. A proto-family is indicated by the Final Romance and wedding, but this, as becomes even clearer in the sequels, is collapsed into the metafamily – the familial and heterosexual relationships being a source of humour rather than a counterpoint to the familialised police grouping.

1986

Back to the Future

Robert Zemeckis (UIP/Amblin Entertainment for Universal) 1985

Michael J. Fox (Marty McFly)/Christopher Lloyd (Dr Emmett 'Doc' Brown)/Lea Thompson (Lorraine Baines)/Crispin Glover (George McFly)/Claudia Wells (Jennifer Parker)

Disappointed by the failures of his family, Marty strikes up a friendship with Doc, a mad inventor. When he is mistakenly catapulted into the past by his mentor's time machine (the DeLorean), he 'remakes' his family, re-engineering his parents' relationship and creating the perfect model. He returns to the present, and finds that Doc heeded his warnings and avoided the murder depicted at the opening of the film. All neatly resurrected, Marty, Doc and Marty's girlfriend, Jennifer, set off into the future to sort out *their* children.

Foregrounded dystopian, absent metadystopian.

Despite the utopian 'recreation' of Marty's family at the close of the film, the family is represented as constantly under threat, never stable and never fully achievable. More importantly, however, the family is the product of the son's endeavours, rather than the father's and Marty is represented not only as the father-figure to his own father but also as potential suitor to his mother and father of himself. More complex than a simple Oedipal passage, Back to the Future *builds in an autogenerative loop which invests all utopian reproductive capability in the son.*

Rocky IV
Sylvester Stallone (UIP/Universal) 1985

Sylvester Stallone (Rocky Balboa)/Talia Shire (Adrian Balboa)/Carl Weathers (Apollo Creed)/Dolph Lundgren (Ivan Drago)/Brigitte Nielsen (Ludmilla)

Against Rocky's advice, close buddy and sparring partner Apollo is hyped into a fight with the new Russian champion, Drago, and is killed. Rocky sets out to avenge him, in defiance of his wife Adrian's protests and defeats Drago in Russia after a gruelling training regime in which his wife eventually joins him.

Present utopian, foregrounded meta-utopian.

Essentially a film about utopian transformation through rampant individualism, the film constructs a diegesis in which all families can be resolved (meta-familial nations, the boxing community and Rocky's own family) through individual effort. The family (represented here most powerfully as the father–son continuity) is achieved and sustainable, nations can be brought together through personal enterprise. (The extra-diegetic discourses make this movie even more interesting: Lundgren was one of the new pretenders to the Stallone–Schwarzenegger muscle-action star crown and Brigitte Nielsen was Stallone's ex-wife.)

Out of Africa
Sydney Pollack (UIP/Universal) 1985

Meryl Streep (Karen Blixen)/Robert Redford (Denys Finch Hatton)/Klaus Maria Brandauer (Bror von Blixen-Fineckel)/Michael Kitchen (Berkeley Cole)

Tired of her lover's infidelities, Karen elects for a friendly marriage with his brother, Bror, to start a new life on her farm in Africa. There she encounters Berkeley Cole, who remains a constant friend, and the maverick hunter, Denys. Bror, too, is unfaithful to her and when they finally part after Karen contracts syphilis from him, she starts a long, but unsettled relationship with Denys. Dissatisfied by this, she breaks it off and when the farm burns down, decides to return home. Denys is killed in a flying accident just before their final flight together.

Absent dystopian, absent metadystopian.

There are no familial frameworks in which these central characters operate. Karen's home and mother are represented as havens when she is in trouble, but the mother is never shown on screen. The only successful family is the exoticised Somali community.

Top Gun
Tony Scott (UIP/Paramount) 1986
Tom Cruise (Pete 'Maverick' Mitchell)/Kelly McGillis (Charlotte 'Charley'
Blackwood)/Anthony Edwards (Nick 'Goose' Bradshaw)/Tom Skerritt (Commander
Mike Metcalf)
Maverick arrives at the Top Gun training school, determined to prove himself by
his skilful and dangerous exploits in order to compensate for the apparent disgrace
of his dead pilot father. His close relationship with his buddy Goose and his family
is not enough to prevent him constantly risking Goose's life in wild rivalries.
Having seduced his instructor, Charley, he abandons her when Goose is killed in
a flying accident after their graduation. Father-substitute Metcalf informs him of
the true nature of his father's heroism and Maverick goes on to prove himself on
a live mission. Returning to Top Gun as an instructor, Charley joins him in the
final sequence.
   Absent dystopian, foregrounded meta-utopian.
   All the central families represented (Maverick's, Goose's) are fractured by loss
   and the familial relationship is represented as a distraction from the true uto-
   pian project – forging the naval pilot (specifically the Top Gun) community.
   Maverick can only achieve maturation through the intervention of a metaphor-
   ical father and the redemption of his natural father is achieved through learning
   of his courage in battle, not his affection for his son. Goose, too, is punished
   for his attention to his family, as is Cougar at the opening of the film. Despite
   the Final Romance, the narrative drive is to convene the metaphorical, not the
   actual, family unit. A film about transgression, the film constantly tests the
   boundaries of what is permissible: physically, psychically and emotionally.

Police Academy 3: Back in Training
Jerry Paris (Columbia–Cannon–Warner/Police Academy Productions) 1986
Steve Guttenberg (Carey Mahoney)/Bubba Smith (Hightower)/Howard Hesseman
(Capt Pete Lassard)/Art Metrano (Lt. Mauser)/George Gaynes (Commandant
Lassard)
Lt Mauser now heads a second training academy but Governor Nielson plans to
close one. While Mauser plants undercover agents to disrupt his rival's new training intake, Lassard brings back his favourite squad of ex-recruits to ensure things
go smoothly. Trailing Mauser's team, Hooks and Mrs Fackler expose the infiltra-
tors and when Nielsen is abducted at a charity regatta, Lassard's recruits rescue
him and arrest the culprits.
   Absent dystopian, foregrounded metadystopian.
   The same formula as in Police Academy 2 *reworked in a slightly different*
   context. The older siblings are brought back to ease the passage of the new
   arrivals as the feuding fathers again fail to ensure a safe maturation passage
   to policehood.

1987

Beverly Hills Cop II
Tony Scott (UIP/Paramount) 1987
Eddie Murphy (Axel Foley)/Judge Reinhold (Billy Rosewood)/John Ashton (Sgt
John Taggart)/Ronny Cos (Andrew Bogomil)

When Lt Bogomil is shot while working on a big investigation, Foley drops an important case in Detroit to return to LA. He reprises the maverick skills he displayed in *Beverly Hills Cop* to solve the crime, enlisting Billy and Taggart in a close buddy formation to do so.

Present dystopian, foregrounded metadystopian.

The dynamics of the familial relationship are similar to those in the previous film, although this text attempts to introduce greater familial depth through the introduction of Bogomil's daughter and Taggart's (absent) wife. These family forms are explicitly rejected throughout the narrative by Foley whose only interest is avenging Bogomil and achieving closer bonding with Billy and Taggart.

Police Academy 4: Citizens on Patrol

Jim Drake (Columbia–Cannon–Warner/Warner Brothers) 1987

Steve Guttenberg (Carey Mahoney)/Bubba Smith (Hightower)/Howard Hesseman (Capt Pete Lassard)/G.W. Bailey (Captain Harris)

Commandant Lessard introduces COP, a neighbourhood patrol scheme, which attracts all kinds of unlikely civilians. Announcing the success of the scheme at a London conference, many multi-national delegates travel back with him to see it. Meanwhile, the jealous Captain Harris tries to sabotage the scheme but the resulting chaos is resolved by Mahoney and his peers.

Absent dystopian, foregrounded metadystopian.

Again, the fathers fail to ensure the protection of the community and it is left to the errant, but redemptive children to come to the rescue.

The Golden Child

Michael Ritchie (UIP/Paramount) 1986

Eddie Murphy (Chandler Jarrell)/Charlotte Lewis (Kee Nang)/Charles Dance (Sardo Numspa)

The Golden Child is a supernatural entity made vulnerable when given blood upon which event his death will cause hell on earth. Chandler, investigating the death of a teenager, is informed by Kee Nang that the missing girl was murdered to provide blood for the Child and that he is the one 'chosen' to effect a rescue. The Child has been kidnapped by a demon, Sardo Numspa, whom Chandler eventually defeats and kills by various magical means. Kee Nang's father also intervenes before Chandler is finally able to rescue the Child and revive the injured Kee Nang. The three plan their future together in the final sequence.

Foregrounded utopian, foregrounded metadystopian.

Here the American 'family' is counterpoised against the demonic forces of the other. The solution to the supernatural evil is represented as the all-American nuclear family unit, reinvigorated by love and purity and blessed by the Tibetan wise-man patriarch.

Superman IV: The Quest for Peace

Sidney J. Furie (Columbia–Cannon–Warner/Cannon Films–Warner Brothers) 1987

Christopher Reeve (Superman/Clark Kent)/Gene Hackman (Lex Luthor)

After a request from a schoolchild, Superman intervenes in the escalating arms race by destroying all nuclear weapons. However, the arch-villain Lex Luthor has escaped from his chain-gang and, in concert with arms dealers, creates Nuclear Man from one of Superman's hairs. Meanwhile, Warfield has bought up the *Planet*, the newspaper on which Superman's alter ego, Clark Kent works, and installed his daughter, Lacy, whom Superman double-dates with Lois. After Superman is wounded in a battle with Nuclear Man, Lois restores his confidence and he defeats his enemy with a solar eclipse. Perry White returns to the *Planet* and Superman returns Lex to his chain-gang.

Absent dystopian, absent metadystopian.

The only family relationship represented is the unsatisfactory nepotistic one of Warfield and his daughter. Superman cannot resolve the metafamilial hermeneutic which is constantly jeopardised by internal dissent and by himself (Nuclear Man is created from Superman). The metafamily (the human race) never coalesces into a stable entity, but its absence provides the motivation to restitution. In this scenario, it is a child who is privileged as the instigator of the narrative and the bringer of peace.

The Untouchables

Brian De Palma (UIP/Paramount) 1987

Robert de Niro (Al Capone)/Kevin Costner (Eliot Ness)/Sean Connery (Jim Malone)/ Andy Garcia (George Stone)/Charles Martin Smith (Oscar Wallace)

Treasury Department Special Agent Eliot Ness arrives in Chicago to investigate the crime-ring of Al Capone. Discovering widespread corruption, he creates a special investigation team of Malone (rough diamond, straight cop), George Stone (streetwise, sharp shooting rookie) and accountant Oscar Wallace. Under threat when he begins to make progress, Ness is forced to hide his family and suffers the deaths of both Malone and Stone. He finally brings Capone to trial on tax charges and, persuading the judge to change the corrupted jury, Capone is convicted. On his way home, he learns that Prohibition has been ended.

Present dystopian, foregrounded metadystopian.

Despite the narrative drive to achieve both actual (Ness's own) and the meta-families (police and City Authorities), both are fractured by Ness's obsession with restoring the law and redeeming the meta-fathers. The nuclear family is desirable, but unachievable because of the meta-family; the solution is the male bonding, which must be fractured in order to achieve any kind of resolution.

1988

Fatal Attraction

Adrian Lyne (UIP/Paramount) 1987

Michael Douglas (Dan Gallagher)/Glenn Close (Alex Forrest)/Anne Archer (Beth Gallagher)

Staying in town for a business meeting while his wife goes to the country, Dan enjoys an adulterous weekend with Alex. However, she becomes increasingly obsessed with him, finally kidnapping Dan's child, Ellen, when he calls her bluff and tells his wife. When Alex breaks in and tries to kill Beth, Dan fails to protect her and Beth is forced to shoot Alex. [The ending was changed from the original one depicting Alex's suicide, after an unfavourable response from audiences.]

Foregrounded dystopian, present metadystopian.

It is the threat posed by the metaphorical family (the publishing house) which tempts Dan to his fatal act of transgression. Playing continually with sexual discourses, the text constructs a castrated, failing meta-father in Dan's boss and his wilful 'children' who cannot be fully trusted. It is Beth, the good mother, who must move outside the law to save her family from the threat posed to it by Dan.

Three Men and a Baby
Leonard Nimoy (Warner Brothers/Touchstone) 1987
Tom Selleck (Peter Mitchell)/Steve Guttenberg (Michael Kellan)/Ted Danson (Jack Holden)/Nancy Travis (Sylvia)
Jack leaves for Turkey, warning flatmates Peter and Michael that a package is due to be delivered. However the intended package of heroin is preceded by a baby which Jack's ex-lover, Sylvia, abandons for him to look after. Confusion reigns once the package does arrive and both the narcotics squad and the heroin dealers try to recover it amidst Peter's and Michael's chaotic attempts at childminding. On Jack's return, the three set a trap for traffickers Vince and Satch, who are arrested. When Sylvia returns to collect the baby, she relents and the four agree to look after the baby together.
Foregrounded utopian, absent metadystopian.
A fragile utopian family is created by the end of the film, with parents (Jack and Sylvia) together under one roof, however uneasily. Yet the film is shot through with transgression and illicit confusions, centring on male desire for the baby and incompletely contained by the techniques and tropes of comedy. The external world is highly dystopian – one from which all retreat to the domestic Eden.

Coming to America
John Landis (UIP/Paramount) 1988
Eddie Murphy (Prince Akeem)/James Earl Jones (King Jaffa Jeffer)/Arsenio Hall (Semmi)/Shari Headley (Lisa McDowell)/Madge Sinclair (Queen Acacia)
Forced into marriage by his father, Prince Akeem resists and insists on going to America to find true romance and learn how to survive in the 'real world'. Accompanied by close buddy Semmi, he takes a job in a fast-food restaurant and falls in love with the owner's daughter, Lisa. After many reversals, his persuades his father to accept Lisa and they are married in Africa.
Foregrounded utopian, absent metadystopian.
As in Rocky, *all is possible through one man's personal efforts. Prince Akeem succeeds in marrying African and American cultures to restore his dynasty and create the utopian extended family.*

Good Morning, Vietnam
Barry Levinson (Warner Brothers/Touchstone) 1987
Robin Williams (Airman Adrian Cronauer)/Chintara Sukapatana (Trinh)/Forest Whitaker (Private Edward Garlick)/Tung Tanh Tran (Tuan)
Saigon 1965. Cronauer is the anarchic host of the Armed Forces Radio Network morning radio show in Vietnam. Angering his superiors Lt Hauk and Sgt Dickerson by his irreverent broadcasts, he is protected by General Taylor who believes he is good for morale. Meantime, he becomes increasingly involved with Trinh, a local English teacher, whose brother, Tuan, is revealed as a Vietcong saboteur. When Tuan saves his life, Cronauer is shipped out in disgrace.
Absent dystopian, foregrounded metadystopian.
The metafamily of the Army and American nation is revealed as cynical and

ruthless – harshly dystopian. Even the Final Romance is prevented by the failed meta-fathers.

Beetlejuice
Tim Burton (Warner Brothers/Geffen Film Company) 1988
Geena Davis (Barbara Maitland)/Alec Baldwin (Adam Maitland)/Michael Keaton (Betelgeuse)/Winona Ryder (Lydia Deetz)
Killed in a car accident, Adam and Barbara return to haunt their former house, now inhabited by the objectionable Deetzes. Trying to drive them out, they enlist the help of the daughter, Lydia, but only manage to be hailed as a potential tourist attraction when revealed to the parents. Desperate, they call in human-exorciser, Betelgeuse. However, when the Maitlands are themselves accidentally exorcised, Lydia has to agree to marry the foul Betelgeuse. Restored, the Maitlands fight him off and dispatch him to Juno's eternal waiting room. The Maitlands and Deetzes settle down to accommodate each other.
Present dystopian, foregrounded metadystopian.
The human-spiritual metafamilial axis is never fully resolved and the familial representation of the Deetzes is not represented as achievable or desirable. Although the film closes on an extended family, it is an uneasy relationship of un-likes and opposites.

1989

Indiana Jones and the Last Crusade
Steven Spielberg (UIP/Lucasfilms for Paramount) 1989
Harrison Ford (Indiana Jones)/Sean Connery (Dr Henry Jones)/Denholm Elliott (Marcus Brody)/Allison Doody (Dr Elsa Schneider)/John Rhys-Davies (Sallah)
Wealthy collector Walter Donovan reveals that Indiana's father disappeared to look for the Holy Grail and Indiana agrees to follow the clues in the old man's notebooks. He travels to Venice with Brody where Dr Elsa Schneider offers assistance. However Elsa, who has slept with both father and son, is, with Donovan, revealed as a Nazi sympathiser, and sends the notebooks to Berlin where father and son infiltrate a Nazi rally before escaping. Meanwhile Brody follows clues leading him to the Middle East to meet Sallah, an ally from *Raiders,* but they too are captured by Nazis. Donovan forces Indiana to lead him to the Grail but Elsa finally deceives him, saving both Indiana and Dr Jones. Elsa and the Nazis die trying to remove the Grail, leaving father, son, Brody and Sallah to ride off into the sunset at the close of the film.
Foregrounded dystopian, present dystopian.
Indie's true quest is here revealed of which the absent father is represented as the object and equivalent to the Holy Grail. The nuclear family is neither desired nor achievable, the only potential new family jettisoned fairly early in the shape of the treacherous Dr Schneider.

Who Framed Roger Rabbit
Robert Zemeckis (Warner Brothers/Touchstone–Amblin Entertainment) 1988
Bob Hoskins (Eddie Valiant)/Joanna Cassidy (Dolores)/Voices : Charles Fleischer (Roger Rabbit)/Christopher Lloyd (Judge Doom)/Kathleen Turner/Amy Irving (Jessica Rabbit)

Eddie Valiant, private investigator, is gradually persuaded to help Toon star, Roger Rabbit, when he is framed for the murder of studio head, Marvin Acme. Eddie's reluctance is due to his belief that Toons killed his brother, but both this crime and the murder are discovered to be linked to Judge Doom's dastardly plot to build a freeway through Toontown by disgracing Toons utterly. Doom is liquidated and Eddie is reconciled both to the Toons and to his long-suffering sweetheart, Dolores.

Absent dystopian, foregrounded meta-utopian.

The Toon meta-family are euphoric and integrated, counterpoised against the sour, bitter and fractured family represented by Eddie and his dead brother.

Rain Man

Barry Levinson (UIP/United Artists) 1988

Tom Cruise (Charlie Babbitt)/Dustin Hoffman (Raymond Babbitt)/Valerio Golino (Susanna)

Estranged from his widowed father, the successful, driven Charlie learns of the existence of an autistic brother, Raymond, to whom his father has left his fortune. Frustrated by the terms of the will, Charlie kidnaps Raymond with his unwitting girlfriend, Susanna, who finally tires of Charlie's selfishness and leaves them. Slowly they build a relationship as Charlie relinquishes his business to concentrate on his brother and Susanna rejoins them in Las Vegas. Finally, after a hearing, Charlie is forced to admit Raymond cannot be cured and is persuaded to return him to the hospital.

Foregrounded dystopian, present metadystopian.

Although the drive of the narrative is to restore the nuclear family, it can only be reconstituted in the form of the sibling relationship. This, too, is represented as impossible – the communication which was impossible between father and son is the real legacy left to the brothers. The Final Romance (Charlie–Susanna) is unstable, Susanna utilised as barometer of Charlie's transformation rather than represented as a future wife and Charlie is depicted as completely alone at the close of the film.

The Naked Gun: From the Files of Police Squad!

David Zucker (UIP/Paramount) 1988

Leslie Nielsen (Lt Frank Drebin)/Priscilla Presley (Jan Spencer)/Ricardo Montalban (Vincent Ludwig)/O.J. Simpson (Nordberg)

Taken from the hit TV series, this is a surreal comedy in which the intrepid Frank Drebin of Police Squad finally foils arch villain Vincent Ludwig's plot to kill the visiting Queen of England through the use of 'hypnotic assassins'. Discredited by his anarchic failures, Frank is sacked and has to operate outside the police structure to kill Vincent and achieve a Final Romance with Jan.

Absent dystopian, foregrounded metadystopian.

Headed by a female mayor, the police community is explicitly familialised – a family which Frank jeopardises by his inability to respect boundaries or rules, whether psychic, social or professional.

Lethal Weapon 2

Richard Donner (Warner Brothers/Warner Brothers) 1989

Mel Gibson (Martin Riggs)/Danny Glover (Roger Murtaugh)/Joe Pesci (Leo Getz)/ Joss Ackland (Arjen Rudd)

Against the orders of their boss, Riggs and Murtaugh find themselves in a war with
the South African consulate, led by Arjen Rudd, who is fronting a drugs ring.
Assigned protected witness Getz to look after, they use him for information and
he accompanies them throughout their battles. While Murtaugh is forced to send
his family away when Rudd's henchmen break into his house, Riggs develops a
relationship with Rika, one of the workers in the Consulate, who is subsequently
killed by her bosses. At the same time, he learns that the same men were responsible for his own wife's death. Maddened, he swears revenge which he achieves in
a spectacular final showdown. Badly wounded, he revives in Murtaugh's arms.
   Present dystopian, foregrounded metadystopian.
   Murtaugh threatens the well-being of his family through his allegiance to Riggs.
   Nor can the meta-family of the policy provide much compensation. The key
   relationship, and solution, is the buddy-bonding between the two men.

1990

Ghost
Jerry Zucker (UIP/Paramount) 1990
Whoopi Goldberg (Oda Mae Brown)/Patrick Swayze (Sam Wheat)/Demi Moore
(Molly Jensen)/Tony Goldwyn (Carl Bruner)
After moving into a new apartment with Molly, Sam is murdered. On learning that
the killer, Lopez, was hired by his old friend Carl, who has been laundering
money, Sam enlists the help of medium Oda Mae to warn Molly who is now
confiding in Carl. Oda Mae is unable to convince the police of Sam's story and
Sam begins to learn how to intervene in the physical world himself. He rescues
Oda Mae from Lopez who is killed by a truck as he flees. Together Sam and Oda
Mae restore the lost millions on the bank's computer and fight off Carl in Molly's
flat, causing his death. Sam and Molly reaffirm their love through Oda Mae before
Sam moves on to the next world.
   Absent dystopian, absent metadystopian.
   Familial structures are entirely missing from the text – although the film com-
   mences with an incipient family unit, this is immediately fractured by Sam's
   reluctance to marry and his subsequent death. The romance sequences are
   problematically played out through the body of Oda Mae, a black psychic with
   a criminal record. Thus the two WASP lovers depend on a social outsider for
   any form of communication or intimacy. Sam, the proto-father, fails in his
   reluctance to father children and by introducing Carl to the familial home.

Pretty Woman
Garry Marshall (Warner Brothers/Touchstone Pictures) 1990
Richard Gere (Edward Lewis)/Julia Roberts (Vivian Ward)/Ralph Bellamy (James
Morse)
Ruthless business man Edward picks up hooker Vivian one night and is so attracted to her that he pays her to stay the week. In a Pygmalion transformation, he
falls in love with her and completely recreates her, slowly humanising himself in
the process. By the end of the film, Edward proposes to Vivian and relinquishes
his tycoon lifestyle to go into business with James Morse, one of his takeover
targets.
   Absent dystopian, foregrounded meta-utopian.

Edward's business ambition is represented as compensation for the infidelity of his father. The narrative drive is to restore the lost father, eventually substituting meta-father Morse for the absent actual patriarch. The Final Romance is an index to Edward's own maturation from the narcissistic ruthlessness of mergers and takeovers, to the actual industrial production he enters by the close. Actual families, both Vivian's and Edward's, are by contrast unsatisfactory, yet father-figures Morse, the hotel manager, even Edward himself, are important to Vivian, easing her passage into the social world of the middle classes.

Look Who's Talking
Amy Heckerling (Columbia-Tri-star/Tri-star Pictures) 1989
John Travolta (James)/Kirstie Alley (Molly)/George Segal (Albert)
Molly becomes pregnant by Albert, one of her married clients, who subsequently abandons both her and his wife to live with someone else. James, who drove her to the hospital in his cab on the birth of her baby, grows increasingly attached to Molly and her 'talking' baby, Mikey, but Molly is insistent on finding the perfect father for her son. Eventually, after a series of reversals, James and Molly are united, with Mikey's blessing.
Foregrounded utopian, present metadystopian.
The business meta-family, headed by Molly's hectoring boss and the infantile, treacherous father of her child, is represented as a dystopian distraction from the utopian vision of the nuclear family. Molly is gradually trained into her 'proper' maternal role, away from her career, and into accepting the proper father for her child.

Honey, I Shrunk the Kids
Joe Johnston (Warner Brothers/Walt Disney) 1989
Rick Moranis (Wayne Szalinski)/Matt Frewer ('Big' Russ Thompson)/Marcia Strassman (Diane Szalinski)/Amy O'Neill (Amy Szalinski)/Robert Oliveri (Nick Szalinski)/Thomas Brown (Little Russell Thompson)/Jared Rushton (Ron Thompson)
Failed inventor Wayne has invented a shrinking machine which is ridiculed by the scientific community. Meanwhile, both his own two children, Amy and Nick, along with the neighbours, Russell and Ron Thompson, are shrunk by the machine and have to battle their microscopic way back to their house through the back garden. In the children's absence, both sets of parents re-appraise themselves and the children are finally restored to a utopian celebration.
Foregrounded utopian, present metadystopian.
The scientific community and mother's workplace are malign distractions from the utopian family environment which is magically restored by their rejection and the restoration of the nuclear family by the end of the film.

Total Recall
Paul Verhoeven (Guild/Carolco) 1990
Arnold Schwarzenegger (Hauser/Doug Quaid)/Rachel Ticotin (Melina)/Ronny Cox (Cohagen)/Michael Ironside (Richter)/Sharon Stone (Lori Quaid)
In a dystopian future world, Quaid has been reassigned to earth, having been brainwashed out of his previous existence as Hauser, in order to fulfill Hauser's and Cohagen's malign plot to defeat the rebels on Mars and maintain their own powerbase. On being told of the plot, he rebels along with his lover, Melina,

killing Cohagen, restoring the atmosphere on Mars and liberating the oppressed mutants.

Absent dystopian, foregrounded metadystopian.

A complex generative relationship constructs Hauser/Quaid as auto-generative, siring each other and the Martian colony.

Appendix 3:
Selection of Texts

The films analysed in this book were selected on the basis of their popularity. That is, they were the most successful Hollywood films in the UK during the eighties. This appendix outlines the basis on which my selection decisions were made.

HOLLYWOOD CINEMA – DEFINITIONS

I elected to look at Hollywood cinema because of its universality and persistent popularity in Britain. It is because socioeconomic discourses in the UK and the US possess important similarities and distinctions (shared language, the upsurge in family-centred discourse and common economic structures, political and military interests) that I wanted to examine the operation of US-produced representations within a UK context. Throughout the 1980s, despite the acclaimed resurgence of British cinema, it was difficult to find many commercial cinemas showing domestic or foreign-language films in any one week, let alone for consecutive weeks throughout the year. Over half of Hollywood's profit from theatrical rentals is derived from export markets and Britain has consistently been one of the top five countries generating this profit. Yet the definition of Hollywood cinema is frequently assumed as a given. In practice it is more complicated. While the studio system of the so-called 'classical period' permitted a fairly straightforward definition of Hollywood cinema, this position changed with the divorcements of the major studios in the forties. Chapter 2 outlines how their powerbase has shifted from production to distribution, but the big studios still, literally, call the shots. My definition of Hollywood cinema therefore includes all those films listed as being either produced or distributed by one of the major Hollywood studios with a UK release within the decade which did well at the UK box office. A study of financing and ownership structures revealed 25 distributing companies which were owned by, or linked to, the major studios and could thus be used to designate a Hollywood film. These were:

Barber International	Miracle
Brent Walker	New Realm
Cannon	New World
CIC	Palace
Cinegate	Rank
Columbia	Sunn Classic
Columbia–Cannon–Warner	Tri-Star
EMI	UIP
EMI–Columbia–Warner	UK
GTO	United Artists
Guild	Virgin
ITC	Walt Disney
Mainline	

I have used *Monthly Film Bulletin*, Vols 47–57 to identify film titles, dates, production and distribution companies. Appendix 2 lists all those films selected along with their US and UK release dates.

HOLLYWOOD AND ITS POPULARITY

The Hollywood film is simultaneously tarnished and strengthened by its popularity. 'Popular' is a word commonly used to connote divisions between high and low culture, between art and the mass market and, as such, has accreted derogatory connotations. However it also denotes entertainment with which large numbers of people have been engaged and therefore offers a rich resource for investigation. I have therefore selected Hollywood cinema as a vehicle for studying cultural representations because of its ubiquity, availability and popularity (in a quantitative sense) – due to the sheer volume of people who have been exposed to, elected to watch or been involved in producing, its texts. This choice also reflects the now almost universal practice of alternative cinemas being defined, and defining themselves, in opposition to Hollywood practice. In this sense, the representations so produced demand investigation. They are ones in whose terms other texts are articulated and circulated. They are a cinematic reference point and are themselves, therefore, representational; they speak or act on behalf of, a category of texts which is both perceptually and empirically, dominant. I have therefore used the films' popularity rather than their canonical status as the criterion for selecting films for analysis.

The latinate root (*popularis* = belonging to the people) leaves its residue in the use of the term today. Although now more strongly associated with the sense of being made for, and consumed by, the greatest possible number of people, this sense of ownership still lingers. Any cultural production, released into, and embraced by, the mass-market of communicating consumers, is immediately appropriated into the discourse and imaginative universe of those consumers. For audiences and individuals, reviewers and critics, films mobilise overlapping, extensive, even contradictory layers of meaning which both attach to it, and attach it to, the discursive formations in which they circulate. The consumption of a film text empowers individuals to speak about it, to generate their own meanings, interpretations, elucidations which capture the film and hold it in memory. It thus becomes part of the fabric upon which consciousness operates and is both embedded and individuated. The financial transaction of 'buying into' the exhibition of the text consolidates this process. Clearly, when large numbers of people have seen the same film, it can genuinely be said to be popular in this original sense. Not because each individual will interpret or remember the film in the same way, but because it forms part of a collective participation and ownership in both public and private cultural production. Such production is, of course, very specific in its scope, nature and output. A tiny fraction of a percentage of the UK and US populations are actually involved in the industrial production of feature films. The production I am describing here is looser, less defined and informal. It has to do with social, cultural and psychic interactions – not all of which are observable – and about which it is difficult to make empirically based generalisations. It is, however, possible to theorise these operations and it is the articulation between observable phenomena (society, audience, film text) and theoretical operations (spectatorship, ideology, consciousness) which I have explored in the book.

I have used the term 'popular' to relate strictly to the number of people who have seen a particular text. This number is not absolute – there is no precise benchmark above which a film can always, in any place at any time, be said to be popular – it is a relative term and needs to be defined in relation to other comparable, valid bases. As Janet Thumim (1992) has shown in her research into the nature and form of popular cinema between 1945 and 1965, the notion of popularity itself is a complex one. Despite the paucity of available box-office data, she established a paradigm for determining popularity in that period. The picture in the 1980s is equally, but paradoxically, complicated: there is a proliferation of data available, but much of it is inconsistent and impossible to compare over time. The cessation of the Eady levy in the mid-eighties, for example, meant that the DTI stopped collecting box-office returns on specific films. Although *Screen International* publishes the top ten box-office films in any one week in London and provincial cinemas with their receipts to date, films which fail to enter or drop out of this limited frame are no longer listed. These films' total box-office receipts are therefore not recorded and a total figure after a determined timescale is impossible to determine for all films released. Taking the first-week returns is a dangerous option, as many films enjoy a more widespread distribution on their release date which is not dependent on forecast profitability. Another source, the Cinema and Video Industry Audience Research (CAVIAR) reports (collated and published by the Cinema Advertising Association (CAA), only record box-office takings in cinemas which accept advertising. These reports, focused as they are on UK markets, are integrally valid and comparative, but again are for selected films only (just taking 24 for detailed analysis in their *Film Monitor*).

Distribution and exhibition practices have also become correspondingly more complicated as social and technological change has accelerated. A 'best possible' measure of popularity would need to take account of box-office receipts, critical reception, cable, satellite and broadcast TV exhibition (and audience figures), video purchase and rental, and industry awards. An algorithm could then be developed to fully determine popularity. There are inherent difficulties in developing such a formula. A decision would need to be taken as to whether to record actual or financial numbers, attendance figures versus box-office receipts, for example. The latter would be difficult to ascertain in relation to television purchases as most films are bought as part of a package. There are difficulties in asserting TV audience numbers for particular films and while ratings figures took account of off-air domestic VCR recordings from 1992 they did not record this through the 1980s. Critical reception (the verdict of press and TV reviewers) and industry awards would need to be recorded as a points system and aggregated into the algorithm. However, with this complexity in the formula, any such 'points system' would contain more subjectivity than is desirable and would be impossible to verify independently.

Such a task, although valuable, is outside the scope of this book and I have therefore elected for a cruder benchmark than an equation of variables. I have selected the ten most popular films appearing in the annual 'top twenty' tables printed in *Screen International* for the previous year. This gave a sample of 55 films for the period 1980–90. It should be noted that up to 1986, the *Screen*

International data were based on the calendar year. From 1986, the data covered the twelve months between 1 December and 30 November. Up to 1987, the positions in the chart were derived from the distributor's shares of the film's box-office takings between these dates; after 1987, it was based on gross box-office revenues for the period for which each film was tracked by its distributor. From 1988, the tables showed the gross box-office takings for the film in the UK.

The data has the merit of being simple and accessible – reflecting back on the concept of popularity itself. While the definition admittedly ignores the success of the film as a video or televisual product, I am critically concerned with the *theatrical* experience of film; the very particular experience of viewing film in the cinema – the intense, unitary relationship a text solicits with the spectator and which cannot be guaranteed in video/small-screen viewing. I have therefore excluded any form of exhibition other than the cinematic for consideration.

Genre

Within this grouping, the films are also referred to generically. Identifying generic categories, in itself, is not an easy task; they are constantly in process and evoke responses and expectation in both the social and psychic realms, posing conceptual and practical difficulties. How does one establish a framework and a set of boundaries using categorisations or taxonomies which are, by their very nature, in flux? Again, I have returned to the notion of the popular and have employed it in a qualitative sense. I developed a 'generic list' drawn from the vocabulary of popular reviewers and the classification systems used by video shops and film guides. This had the merit of being a system which is contemporaneous with the objects it was classifying, which was consumer-led and which tapped a vein of popular comprehension and discourse. That those using the terminology rarely attempt a definition or explanation suggests that the definitions are both in process and commonly understood by consumers as well as producers. They are thus 'commonsense' and, therefore, ideological categories. This method therefore meets the exigencies of both my particular ascription of genre and my particular criteria for defining the popular.

This methodology has certain features which should be noted in considering my textual interpretations. The categories are very broad – films which are in both substance and style very distinct, often fall into the same category. In contrast, see, for example, the more extensive categorisation used by CAVIAR (CAA). I did not use these categories (although it would offer a more comparative base for marketing data) because they imply exclusivity by their very extensiveness. Such a detailed breakdown suggests a film can belong to one category and one category only and occludes overlaps and tensions. I did, however, group the CAVIAR data to dovetail with my own framework in order to undertake certain comparisons and analyses. My categories are therefore not exclusive – there are huge areas of overlap and some films fit equally well into several generic modes (indeed my analysis showed how these different generic pressures worked in tension within and between texts). For the purposes of my own categorisation, I identified what I considered to be the *primary* mode of address to determine the genre to which I assigned the film and where I have carried out quantitative breakdowns by genre, as in Chapter 3, all films are counted in one genre and one genre only.

ENDOTE: FURTHER CATEGORISATIONS

I rejected a further breakdown by certification. This clearly has merit as a criteria for categorisation but would lead more productively into study of the institutional regulation of film texts and the specific relation of audience to text and my intention was to be text- rather than industry-oriented. While such classifications raise interesting questions around the definitions, organisation and expectation of the intellectual and emotional development of individuals generically grouped by age – and, extrapolating from that, the social and mutual responsibilities of family members – it is properly the subject of another book. In so far as a film's certification imbued meanings within a particular film text, I have noted it in my detailed textual analyses. I have also elected to defer other forms of structural categorisation such as production and distribution companies, producers, technical staff, exhibition outlets, stars and so on, for the same reason. The remaining categorisation to be considered which ineluctably bridges the psychic/social divide is that of the director. Auteurism has been derided as ignoring the industrial – and collaborative – nature of film-making. It is, however, impossible to deny that specific directors do bring particular motifs and meanings to the texts on which they work. Whether these imprints lie in the gift of the director, the audience expectation or the marketing machinery is, of course, endlessly debatable. What I absolutely refute is any notion of the tendentious text in which it is possible to read, unproblematically, the directors' intention for the film. As a marketable commodity in the same way as its stars and its genre – existing both in the 'mental machinery' of the spectator and the industrial machinery of cinematic marketing – the director plays a key part in distinguishing film texts and, where this is significant to the understanding of a specific text, I have noted it.

Notes

INTRODUCTION

1. In common with other feminist theorists, Linda Williams has noted that 'the female spectator tends to identify with contradiction itself' (1984: 17). While I would not necessarily agree entirely that this is the only way in which women can identify with a text, I would suggest that any socially marginalised group, including women, are better disposed to identify with contradiction. The female spectator is peculiarly privileged in relation to such potential for mobility by virtue of two specific reasons. Firstly, in her own psychic development and her subsequent precariousness within the symbolic order. Secondly, in relation to the social, lived experience which structures her cognitive and psychic activity. Women always occupy a dislocated position in culture because of their relation as other within the symbolic realm and can thus identify more easily with fractures and dislocations within the text as well as occupying a more fluid space for spectatorship. This fluidity permits women to take up bisexual positions in relation to the text which are not biologically determined but which will be determined by sociocultural and psychic structures, among which will be gender. As Tana Modleski succinctly comments, 'A discussion of bisexuality as it relates to spectatorship ought, then, to be informed by a knowledge of the way male and female responses are rendered asymmetrical by a patriarchal power structure' (1988: 10). Thus gender plays a crucial, but not the only, part in shaping the psychic and cognitive processings of spectatorship and viewing competence.

2. *Fatal Attraction* made $70 million at the US box office alone and was ranked 26th in the US top grossers of the 1980s.

3. 'Ideology has no history, which emphatically does not mean that there is no history in it (on the contrary, for it is merely the pale, empty and inverted reflection of real history) but that it has no history *of its own*' (Althusser, 1984: 34). I have taken the term 'ideology' in its strictly Althusserian sense; that is, of 'a "Representation" of the Imaginary Relationship of Individuals to their Real Conditions of Existence' (ibid.: 36).

4. Carr, 1990: 30.

5. Bhaskar theorised a core distinction between historical events and what he called 'generative' or causal 'mechanisms' which never operated in isolation, interacting to produce 'the flux of phenomena that constitute the actual states and happenings of the world' (1978: 47). He also proposed the analytical tool of 'causal analysis' or redescription as the method for accessing the 'real' through the structures which frame it; a method I have followed in the textual analyses in Part 2.

6. See, for example, Guback (1969 & 1985); Schiller (1969); Ray (1985); and Ellis (1985).

7. Recently critics have begun to challenge the inevitability of Hollywood practices, and practitioners working in the art cinemas of America have always demonstrated the alternative possibilities available, but this teleological

perspective still remains both current and dominant in popular discourse. The production process, distribution and exhibition practices have, since the original settlement of the Hollywood ranch in 1887 and the construction of the first movie studio in 1908, become a universal (and thus seemingly both an inexorable and 'natural') model for cinematic operations throughout the world. Although some domestic cinemas, such as those of India, parts of Africa and China, both thrive and are clearly distinct from the US product, nearly all are now competing in their domestic and export markets with Hollywood texts and distribution networks. The popularity of Hollywood cinema is incontestable as is its contribution to the US economy from both its domestic and export performance. Earnings from foreign distribution (most notably in Europe and Canada) equalled or exceeded earnings from domestic distribution throughout the decade.

8. Byars, 1991: 10.
9. Gledhill, 1987: 32.
10. Weekend section on eighties cinema in *The Guardian* (20 February 1993).
11. Tasker, 1993: 3.
12. David Bordwell has definitively analysed how heterosexual romance functioned as a first or secondary plot line in the bulk of classical Hollywood films (95 per cent of the sample; 1988: 16–17). See also Wexman (1993) for an analysis of the centrality of romance and the heterosexual coupling to Hollywood film.
13. Ray, 1985: 20.
14. I have distinguished between the epistemological use of the term Realism and the aesthetic mode of realism by capitalising the former term while the latter appears in lower case.
15. Modleski, 1988: 15.
16. This approach draws on the principle of non-contradiction which was originally theorised by Benton (1977: 196) and developed by Robert Allen and Douglas Gomery in their important and polemical work on film history (1985).
17. Modleski, 1991: 13.
18. Traube, 1992: 3.

1 BRITAIN IN THE EIGHTIES

1. In his historical survey of the postwar years, Arthur Marwick noted the common currency of 'crisis' by the eighties: 'Most commentators writing at the end of the [seventies] were concerned with "crisis": crisis in the economy, crisis in law and order, crisis in racial and industrial relations' (1990: 268).
2. Roland Barthes analysed how mythologies turn 'culture into nature' in an attempt to hide their ideological function (1972). Barthes later developed his work on mythology to propose 'idiolectology' as a more exact way of distinguishing the operations of ideology (1984: 165–9). Structural anthropologist Lévi-Strauss, too, explored this function of myth (1975) and Bourdieu's concept of 'doxa' also defines how the constructions of culture work to describe and efface the material world, making ideology 'natural' (1994). Robert Ray drew upon a Barthesian, as opposed to a Jungian,

formulation of myth to analyse what he called a 'certain tendency' in Hollywood cinema (1985).

3. Reagan's presidency spanned almost the entire period that Thatcher was in office. Reagan left the White House at the end of 1988, Mrs Thatcher resigned on 21 November 1990. Ronald Reagan's comments demonstrate how close both countries had become and how far this was personalised: 'Ours is a friendship that I treasure very much . . . It's just a wonderful relationship.' (Ronald Reagan of Margaret Thatcher, 1988).

4. Parsons in Kavanagh & Seldon (eds), 1989. He went on to state baldly that 'Britain is no superpower.'

5. A *Newsweek* poll conducted in 1989 indicated American anxiety over Pacific Rim competition: 'More than half surveyed now consider Japan's economic might a bigger threat than the military power of the Soviet Union.' A symbol of this national anxiety was the continual reprise of the Vietnam War (the first war to be comprehensively represented on broadcast TV) which was constantly visited and re-presented through the eighties. The war was rehearsed in films such as *Born on the Fourth of July, Good Morning, Vietnam, Casualties of War, Full Metal Jacket, Platoon, BAT 21* and in Michael Herr's postmodern memoirs, *Dispatches*. See also Gilbert Adair's comprehensive filmography of Vietnam in Hollywood cinema (1989).

6. 'I was brought up by a Victorian grandmother. We were taught to work jolly hard. We were taught to prove yourself; we were taught self reliance; we were taught to live within our income. You were taught that cleanliness is next to godliness. You were taught self-respect. You were taught always to give a hand to your neighbour. You were taught tremendous pride in your country. All of these things are Victorian values. They are also perennial values. You don't hear so much about these things these days but they were good values and they led to tremendous improvements in the standard of living.' (Mrs Thatcher, radio interview on LBC, 15 April 1983).

7. The Establishment position was most neatly encapsulated in the Arts Council 'manifesto' published in 1985 which stressed the importance of the arts as 'an important strand in our export drive, both producing real profits and preparing the way for further enterprises. The arts matter.' The object of the manifesto was to plead for 'the nation to invest in this well-proved "product"'; to provide the cash to ensure that past glories do not become insubstantial memories, and that present achievements can be built upon for even greater returns in the future'.

8. Institutionally, many cultural bastions were brought into question. The BBC, in earlier decades represented as a pillar of the establishment, analysed and attacked for its right-wing bias by the left, was represented as the mouthpiece of socialism and programmes were frequently censured, or even censored, by politicians. In the early eighties, much arts activity depended on public funding but the ethos of self-sufficiency was quickly introduced and subsidy was largely discredited, resulting in the collapse of many regional and fringe exhibition outlets as local authorities themselves became subject to rate capping. The theatre was sharply polarised between heavily subsidised 'heritage' productions (through the Barbican, RSC and National Theatres) and the commercial West End venues – although ironically the great resurgence of opera during the decade mainly rested on subsidy.

9. Symptomatised by the creation and adulation of the new 'Supermodels', the body beautiful became an essential accessory for the successful individual and it was the masculine shape which was privileged. For the first time outside body building and health publications, the male body was actively displayed and eroticised. While women had attended aerobics classes in droves in the seventies, men joined in to reconstruct themselves as 'hard bodies', hitherto derided as the freakish province of bodybuilding. Women stripped their bodies of fat and then packed them into 'power-dressing' suits with padded shoulders and tight, short skirts, emulating the narrow hipped, broad shouldered look of the male physique. Health denoted virtue and enterprise and the nutrition and fitness industries thrived on it.

10. The Conservative government lowered top tax rates from 83 per cent to 40 per cent and gradually shifted the burden from direct to indirect taxation throughout the decade.

11. These were popularly known as quangos (quasi-autonomous non-governmental organisations). They were allocated huge sums of public money to spend in the private sector, money previously administrated by elected bodies such as local authorities.

12. Only 9 per cent of Britons put their primary goal in life as getting rich, compared to 38 per cent in Japan and 15 per cent of Americans. For Britons, the primary goal was to 'live as I like' (77 per cent). *Social Trends* No. 19 (1988) stated that 'inflation and unemployment are seen as everpresent threats and a sizeable minority of the population, largely concentrated in the lowest income groups seem to be sceptical that any general improvements in the economy will actually benefit them'. Ivor Crewe provides an incisive analysis of the gap between public and individual value systems in Kavanagh & Seldon (eds) (1989: 239–50).

13. The eradication of the Welfare State was never seriously on the agenda but the 1970s moral panic about 'scroungers' was resurrected in various guises throughout the decade in the tabloid press. However, although Thatcher herself assured the nation that the National Health Service, a key signifier of the state in the eighties, was 'safe in our hands', this assurance could not be so secure within the tenets of Thatcherism. In 1985, a White Paper, *Reform of Social Security: Programme for Action*, spoke of giving 'greater responsibility and greater independence to the individual' – an ambition which was enacted in the Social Security Act of 1986, separating Social Security from Health.

14. The number of those in work declined from over 23 million in 1979 to between 21 and 22 million up to 1989 before falling again in 1991. However a gap of around 2 million between those in work and those claiming benefit opened up in 1981 and continued to hover between 2 and 3 million despite the continual adjustment of unemployment criteria throughout the decade. Although average working hours have been steadily decreasing through time, men in the UK worked longer hours than in any other country in the rest of Europe – 44 hours per week as compared to a European average of 40.4. Women, by contrast, worked fewer hours than any other country except the Netherlands (30.5 compared to an average of 33.1). This can be explained by the high proportion of women in part-time work (45 per cent of those employed).

15. Four particular types entered common discourse; the 'yuppie', the 'lager lout', the '*Sun* reader' and the 'chattering classes'. The second was most obviously a term of denigration, but the others were more ambivalently used. The yuppie (young, upwardly mobile person) was ambitious and highly paid, frequently employed in the newer service industries, particularly finance. There were specific accoutrements that became associated with the yuppie, notably the new personal organiser, the filofax and the mobile phone, all signifying the importance of new technology, time and communication; hallmarks of enterprise and service. The lager lout was most strongly associated with the increase in football hooliganism, particularly with the English football fan abroad, and can be interpreted as the working class left behind – those who did not become yuppies. A further cultural typing distinguished between *Sun* Readers (a largely commonsense, 'salt of the earth', if ill-educated grouping) and the chattering classes. The latter was a derogatory reference to the section of the middle classes who talked rather than acted and who, it was claimed, dominated the much derided public sector broadcasting.

16. The list of these 'battles' conjures both the social categorisations and the oppositional forces in play: Southall (Asian, white youths and police; 1981), Brixton (West Indian/Afro-Caribbean community and police; 1981 and 1985), Toxteth (West Indian/Afro-Caribbean community and police; 1981 and 1985), Orgreave (striking miners and police; 1984), Handsworth (Asian/black communities and police; 1985), Broadwater Farm, Tottenham (West Indian/Afro-Caribbean community and police; 1985), Hysel (football fans; 1985), Wapping (striking print-workers and police; 1986/7), Enniskillen (IRA and British state as represented by Remembrance Day ceremony; 1987) and Trafalgar Square (poll-tax protesters and police; 1989).

17. For an incisive and comprehensive analysis of these developments, see Hutton (1995), especially Chapter 1.

18. Fredric Jameson proposed that a utopian postmodernism, 'the political form of postmodernism, if there ever is any, will have as its vocation the invention and projection of a global cognitive mapping, on a social as well as a spatial scale' (Jameson, 1992: 54). It was the crisis of positionality and subjectivity which constructed dystopia.

19. The movement originated in the 1960s, specifically in the field of architecture, but its moment of entry to popular cultural discourse and practice was the eighties. Postmodernism attempted to address a perception that, once modernist praxis had entered the academy, it was co-opted, appropriated for commercial and/or aesthetic appreciation. The 'shocks of the new' were therefore no longer available to the radical politics and philosophies, specifically the praxis of modernism, feminism and gender politics, to which they had been wedded, leaving a vacuum for new theoretical forms and discourses. The new theory was postmodernism which, as Fredric Jameson so elegantly put it, expressed the logic of late capitalism. The new cultural forms and ideas were understood to be expressed in, and effacing the boundaries of, high and low culture, in which previously marginalised cultural discourses suddenly demanded to be taken seriously.

20. 'Family values' were foregrounded in the United States even more prominently than were the 'Victorian values' of the Tory Party. It is possible to

chart almost simultaneous public debates on both sides of the Atlantic, sparked by the same, or parallel, events around such issues as abortion, surrogacy, artificial insemination and child abuse. Barrett & McIntosh argue, for example, that 'political dispute over the family is considerably less sharp in Britain than it has become in the United States, where issues of family and sexual politics have a very high profile in public debate' (1991: 13). Susan Faludi argues a similar point in her very comprehensive overview of sexual politics during the decade (1992).

21.   Magazines, specifically *Hello*, were launched and flourished on the back of these royal dramas. In 1986, NBC networked its popular soap series *Days of Our Lives* to dovetail an English-set wedding with Andy and Fergie's real-life event. The story did not turn really sour until the 1990s when the respective marriages started to break up. The 'fairy-tale romance' of the marriage and offspring of Prince Charles and Lady Diana Spencer had lost its gloss by the time that Prince Andrew and Sarah Ferguson were married.

22.   The most prominent of these, *EastEnders, Coronation Street, Crossroads, Dallas* and *Dynasty* routinely swept the majority of the top ten viewing table slots. Christine Geraghty has explored how both British and American soaps are structured by familial ideology and construct a familial audience although the ways in which they strive for narrative resolution is very specifically and intriguingly different. While British soaps are matriarchal in structure, portraying open family frameworks concerned primarily with moral and practical issues, the US soap is generally patriarchal and obsessively concerned with constructions of masculinity, boundaries and inheritance. While in US soaps, the woman is often a threat to family unity, specifically in her ability to break the closed lineage structure through illegitimate reproduction and representing illicit competition in the board room, in UK soaps it is the woman who bears the burden of responsibility for uniting the family. Threats are external rather than internal and the family deals with them by incorporation rather than exclusion. Geraghty suggests that the specific family type constructed at the heart of the new British soap operas was the white, working-class nuclear family – a nostalgic throwback to a mythical heart-of-gold turn-of-the-century ideal represented in the old Ealing comedies. This family type was the resolution to all the problems thrown up by the broader social canvas that all the soaps struggled over – and were celebrated for – portraying (1991 & 1992).

2   HOLLYWOOD CINEMA IN THE EIGHTIES

1.   See Jim Hillier (1993), Thomas Schatz (1993) and Douglas Gomery (1992) for more extensive overviews of Hollywood's industrial landscape during the decade.

2.   For an excellent analysis of Hollywood's contemporary domestic performance, see Douglas Gomery (1992) or Guback (1985). Joel Finler has also collated an impressive historical overview of Hollywood's financial performance (1992). Kristin Thompson's book *Exporting Entertainment* (1985) offers a comprehensive historical background to Hollywood's export drive.

3.   American films financed abroad rose to about 60 per cent of the total output

of US producers in the 1960s. In the UK between 1962 and 1971 around two-thirds of the 489 British feature films exhibited in the two main distribution circuits were financed in total or partially by US interests. Although these figures have declined due to the devaluation of the dollar and rising overseas costs, they are indicative of a continuing trend. See Balio (ed.) (1985: 479).

4. In 1990, for example, Matsushita bought Universal and Sony bought out Columbia in 1989. The neo-Indies showed even more cosmopolitan funding structures. Carolco, for example, was owned by Pioneer Electronics (Japan), Canal Plus (France), Carlton Communications (UK) and Rizzoli/Corriere della Sera (Italy); Morgan Creek was formed in 1987 with Japanese finance.

5. Parretti's Pathe company took over MGM in 1990, renaming it MGM/Pathe Communications; financier Kirk Kirkorian and MGM bought United Artists in 1981 to rename it MGM/UA; oil tycoon Marvin Davis bought Twentieth Century-Fox in 1982, retaining its name.

6. Paramount, for example, were taken over by Gulf & Western in 1966, United Artists by Transamerica and then MGM. Columbia, Home Box Office and CBS set up Tristar in 1982. Warner Communications and MCA substantially extended their operations in the leisure industries (toys/video games and publishing houses and a Coke bottling plant respectively) and Twentieth Century-Fox became a conglomerate in its own right, purchasing Coca-Cola Bottling Midwest, Aspen Skiing Corporation and the Pebble Beach Corporation. Like any large business, these ventures enjoyed mixed fortunes – Twentieth Century-Fox and Paramount were well served by this development, United Artists were not.

7. For example, Warner Brothers were purchased by Time Inc. who became Time Warner Inc. in 1989; Gulf & Western became Paramount Communications in 1989.

8. In describing his company's bid to become a 'citizen of the world', Akio Morita, co-founder and chairman of Sony, tellingly revealed the prevailing paranoia about such global, particularly Japanese, penetration into American markets. 'In choosing our name, we did not purposely try to hide our national identify but we certainly did not want to emphasise it.'

9. Paradoxically, this prompted an oscillation between experimentation and commercial caution by the biggest names. Directors such as Scorsese and Coppola used commercial success (such as *Cape Fear* and *Bram Stoker's Dracula*, respectively) to subsidise more experimental and personal work.

10. Roger Birnbaum, Head of Production at Fox, for example, acknowledged audience fragmentation when he asserted that 'it makes it exciting that a studio can develop a slate of pictures that doesn't just cater to one demographic. It used to be that we only made pictures for teenage boys. Now, all the demographics are broader and deeper than that' (quoted in Hillier, 1993). By 1990, producers Simpson and Bruckheimer noted that 'for the first time in their history, movies have become more marketing driven . . . without exception the pictures fall into line relative to their expenditures' (quoted in Kent, 1991). See also Traube (1992) and Tasker (1993) for explorations into how Hollywood deployed the demographics of class and gender at a textual level to segment the product portfolio during the decade.

11. Although the sequel had been popular in specific genres, notably horror, in

earlier decades, the eighties was the period in which it substantially entered mainstream production. Among the top box-office hits of the decade, a high proportion were sequels. These included, for example, the following series: *Police Academy, Star Wars, Ghostbusters, Beverly Hills Cop, Lethal Weapon, Rocky* and *Rambo*.

12. Murphy, 1983: 250.
13. Gomery (1992) charts the rise of the multiplex in America through the seventies and eighties, providing a useful case history of Cineplex.
14. From the first ten-screen multiplex built at Milton Keynes in 1985, the number of screens had leapt to 387 on 41 sites by the end of 1990. The largest growth spurt in audience figures was in 1985 when cinema audiences rose by a third and again in 1989 when another spurt of over a sixth was recorded.
15. Bordwell *et al.*, 1988: 3.
16. Scholars have explored how such elements as genre, directors and stars have contributed to the marketing process. See for example, Dyer (1987) and Gledhill (ed., 1991) on stardom or Hillier (1992) on the development of the director in the marketing process of New Hollywood.
17. The camera's entry into virtual space would be developed in the nineties with films such as *Lawnmower Man* and *Strange Days*.
18. Ray, 1985: 32.
19. Schatz, 1993: 23.
20. Bordwell *et al.*, 1988: 377.

3 FAMILY REPRESENTATIONS: THE FAMILY IN CRISIS

1. Gittins, 1993: 1.
2. Robertson, 1991: 7.
3. Theorists who have worked on distinguishing the social and ideological family include, for example, Althusser (1984); Barrett & McIntosh (1991); Stone (1977); Gittins (1993); Flandrin (1980); Donzelot (1979); Aries (1973). These theorists differ, for example, from those who would take a straightforwardly positivist approach in providing 'pure' demographic analyses of family history.
4. Three-quarters of children born outside wedlock were registered by both parents while half had their parents living together at the same address. Live births outside marriage increased from around 11 per cent of all births in 1981 to 30 per cent in 1991.
5. By 1981, the majority of those remarrying were widowers or divorced men while far fewer widows and divorced women remarried. In 1982, US government demographer Jessie Bernard stated baldly that 'Being married is about twice as advantageous to men as to women in terms of continued survival' (1982: 25). In the US the documented suicide record for married men is half that for single men and single men suffer double the mental-health ailments than do single women (see, for example, Schaffer, 1980).
6. A Virginia Slims poll carried out in America in 1985 found that 70 per cent of women felt their lives could be 'happy and complete' without marriage. The US national survey detected an increasing 'happiness' quotient in women

between the age of 20 and 40 and a corresponding decline among married women in the same age bracket through the 1980s. The reluctance to marry increased in proportion to salary and job satisfaction (Simenauer & Carroll, 1982: 15). In the UK, *Cosmopolitan* magazine found that 81 per cent of their readers enjoyed being single (quoted in Faludi, 1992: 33–4).

7.   Divorces increased in the UK from 157 000 decrees absolute in 1981 to 168 000 in 1990, stimulated by the Matrimonial and Family Proceedings Act in 1984.

8.   Jameson, 1989: 28.

9.   Robertson neatly summarises this process in relation to his anthropological study of the Balinese, 'By such cultural devices time is, so to speak, looped back on itself: birth and death are elided, and social structure is given an appearance of timelessness which defies reproductive reality' (1991: 24).

10.   Robertson, 1991: 7

11.   Gittins, 1993: 153.

12.   Graham Webster-Gardiner, press conference, 1986 (quoted in Gittins, 1993: 1). Interestingly, this explicitly contrasts with the demographers' stance. In 1990 the US Census Bureau ruled that the head of the household could no longer automatically be defined as a husband.

13.   In working with this concept of familialisation, I am anxious not to transgress David Bordwell's stricture of 'the ability to be disconfirmed' (1991: 253) within a theoretical proposition and be confident that these paradigms must be empirically falsifiable. The danger of throwing the familial net wider than the actual family form is precisely the problematic identified by Barrett and McIntosh in their polemical analysis of the contemporary family. They draw on the concept of 'familialization' – 'the rendering of other social phenomena like families' – to endorse their theory of the hegemony of the family form and the stifling of alternative social structures and affiliations (1991: 26). The extreme pole of this theoretical expansion is that, if we are not careful, everything can be explained as a family and families can explain everything. This expansion, Barrett and McIntosh convincingly argue, is a contemporary sociocultural malaise and we must recognise the dangers in attempting to plot how non-family organisations are familialised without ourselves familialising them by rendering every social phenomenon as a family. The following chapters represent a preliminary attempt to avoid such elisions by mapping both familial and familialised structures through the identification of 'metaphorical' families in Chapter 4.

14.   Ibid.: 130.

15.   In the words of Ned Tanen, ex-head of Universal and Paramount, in 1991, Hollywood itself was represented in (ambivalently) familialised terms. 'It's a kind of love–hate family relationship where [Hollywood people] are not necessarily wishing their best friends well, but they cling to each other in some form of desperation.'

16.   In addition to this familialisation within the workplace, it is interesting to note that the vast majority of commercial enterprises in the UK were family-owned in the eighties, employing over 50 per cent of the workforce and that the inheritance of, and succession in, such businesses has been identified as one of the key reasons for the UK's commercial stagnation at the small/medium-enterprise level.

17. Barrett & McIntosh, 1991: 130.
18. The exception to this is the legislative concern with the containment and regulation of women, particularly in relation to their sexuality and reproductive capacities. However, in these instances, regulation was particularly concerned to relocate offenders within a family or familial context. Once they were contained, the law was content to leave them to their fate. See Smart (ed.) (1992) for more detailed analyses of this phenomenon and a lucid overview of the historical controls exercised over women by the medical and legal communities in both Britain and America, particularly in relation to their reproductive capacities.
19. All these paradigms broadly assume a functionalist model of the family which, from Althusserian reproduction to contemporary feminists' replications of gendered power relations, all necessarily assume a universal family type. See Morgan (1975) and Gittins (1993) for insightful critiques of functionalist analysis.
20. For an incisive analysis of the damage done to the women's movement by 'post-feminism', see Modleski (1991).
21. See, for example, Lawrence Stone's work on patriarchal paradigms (1990, particularly Chapter 5) and Barrett & McIntosh for analysis of the patriarchal role of provider (1991).
22. By the eighties, the definition of individual poverty was still based on supporting a family, pitched just below the level of social security benefit for two adults and two children.
23. The number of working women grew by one million between the middle and end of the 1980s in the UK. By the early eighties over 50 per cent of women were working in the US, including more than half of all married women (see Johnston & Packer, 1987: 85).
24. See, for example, Beatrix Campbell's account of the Cleveland case (1988: 113–93).
25. Chesler cites the findings of the New York State Task Force on Women and the Courts that 'mothers are losing custody on grounds unrelated to the child's best interests ... substantial evidence exists that when fathers do litigate custody, they win at least as often as mothers do.' Further studies suggest that fathers who contest custody win between 62 and 70 per cent of the time at trial level (Chesler, 1990: 15).
26. Institute for Social Research, University of Michigan Report, 1984.
27. Bernard, 1972: 16–17.
28. Feminists preoccupied with recuperating the maternal role came from many disciplines, including theorists as diverse as Kristeva (1982); Chodorow (1978); Kaplan (1992) and Griffin (1984).
29. E. Ann Kaplan has linked these dimensions to textual positions in her study into paradigms of maternal representations over time. She proposes three dominant models characterising the modern, high modern and postmodern periods as divided between 'complicit' and 'resisting' paradigms to show how texts might be recuperated for feminist interpretations and more positive representations of the mother. Unfortunately these paradigms assume the primacy of the text in the process of making meaning and that a text can control its own readings (1992: 12–13).
30. Faludi, 1992: 55–65.

31. Ibid.: 462.
32. See Chesler (1990) for a detailed, if polemically presented, analysis of the case.
33. Shirley Conran's *Superwoman* was published in 1975 and *Superwoman 2* in 1977.
34. Philips, *Marxism Today*, March 1990: 64.
35. See, for example, Aries (1980) and Donzelot (1980) for a more expanded treatment of the developments in childhood formations.
36. The concept of child as blank slate was developed in Locke's treatise *Some Thoughts On Education*, in 1693.
37. Gittins also noted the enormous social pressure for reproduction in the eighties. 'Having children has certainly become intimately linked in cultural values to the idea of forming and of being a family, to the extent that married couples without children are persistently asked by kin and friends "when are you going to start a family?" as though only by having children can one claim to be part of a family' (Gittins, 1993: 110).
38. See, for example, Smart's and Hooper's essays in Smart (ed.) 1992.
39. The use of videotape was admitted as evidence for the first time in a British court, specifically to permit children to testify in the Family Courts. The body of the child was itself a site of conflict during the decade, giving rise to discursive clashes as to its appropriate examination and interpretation (the famous anal dilation debate) and its proper location. These debates were initiated by professional interventions into the family home (involving primarily the police and social work communities and later involving the medical profession) and given wide circulation and currency through the media, particularly the press.
40. One episode of the popular British TV series, *Rumpole of the Bailey* (tx 29/10/92 C3) exemplified one discursive position in this debate by indicting the professionals and positioning the 'abused' child firmly back in the parental home – even one tarnished by a dynastic history of criminality. The episode was additionally complicated by its sexual representations – the case was represented and won by the male defender (the series' hero) whose prosecuting opponent was not only a woman but a former pupil. This characterises the public debate where opposing positions were frequently represented as gender-specific and the women who were vilified for presenting them, were also charged as iconoclasts in the profession which trained them. This latter debate is best exemplified by the Cleveland child abuse and Wendy Savage cases.
41. Quoted in Marwick, 1990: 367.
42. Defined as 'those feature films that contain scenes of such violence and sadism involving either human beings or animals that they would not be granted a certificate by the British Board of Film Censors (BBFC) for general release for public exhibition in Britain. Such films may be liable to prosecution by the Director of Public Prosecutions under the Obscene Publications Act 1959 Section 2' (Barlow & Hill (eds), 1985: 171).
43. See, for example, Modleski (1988 & 1991); Clover (1992); Williams (1990); or Pribham (ed.) (1988) on issues of spectatorship. In relation to children's ability to distinguish actuality and fiction, see Hodge and Tripp (1986).
44. Barlow & Hill (eds), 1985: 5.

45. Ibid.: 166.
46. 'The violence emanates mainly from men but an increasingly conspicuous feature of the "video nasties" has been the return of the violence with a vengeance, by the women and in some cases they are the initiators of vicious and sexually brutal behaviour towards the opposite sex' (Ibid.: 3).
47. Ward, 1984.
48. An earlier crisis of child abuse occurred in the 1960s – the epidemic of 'baby battering' which was explained by Kempe and Kempe (1983) as symptomatic of dysfunctional families. Other studies have suggested a far stronger correlation with poverty (Parton, 1985; Gordon, 1989).
49. See Campbell (1988) for an interesting, oppositional analysis of the entire episode.
50. Gittins, 1993: 167.
51. Social scientist Kingsley Davis wisely pointed out the pathologising nature of much social science as early as 1948, in his admonition that 'most social research into the family has had an immediate moral purpose – to eliminate deviations like divorce, desertion, illegitimacy and adultery – rather than a desire to understand the fundamental nature of social institutions' (1948: 393).

4   FAMILY FORTUNES: KEY REPRESENTATIONAL PARADIGMS

1. This trend characterises the work of the *Indiana Jones* director, Steven Spielberg, who as we shall see in Chapter 9, was routinely represented as the 'father' of his films, searching for his own father in the process of making them. He was also the most commercially successful director of the eighties. It is certainly possible to chart a quest for the absent father in such of his films as *Empire of the Sun, The Color Purple* and *E.T.*
2. See Appendixes 1 and 2 for detailed analysis of how each film has been assigned to a specific family paradigm. To analyse these paradigms, I have drawn on the categories constructed by Richard Dyer in his analysis of the musical (Dyer in Altman (ed.), 1981) and which Linda Williams also drew on in her brilliant examination of the structure and cultural function of pornographic films (Williams: 1990). These broadly correspond to the structuring dimensions identified in this chapter. Dyer posits a utopia as a culturally and historically determined sensibility which is related to specific inadequacies in a represented social field. This utopia is represented as the sociocultural state which can liquidate inadequacies such as scarcity by abundance, exhaustion by energy, dreariness by intensity, manipulation by transparency and fragmentation by community. While Dyer's own analysis relates specifically to the narrational form and *mise-en-scène* of the musical, the utopian sensibility, its sociohistorical specificity and its capacity as resolution can be productively extrapolated to analyse the family. Dyer's analysis also constructs a version of the relational field utilised here to identify how the narrative of the musical constructs its utopian solutions. Dyer analyses the narrative in terms of the locus of the musical numbers – whether they are separated, integrated or dissolved to identify the manner in which the musical exhausts its utopian sensibility. In the separated musical, the narrative

presents the problem, while the numbers are an escape mechanism; in the integrated musical, the numbers seek to efface the narrative problem within the narrational field; in the dissolved musical the narrative is always (already) utopian.

3. I have deliberately chosen to use the word 'actual' rather than 'natural' to describe the reproductive family unit as I want to indicate the constructedness of all the family types which are represented.

4. Thirty-five of the top 55 films close on the Final Romance. In 23 of these, the romance was not represented at the beginning of the film, or is between different characters by the end. In other words, one narrative thread of these films is the building of the Final Romance, a conventional narrative structure in classical Hollywood cinema, but differentially inflected by familial paradigms by the eighties.

5. Some basic elaborations may help to clarify the key variables in play. In the absent utopian film the family is aimed for but is never fully achieved within the narrative whereas in the absent dystopia, the family is to be avoided, it is missing from the narrative, but not sought after. In the present utopia, the family is a positive environment for the narrative to unfold and the maintenance or creation of a family is a necessary condition for resolution. In the present dystopia, the family is a negative environment for the narrative and the maintenance or creation of a family is an active barrier to resolution. In the foregrounded utopia, the family is a central driver of the narrative – both its motivation and its resolution, whereas in the foregrounded dystopia, the family is both the subject of the narrative and a dystopian resolution. This is characterised either through its undesirability as an organising structure or its unattainability in any satisfactory form. Where metaphorical families are not present and actual families are, they are marked as dystopian if they are not represented as a solution to a dystopian actual family. These categories apply to both actual and metaphoric family forms.

6. From this point on, any paradigm which is not qualified as a metaphorical paradigm can be assumed to be actual. Metaphorical paradigms will be referred to as meta-utopias and metaphorical dystopias will be referred to as metadystopias.

7. One study which looks most specifically at textual anxiety over familial representation at the level of its absence from the text is Sylvia Harvey's consideration of *film noir* (Harvey in Kaplan (ed.), 1980). Harvey argues that the 'transformation' of romantic union at the close of the narrative into an extra-diegetic, 'unspoken and usually invisible metamorphosis that is implied to take place at the end of every happy ending' – the generation of a family – is subverted in the *noir* genre. This disruption, she posits, is directly reflective of the contemporary 'changing economic and ideological function of the family' (ibid.: 25). Harvey, however, conflates social and fictional realms, stipulating that 'it is through the particular representations of the family in various movies that we are able to study the processes whereby existing social relations are rendered acceptable and valid' (ibid.: 24). This elision enables her to propose that it is a social ideology produced by capitalism which identifies the absent family of the text for the spectator and by its 'absence or disfigurement', opens up the possibility of oppositional readings. The unproblematic assertion of family as site of social oppression

and as an ideological determinant for fictional representation and textual readings poses some difficulty for more rigorous analysis. However, Harvey has brilliantly located the absent family as narrative function and begun to expose its agency within the symbolic realm, within the extra-diegetic space governed by spectatorial activity and in its engagement with contextual discourses.

8. See, for example, *Indiana Jones and the Temple of Doom, Total Recall, Good Morning, Vietnam, The Naked Gun, Rambo: First Blood Part II*, the *Police Academy* series, *Sudden Impact, Beverly Hills Cop* and *Beverly Hills Cop II*.

9. Zaretsky, 1973: 127.

10. The absent metadystopian texts in this paradigmatic construction are: *Three Men and a Baby, Coming to America, Gremlins, Arthur, Back to the Future, Terms of Endearment* and *The Blue Lagoon*. The utopian present meta-dystopian texts are *Honey, I Shrunk The Kids* (the scientific community), *Look Who's Talking* (accountancy), *Fatal Attraction* (publishing), *Kramer versus Kramer* (advertising), *Annie* (the orphanage) and *Rain Man* (entrepreneurial commerce). The utopian foregrounded metadystopian texts are represented by just *The Golden Child* (religion – good versus evil).

11. If the actual family is foregrounded, then the metaphorical family is always dystopian. The metafamily is only utopian if it is foregrounded. Similarly, if the metafamily is present, then the actual family is more likely to be utopian than if the metafamily is absent or foregrounded. Actual dystopian paradigms represent 47 of the 55 top box-office films and metadystopian paradigms characterise 48 of the 55. Just eight films represent a central character's family as utopian and six of these are foregrounded. Seven are meta-utopian and these are all foregrounded paradigms. In the majority of these, the actual family is also dystopian. Twenty-two out of the top 55 films foreground the actual family. Twenty-five out of the top 55 films represent it as an absence.

12. Seven meta-utopian films in all – *Pretty Woman, Top Gun, Who Framed Roger Rabbit, Star Trek, Ghostbusters, Rocky III* and *Rocky IV*.

13. *Out of Africa, '10', Ghost, The Fox and the Hound, Trading Places, Superman IV, Gremlins, Arthur, Back to the Future, Terms of Endearment* and *The Blue Lagoon*.

14. Twenty-six of the top 55 films represent a close male bonding. In ten of these, the buddy bonding is proposed as a resolution to the narrative, subordinating or occluding any romantic alliance. All but one of these films construct actual dystopian paradigms, the exception being *Look Who's Talking* in which one of the male buddies is a baby and therefore non-threatening to the final utopian resolution. In the remaining 16 films, the buddy is killed off (often literally, as in *Top Gun, An Officer and a Gentleman, The Untouchables* or *Arthur*) or displaced by a female romantic interest (as in *Three Men and a Baby, Any Which Way You Can* or *Coming to America*).

15. The films within this paradigm (foregrounded metadystopian, absent actual dystopian) are *Indiana Jones and the Temple of Doom, Total Recall, Good Morning, Vietnam, The Naked Gun, Rambo: First Blood Part II*, the *Police Academy* series (*I* to *IV*) *Sudden Impact* and *Beverly Hills Cop*.

16. Brooks, 1984: 94.

17. We should not ignore *Ghostbusters'* marketing success. The fastest growing segment of the cinema audience in the 1980s was the mid-teens to early twenties sector. Around the summer and Christmas holiday periods (the release dates in the US and UK respectively) there was the additional 'child/family' market share. Building identificatory strategies for adolescents and children within the text was thus crucial in developing these important market segments.

18. A raft of horror movies from *Halloween* to the *Nightmare* series has employed the suburb as a problematic site for the family from the late 1970s on. A hugely dystopian horror film, *Parents*, takes very particular care to specifically locate the family in a suburban setting from the opening pan across the suburban sprawl thus suggesting that the trouble (in this case cannibalism) begins as a direct cause of the family's transfer into the suburb. *The 'Burbs*, in comic symmetry, also uses the suburb to expose some horrific entity beneath the calm exterior. This moves away from the convention of the urban/rural opposition – as charted by Carol Clover – which had been a central spatial organisation within the horror film. In the popular films that we are looking at, *Gremlins* and *E.T.* both problematise the suburban locus.

19. The main exception to this being *Rain Man*, in which the sibling relationship is constructed more closely as buddy bonding.

20. Medved, 1993: 137.

5 BACKLASH PATRIARCH OR THE NEW MAN? THE ROLE OF THE FATHER

1. Of the 55 top box-office films, 17 represent failed fathers, 12 represent absent fathers, 10 feature fathers whose masculinity has failed, 8 represent traitors and 8 films feature failed patriarchs.

2. *The Jazz Singer* makes this particularly clear in the opposition of Ruth and Molly. Jess's wife, Ruth, epitomises the values of the tightly focused Jewish community and actively discourages his singing. Molly literally promotes his work, supports Jess's resurrection after his father 'kills' him, and bears his baby in the new community of showbusiness.

3. The resonance of this scene with a similar sequence in Eisenstein's *Battleship Potemkin* underpins this interpretation. In the earlier film, the sequence is used to counterpoint the brutal deceit of Tsarist Russia (represented by the battleship) against the revolutionaries or ordinary people (as represented in the figure of the mother and child). As in this film, the mother and child are collapsed into the clash of patriarchs.

4. See, in particular *Jokes and Their Relation to the Unconscious* (Standard Edition, 8: Penguin Freud Library, 6: 38, 131 & 237).

5. Hysterical science-fiction films (such as *Return of the Jedi, The Empire Strikes Back* and *E.T.*) interestingly all figure a treacherous father who is the source of the repressed trauma, rather than a failed male, and thus are dealt with in the next section.

6. See in particular, Tania Modleski's fascinating analysis of *Three Men and*

a Baby, which proposes the reproductive aspiration of men as a driving force behind several key films of the decade (1991: 79–90).

7. Intriguingly, Arnold Schwarzenegger who played Quaid/Hauser later starred in *Junior*, a film about a male scientist who becomes pregnant in the interests of research (see Chapter 9 for further analysis).

6 ABSENCE AND LOSS: THE EVACUATION OF THE MOTHER

1. Over two-thirds of the sample, 38 of the 55 top box-office films from 1980 to 1990, do not feature a maternal figure as a key character at either a metaphorical or actual level.

2. For a study of these positions, see, in particular, Irigaray (1977), Kristeva (1980), Hermann (1980) and Cixous (1980). Such film-makers include Marguerite Duras (*Nathalie Granger*) and Marlene Gorris (*A Question of Silence*).

3. See, for example, Kaplan (1992); Faludi (1992); Modleski (1991) and, for a more recent exploration of this paradigm, Tasker (1993).

4. See Rosie Jackson's work on maternal absence and blame for a valuable, if anecdotal, study into the subject (1994).

5. A reference to the highly ambiguous drama of woman-curbing, *The Taming of the Shrew*. This reference is picked up in E.T.'s use of *The Quiet Man*, an allegory of the same tale. (See Chapter 8.)

6. *Daily Mail* (16 March 1984); *Glasgow Herald* (16 March 1984).

7. *Mail on Sunday* (18 March 1984).

8. 'The secret of this film's popularity lies, I suspect, elsewhere – and riding on the last wave of the women's movement, *Terms of Endearment* is ostensibly a study in women's feelings . . . as such it has earned those epithets which unreconstructed psychologists tend to apply to women – it has been described as "caring", "warm", "tender", "sensitive" and other adjectives which swirl around the plastic Magimix bucket of failed imaginations,' *Spectator* (24 March 1984).

9. *New York Times* (4 December 1983).

10. Philip French, *Observer* (18 March 1984).

11. Pauline Kael, *New Yorker* (12 December 1983); *You Magazine* interviewed Penelope Mortimer and Julia Mankowitz (11 March 1984). Two further reviews are typical, both deeply rooted in the realist aesthetic and a straight conflation of social and diegetic. 'The idea is that this is, somehow, real life to which we can "relate" but the fact that such films always need "stars" to sustain them suggests that the film makers have either a very limited or a very fitful interest in what is real', *Spectator* (24 March 1984). An overtly political review bitterly noted the privileging of the private at the expense of the social realm without acknowledging the conventions of fictional melodrama or the politics of representation: 'momentous periods of history and political turmoil pass by her [Aurora] unnoticed, every minute detail of her comfortable yet uneventful life is revealed with unsettling candour', *Morning Star* (23 March 1984).

12. *Daily Telegraph* (23 February 1984); *Guardian* (24 February 1984); *New York Times* (4 December 1983); *Time* (28 November 1983).

13. This feature is noted by Peter Ackroyd in the *Spectator* (24 March 1984) who goes on to draw some interesting conclusions from these representations: 'Mother is sharp, independent, "liberated", she would rather her daughter had multiple abortions than bring up a family in relative poverty ... her daughter is more blowsy and lumpen, concerned with the ancient imperatives of children and household rather than the more recent demands of career and familial independence. One has only to read the reviews of Germaine Greer's latest book to see that this is a phenomenon now being recognised and applauded. The film has cashed in on the right fashion at the right time.' In proposing that these two representations lie at opposite poles of a female spectrum, Ackroyd has defined a rather different discourse than the one he purports to engage. 'Mother' certainly has no career and has herself created a world which is centred entirely around her family. Her 'independence' can only be intended as financial (she is entirely dependent on others for her lifestyle and affections), which must in turn have been inherited from her husband for she has no other visible means of income. Aurora's proposition of abortion to Emma is based far more on her distrust of Flap as father than a desire for Emma to go out to work. Finally, the 'sharpness' may refer to the bitter-sweet and highly barbed exchanges between mother and daughter – a Hollywood convention employed to represent intimacy-despite-themselves in close relationships – see, in particular, the screwball comedies of the forties and fifties and the *film noir*. Interestingly, it is usually used as a signifier of a potential romantic liaison.

14. Cancer and AIDS were the focus of health concern through the 1980s. Both are invasive and have been represented as the body turning on itself. AIDS attacks the immune system and is popularly understood as being introduced through some deliberate and illicit act (aberrant or promiscuous sex, drugtaking and so on); cancer is understood as the deviant cell (the body's own material) which multiplies, transforming and eventually destroying its host. Throughout the 1980s, speculation (alongside the research) grew as to the causes of cancer. One proposition, in particular, took hold: that emotional and physical debility could render someone more susceptible to a cancer. Remedial centres were established (the Bristol Clinic in the UK in the early 1980s) to begin to treat the whole person – mind as well as body. It also became clear that many cancers were curable in the early stages, necessitating more rigorous preventative screening. The responsibility for breast cancer diagnosis (Emma's cancer) was located firmly with the woman and pamphlets were circulated and doctors instructed in the UK to show women how to examine themselves. Death from breast cancer was thus characterised as unnecessary and – by extension – a woman's own fault. Thus the one disease is propagated by deviancy, the other by neglect – both calumnious offences in the self-conscious, health-conscious, achievement-oriented eighties. The fact that it is Emma who contracts cancer may be traced through another discourse of illness located by Doane as a signifier of women's moral and psychic disturbance in the women's films of the 1940s (Doane in Suleiman (ed.) 1986: 152–74).

15. Fascinating work has been undertaken on the gender imbalances in legislation on sexual matters. Ursula Vogel (in Smart (ed.), 1992: 146–65) offers an excellent overview of the inscription of the 'double standard' within

nineteenth-century legislation and its relationship to criminality and punishment. While I would resist any attempt to conflate social women with cinematic representations, the specific resonances between these discursive formations would repay further study – particularly the enshrining concept that women's liberty was the threat which needed regulation.

16. Shaun Usher, *Daily Mail* (15 January 1988). This review was typical also in highlighting the generic conundrums of the film.

17. Fifty-nine-year-old headmistress Jean Harris, who was convicted in 1981 of the murder of Dr Herman Tarnover, author of *The Scarsdale Diet*. In the same interview, Dearden also claimed that a psychiatrist told him that seven out of ten of his patients had talked about the film during their consultation.

18. *Daily Mirror* (15 January 1988).

19. This interpretation of Dan's uncontrollable sex drive was consolidated by contemporary extra-diegetic stories of the star Michael Douglas's 'addiction to sex'.

20. The inability of state agencies – most notably social workers and the police – to adequately contain and adjudicate on intra-family violence – was furiously critiqued in popular discourse throughout the decade, particularly in the UK, over such incidents as the Cleveland child abuse case.

21. These 'rules' are, of course, the old sexual double standard which permits male promiscuity but condemns women for behaving likewise. They also refer to the ordinance of marriage – 'Let no man [or woman] put apart' – Dan may have sex outside wedlock, but Alex may not intrude into it: a one-way movement. Dan may escape both punishment and responsibility, Alex, as she points out, gains nothing. The *Daily Mail* (15 January 1988) underlines this in its review of the film: 'Gradually, in a way fit to make many men break out in a cold sweat of I-was-there empathy, Alex reveals that her promise of no strings disguises great cables of obligation.'

22. This unusual figuration of the Final Girl might prompt a feminist reading by tracing an Oedipal trajectory in which the girl achieves maturation through the transference of her ambiguous passion from the monster-father to the potential lover. Certainly, there is a clear case for arguing that Dan has infantilised Beth and that Alex comes to represent his repressed and 'loose' self (his pre-Oedipal, greedy, orally-oriented consciousness). By destroying this, Beth not only locates Dan firmly and finally within the symbolic realm, but in identifying him as father-repressor, may be able to move past him into another, more nurturing relationship. As Ellen Willis speculates in *The Village Voice* (15 December 1987), the final shot of the photograph may be heavily ironic. Willis also longed for an alternative ending to the film: 'as Douglas' wife begins to figure out what's going on, the spectacle of Close's vengefulness ignites her own feminist anger, long smothered under that sweet nurturing facade. Close then kills Douglas and his wife provides her with an alibi. Or vice versa. After that, the family portrait shot would make sense.'

23. Noted by Alexander Walker in *The Evening Standard* (London; 4 January 1988) – 'it succeeds scarily well in being several types of film'. A strong case can be made that this 'scariness' is derived precisely from the 'several types of film'.

24. *The Evening Standard* (London; 4 January 1988); *The Guardian* (7 January 1988).

25. For example, *Today*'s observation (15 January 1988) that 'It does the lone career woman no favours but *Fatal Attraction* is a timely movie about the wages of casual sex: If disease doesn't put you off, Glenn Close will.' Note, again, the conflation of character and actress.

7 LOOK WHO'S TALKING: CHALLENGING CHILDREN AND PARENTAL INVERSIONS

1. Redeemer-child films include *Indiana Jones and the Temple of Doom, The Golden Child, Rocky IV, Annie, Three Men and a Baby, Kramer versus Kramer, Tootsie* and *Gremlins*.
2. The top box-office films representing the adult child are *Top Gun, An Officer and a Gentleman, Staying Alive, The Jazz Singer*, the *Indiana Jones* trilogy, *Coming to America, Rain Man, Pretty Woman, The Empire Strikes Back* and *Return of the Jedi*.
3. *Monthly Film Bulletin*, March 1983, Vol 50, No. 590.
4. *Ghostbusters* gave Columbia the four biggest weeks of box-office business achieved by a single film in the company's history. It was released as a summer movie in the US and by the date of its UK release for the Christmas market, on 9 December 1984, had grossed $220 million. The film was announced in the US by an extended and mysterious ad campaign using the Ghostbuster symbol and the slogan 'Coming to Save the World this Summer'. In the blockbuster mould, there were a huge number of tie-in products and associated ephemera which were emblazoned with the film logo used in the credit sequence and the group's badge and which actually made an appearance in the final sequence when the crowd wave Ghostbuster T-shirts at their heroes. There were Ghostbuster shops, clothes, badges and a fan club. A music video was released featuring the stars singing along with the film's soundtrack. An International Ghostbusters' Club issued a 'Tools of the Trade' membership kit (badge, Certificate of Paranormal Proficiency, ID Card, stickers and a year's subscription to the Club magazine.) In the UK a wave of articles announced the influx of ghosthunters arriving from the States to plunder our supernatural heritage and the *Sunday Mirror* ran a Ghostbuster competition.
5. In fact, Columbia was clearly unsure about the box-office appeal of the central three actors and instead publicised the filmography of Sigourney Weaver, building her star credibility – and generic dexterity – by stressing *Alien, Eyewitness* and *The Year of Living Dangerously*.
6. *New Statesman* (7 December 1984). Other reviews were also typical: 'costly and calculated industrial product' (*The Times*, 7 December 1984); 'suffers from a nasty dose of diminishing returns. The pricier and pacier the Special Effects . . . the less the plot seems able to keep up with them.'
7. Phillip French, *The Observer* (9 December 1984). Michael Wood, *New Society* (13 December 1984). French went on to contrast this phenomenon with *Gremlins* which he claimed was targeted at the very young despite its 15 certification, thereby ranking the transgressive language of *Ghostbusters* as less suitable for children than the violence of *Gremlins*.
8. The film creates its comedy from a wide repertoire: from the subversion of

norms (the application of business terminology to parapsychology; the 'child' vs the 'adult'; the excessively 'human' behaviour of the ghosts; pitting technology against the spiritual; the impotence of the state apparatus); from classic slapstick (being slimed/marshmallowed); from stereotypes (Lewis the accountant; Venkman's casual womanising); from transformations (Dana to a dog; the Destroyer to a Marshmallow Man); from irony (the constant commentary from Venkman; the mayor's change of heart; the use of Winston) and from parodic intertextual references in the iconography to films as varied as *Metropolis* and *The Blob*. However, the film's generic structuring is interesting. As a comedy, it plunders elements from a variety of generic sources. One critic, indeed, suggested that in coming from the stable of horror movies, it signalled the end of the genre. However, its narrative structure and iconographic field suggests a mode closer to science fiction than to horror. Other generic forms comprise the material that the comedy works on, underlining the folly of attempting a simple dichotomy of form and content for it is these alternative generic structures which themselves become the content of the text.

9. As the star, Sigourney Weaver (Dana) brings her previous persona of Ripley in Scott's *Alien* to the text. She can thus be read as highly suspect in this continuing connection with science fiction and with Maternal Monsters. The impossibility of union and the necessity for repelling Dana from the group is reinforced by the film's sequel, *Ghostbusters II*, in which Dana is now a divorced, single parent – a relationship entirely separate from the brief interlude with Venkman. Her baby is abducted by alien forces and the Ghostbusters re-form (Venkman is now a chat-show host, Ray and Winston entertain at kid's parties and Egon continues his research) to save both her baby and the city. Again, it is humanity's own wickedness that threaten it – people's 'nasty thoughts' have created a river of mucus under New York City. Woman and her vulnerability combine with the general stew of fallibility to provide the material for the Ghostbuster team.

8 FAMILY DRAMAS: THE FAMILY IN *E.T.* – *THE EXTRA-TERRESTRIAL*

1. I have used the italicised title *E.T.* to denote the film's title and the unstopped ET to indicate the eponymous character. The only time ET's name is written is by Elliott in the classroom sequence and this is without full stops. I have therefore used this form of the character's name throughout.

2. If graffiti indeed represent marginal and repressed social desires, then it is fascinating that the discourse of *E.T.* figured so immediately and blatantly at that level, even preceding its institutional form. Many critics noted the mythical status accorded to the film. In *Time*, David Robinson noted that '*E.T.* has passed into the realm of universal mythology, where only the legend itself matters. The great public all over the world have some sense of it: no amount of publicity could have launched the unprecedented popularity of the film' (10 December 1982). David Hughes in *The Sunday Times* commented that ET, the eponymous hero, 'is like a collective unconscious waddling about the domestic scene, acting to communicate race memories

while trying to understand our mad habits' (12 December 1982). Andy Gill in *New Musical Express* remarked that 'It's certainly the only film I can think of to have achieved saturation cliché status before it even opens in Britain' (11 December 1982).

3. *The Sunday Telegraph* observed that 'the extent of Fleet Street's fascination with this fictitious character has resulted in numerous competitions with stickers, badges, posters and dolls as prizes. A fan club was set up. On 9 December one newspaper devoted four times more space to *E.T.* related items than it did to the Home Office barring of Sinn Fein leaders' (19 December 1982): an ironic (and probably unintentional) comparison with the xenophobic practices of the British government throughout the 1980s. *The Daily Express* (24 September 1982) perhaps best exemplified the contradictions inherent in many stories by printing a story with a blatantly dual agenda – firstly to publicise the huge wave of tie-in products available and secondly to appear to castigate manufacturers for leaping on to the bandwagon – which it was, of course, itself doing.

4. For example, almost three months prior to the film's release, *The Sunday Times* featured a story about video piracy and the 'unlimited budget' UIP had been given to track down the pirates (19 September 1982). Similar coverage continued and on 17 December 1982, *The Sun* reported on the prosecution of four pirate companies for selling unlicensed *E.T.* merchandise.

5. Newspapers were full of stories such as that featured in the *Daily Mail* (14 December 1982) which reported that the sole cinema on the Isle of Sheppey actually rejected the film on the grounds that 60 per cent of a sample 1000 of their customers had already seen it on illegal pirate videos. Stories of the pirates' capture and exemplary sentences also caught the public imagination. The intra-textual parallel with this element of the 'social' narrative is an obvious one. In the bedtime story which is read in Scene 17, Peter Pan adjures children everywhere to clap their hands to demonstrate their belief in fairies and thus save Tinkerbell. The enemies against whom they are fighting are, of course, the pirates.

6. *Poltergeist* forms an interesting counterpoint to *E.T.* Not only did it employ the visual excess and generic conventions of horror rather than science fiction, it featured a woman and her daughter as the heroic central characters. The nature and expression of desire is very different in the two films, although the family representations share certain instrumentalities and paradigmatic conventions.

7. Source: *Screen International*. The film was released too late for inclusion in the 1982 list. In Japan, in particular, *E.T.* was phenomenally successful, taking £1.7m from 35 screens in 11 cities in the first two days of its release (4/5 December 1982).

8. Derek Malcolm, *The Guardian* (9 December 1982). Annual UK admissions had dropped by 26 per cent in 1981/2 and by 2 per cent in 1982/3. They were to sink a further 16 per cent in 1983/4 (source: Dept. of Trade; figures published by CAA). The divinity claimed for the film and its hero was rehearsed across the press. Andy Gill in *New Musical Express* (11 December 1982) observed, in common with many other reviewers, that 'the story of ET bears close resemblance to that other Greatest Story Ever Told, of

Jesus Christ and the Crucifixion'. This was of course underpinned by the promotional use of an image taken from Michelangelo's painting on the Sistine Chapel for the film's poster campaign.

9. The film was re-released in 1986, justifiably billed as 'The Story that Touched the World' but was not released on to video until October 1988. Its first UK network broadcast was on Christmas Day 1990 where it was heralded as competing with the Queen for the nation's attention.

10. The *Daily Express* (18 August 1982) quoted an interview with Spielberg in which he recalled the genesis of the movie. 'I remember wishing one night for someone to talk to. It was just like being a child again and wanting that little voice in your mind.' Split identities and a desire to become a child again are, of course, significant elements in the text.

11. Interview with Ivor Davis, *Daily Express* (4 April 1982).

12. *Daily Mirror* (5 November 1982).

13. It was as a result of *E.T.*'s phenomenal box-office success that Universal presented him with Amblin, his studio within a studio at Burbank, allowing him more control over his work – and that of others (Robert Zemeckis and Joe Dante, for example).

14. In a particular validation of this reading, Jean Ritchie of *The Sun* invited 'psychologist', Jane Firbank' to preview the film. In the article she is quoted as saying 'We're all children and this film makes the most of that fact' (14 November 1982). Alexander Walker in *The Standard* (4 December 1982) made the identification even more explicit, writing a spoof letter in the character of ET and making an ironic comment on his own adult–child position as spectator of the film: 'You kids may talk that kind of dirty talk but adults don't like to hear it in my movie. It sort of destroys the childhood innocence that the story gives them back.' (An interesting contrast to the language of *Ghostbusters*. In this interpretation, the adult is the child no one ever was (the phantasy of a child) – in Margaret Hinxman's words, 'a rapturous secret society of childhood that leads a separate life to the world of adults' (*Daily Mail*, 7 December 1982).

15. One exception to this was a review by Russell Baker in the *International Herald Tribune* (6 August 1982) as he speculated acerbically on why ET had 'scored' over *Annie* at the box office: 'Americans these days would rather invest in creatures than tomorrow, a conclusion buttressed by the continuing public support of the Reagan administration and the anaemic condition of the Stock Market.'

16. Reviewers such as Peter Ackroyd in *The Spectator* (11 December 1982) levelled the charge of infantilism at the film but remarked that it was endowed 'with the good fortune of living in a culture that is so debased that it takes such things seriously'.

17. *Rolling Stone* (July 1982).

18. *The Daily Telegraph* (20 January 1983) reported that Swedish, Finnish and Norwegian censors passed the film as unsuitable for young children because 'the film portrays adults as enemies of children'.

19. *The Mail on Sunday* (23 December 1990). The movie is thus essentially 'high concept', that is, it can be pitched to a production executive in one punchy sentence.

20. Many critics have observed that Elliott was ignored and ostracised from the

family. Andrew Sarris, for example, characterises him as 'the hitherto lonely, neglected and repressed Elliott' (*The Village Voice*, 21 September 1982). Yet all the signs are that this ostracism (if such it was) was a deliberate choice made by Elliott himself. His family – even his siblings – make every effort to include and care for him at the beginning of the film while he rejects and hurts them. Even his brother's friends are willing to include him in their game in Scene 2.

21. The boy tentatively probes his index finger towards Mary's bottom as she bends to put dishes into the dishwasher. She is an object of harassment while, or perhaps because, she is doing domestic chores. Servicing is a conventional linguistic conflation for performing both sexual and domestic duties. The action forms an interesting parody of ET's own finger movements which are heavily emphasised through the film.

22. These dramas resonate with contemporary sociological paradigms such as the three outlined by Brigitte and Peter Berger (1984) in which the family is alternatively conceived as the problem, as the solution and as a social form which requires professional surveillance and intervention.

23. Significantly, all the escapes made by the children are from the adult realm of the city to the forest, signifier of wildness and of nature. Flight, which figures in two of the escapes, also functions as a symbol for a fear of sexuality and of maturation.

24. This attempt at locating ET continued in the extra-textual speculations on his origin. Information, such as his home being three million light years away was all provided by the director, distributors or reviewers rather than by the text itself. For example, it was a UIP press release which supplied the following lines: 'He is afraid. He is totally alone. He is three million light years away from home.' Critic Stephen Pile took his investigations into ET's gender to the extent of contacting Universal where a spokeswoman asserted that, 'The whole beauty of the film is that he [sic] is sexless' (*The Sunday Times*, 14 December 1982).

25. *The Quiet Man*, with its 'Taming of the Shrew' narrative of female containment is a fascinating counterpoint to this scene. The sequence depicted is the initial foray made by John Wayne at taming the vigorous Maureen O'Hara. Elliott can only reach to kiss the girl by standing on another boy's back. Elliott not only subjugates the girl but also, by climbing on his back, his male classmate. However, he is also symbolically tied to the pre-Oedipal realm by this scene, in his interdependence on others (ET and the boy lying on the floor) and his defiance of the teacher.

26. The adult scientist-doctors, some of whom surprise the spectator by turning out to be female when they remove their masks after ET's death, were actually played by a mixture of academic and medical doctors – their qualifications meticulously spelled out after each name in the credits.

27. Ruppersberg in Kuhn (ed.) (1990).

28. ET's designer, Carlo Rambaldi, took the concept for ET from a picture he had painted in 1952 (another 'decade of the family') called *Ladies of the Delta*. There were three ET models – one a mechanical version operated by cables, one electronic one for facial movements and one a shell operated by someone inside it. ET required 82 separate controls to work it. Three actors worked inside ET – two were dwarfs and one a schoolboy without legs.

ET's voice was provided by Pat Walsh, a former speech teacher, aged anywhere (according to press reports) between 64 and 82. Even in his material referent, ET inhabited the realm of the marginal and dispossessed.

29. The release of the film was contemporaneous with some of the early developments of virtual reality equipment which was to be subsequently manufactured for games playing.

30. The classroom scene also clearly foregrounds the blurring of representational/real boundaries in the choreographed 'fantastic' sequence which crosscuts between the television scenes of *The Quiet Man* and Elliott kissing the girl in the classroom. An additional doubling is enacted here too as this is a film being screened on television.

31. As noted earlier, ET was constructed as three different models. This accounts for the difference in his size which is apparent between and even within scenes. He is also able to extend his neck to change his eye level to that of any interlocutor. He is assigned gender and a name (significantly in visual form originally in Elliott's drawing of him) by others and is dressed up in both men's and women's clothes. His language learning is a parrot-fashion form of repetition and there is little evidence within the text that he fully comprehends the meaning of any of the words he uses. He eats the favourite food of his guardians and can be killed and resurrected by them. His first activity within the text is to throw a ball back to Elliott, and their first sequence together is characterised by mimicry. It is thus possible to read him as the plastic representation of the other characters' desires.

9 CONCLUSIONS AND FUTURES – STASIS AND CHANGE

1. Modleski, 1991: 7.

2. Source: The Henley Centre, *Planning for Social Change* (1994/5). The survey demonstrated a similar increase in respect and influence for work colleagues and friends. The highest variance was a swing against the government, advertisements and manufacturers who all declined significantly in the amount of respect and influence they could command. In all cases, the same three factors prevailed with those losing respect and influence being seen as impersonal and commercial, as were those where the basis of the relationship was opaque.

3. The Foundation was explicitly established 'to search out the underlying causes of weakness or evil in the community'. The fact that it has diverted its attention to the family in the latter part of the eighties and early nineties is indicative of the popular social and political focus of where that 'weakness or evil' might be located. (Kiernan & Wickes, 1990, quoted in Utting, 1995: 72). The research was based on the premise familiar to eighties family values discourse that 'families are one of the important places where children's behaviour and attitudes are shaped. Through a loving and stable relationship with their parents, they can first be introduced to the balance between personal responsibility and interdependence that enables wider society to function' (Utting, 1995: 7).

4. The report predicted that three-quarters of all men and women will marry

and most will have lived together first, increasingly postponing marriage until after the birth of the first child. Twice as many babies will be born inside wedlock as outside and will average at 2.1 children per family. Nearly half of all marriages will end in divorce and the number of adult carers will rise as the population continues to age (Utting, 1995: 7).

5. Bill Clinton was the most right-wing Democrat President in years and both Labour and Conservative parties wrestled over the centre ground in the first half of the decade.

6. Speech by Rt Hon Tony Blair MP while Shadow Home Affairs spokesman, 15 October 1993. Blair reprised this theme again in a speech to the leaders of Rupert Murdoch's media empire in 1995 when he stated that 'the family unit – the bedrock of stability – is, at least in parts of the West, almost collapsing' (quoted in *The Independent*, 17 July 1995). Although the Anglo-American alliance was weakened in the nineties, Clinton could claim some credit for the Labour Party adoption of the community theme, since Blair visited the States to discover the secrets of the Democrats' election-winning campaign and discussed the emerging 'community' paradigms of responsibilities replacing rights in socialist discourse. The Rt Hon John Redwood MP's speech was given to the Conservative Political Centre Summer School, Cardiff (2 July 1993). In 1995, Redwood mustered a credible challenge to John Major's leadership, culling support from the right of the party for his position on Europe and on home policies.

7. The AFA was founded to 'protect the family. This country was built on the family. In the past 30 years, family values have been under attack. During that time crime has risen, illegitimacy has risen, drug use is all but out of control. That's what happens when the family is weakened. The family is God's way of establishing order in the universe' (Rev. Wildmon, quoted in an interview in *The Independent* by Daniel Jeffreys (27 July 1995). By 1995, AFA had seriously affected the sales of 7-Eleven, ABC TV, Burger King, MatchBox Toys and Clorox bleach through a persistent campaign of corporate boycotts. In the same year, the Rev. Wildmon announced AT & T and Disney as targets. 'Hollywood is the worst, They won't let us in to influence their values so we will just have to take the place by storm.' Issues which primarily offended the AFA's pro-family agenda were sex, violence and homosexuality, all characterised as 'anti-family' and capturing the 'family' agenda firmly for the values and ethics of the right.

8. A video which, incidentally, it was never proved the children had watched. *Child's Play 3* was immediately withdrawn from sale and rental while, paradoxically, excerpts were extracted on national broadcast TV. The judge's comments endorsed the restrictive video legislation introduced in 1984 and paved the way for a new Private Member's Bill to further constrain video distribution.

9. The star of *Terminator 2* and *Junior*, Arnold Schwarzenegger, was playing roles at glancing angles to his pumped up hard-body persona of the early eighties, and throughout the nineties created a portfolio of characters which persistently returned to the role of the parent. The Schwarzenegger persona was perpetually constructed within a familial environment and persistently represented as creating himself, as he himself suggested: 'I only really had a plan when it came to creating and publicising myself' (interview with

Schwarzenegger, quoted in Kent, 1991: 104). His role as perfect father was continually reprised, becoming more and more explicit until he takes over the reproductive function itself in *Junior*.

10. Both producer and scriptwriter affirmed the familial focus of the film. Producer Jordan Kerner felt moved to stress that 'Family in the 90s is really about the taking of responsibility of each other' while, underlining the contradictory discourses and interpretations which circulate around any film, scriptwriter Ronald Bass proclaimed that 'After seeing this film, audiences will want to work harder on their marriage and their parenting.' Perhaps the film evoked such strong responses in these male stakeholders because they saw their work eroding their patriarchal power.

11. The only exception to this embargo on child jeopardy being *The Golden Child* and *The Untouchables*. Other films, such as *Annie* and *The Fox and The Hound* dealt with the aftermath rather than the actual moment of jeopardy and abandonment.

Filmography

Film title	Director	Distributor/Production company	Country of origin	Release date
'10'	Blake Edwards	Columbia–EMI–Warner/Orion Pictures	US	1979
Addams Family, The	Barry Sonnenfeld	Columbia–Tri-Star/Paramount & Orion	US	1991
Addams Family Values	Barry Sonnenfeld	UIP/Paramount Pictures	US	1993
Airplane!	Jim Abrahams, David Zucker & Jerry Zucker	Walt Disney/Walt Disney	US	1980
Alien	Ridley Scott	20th Century Fox/Brandywine	UK	1979
Alien³	David Fincher	20th Century Fox/20th Century Fox	US	1992
Annie	John Huston	Columbia–EMI–Warner/Rastar for Columbia Pictures	US	1981
An Officer and a Gentleman	Taylor Hackford	UIP/Lorimar	US	1981
Any Which Way You Can	Buddy Van Horn	Columbia–EMI–Warner/Warner Brothers	US	1980
Arthur	Steve Gordon	Columbia–EMI–Warner/Orion	US	1980
Baby Boom	Charles Shyer	UIP/MGM–United Artists	US	1987
Back to the Future	Robert Zemeckis	UIP/Amblin Entertainment for Universal	US	1985
BAT 21	Peter Markle	Guild/BAT 21 Productions	US	1988
Batman Returns	Tim Burton	Warner Brothers/Warner Brothers	US	1992
Battleship Potemkin	Sergei Eisenstein	Goskino	USSR	1925
Beetlejuice	Tim Burton	Warner Brothers/Geffen Film Company	US	1988
Beverly Hills Cop	Martin Brest	UIP/Paramount	US	1984
Beverly Hills Cop II	Tony Scott	UIP/Paramount	US	1987
Big Heat, The	Fritz Lang	Columbia/Columbia	US	1953
Bladerunner	Ridley Scott	Warner Brothers/ Ladd-Bladerunner Partnership	US	1988
Blob, The	Chuck Russell	Braveworld/Palisades California Inc.	US	1988
Blue Lagoon, The	Randal Kleiser	Columbia–EMI–Warner/ Columbia	US	1980
Born on the Fourth of July	Oliver Stone	UIP/Ixtlan for Universal	US	1989
'Burbs, The	Joe Dante	UIP/Imagine Entertainment	US	1988
Casualties of War	Brian De Palma	Columbia TriStar/Columbia	US	1989

Film title	Director	Distributor/Production company	Country of origin	Release date
Close Encounters of the Third Kind	Steven Spielberg	Columbia/EMI	US	1977
Color Purple, The	Steven Spielberg	Columbia–EMI–Warner/ Amblin Entertainment	US	1985
Condorman	Charles Jarrott	Walt Disney/Walt Disney	US	1981
Coming to America	John Landis	UIP/Paramount	US	1988
Empire of the Sun, The	Steven Spielberg	Robert Shapiro/Amblin Entertainment	US	1987
Empire Strikes Back, The	Irvin Kershner	20th Century Fox/Lucasfilm for 20th Century Fox	US	1980
E.T.–The Extra-Terrestrial	Steven Spielberg	UIP/Universal	US	1982
Eyewitness	Peter Yates	20th Century Fox/20th Century-Fox	US	1981
Fatal Attraction	Adrian Lyne	UIP/Paramount	US	1987
Ferris Bueller's Day Off	John Hughes	UIP/Paramount	US	1986
Flashdance	Adrian Lyne	UIP/Polygram for Paramount	US	1986
Fox and the Hound, The	Art Stevens, Ted Berman, Richard Rich	Walt Disney/Walt Disney	US	1981
Full Metal Jacket	Stanley Kubrick	Warner/Stanley Kubrick	UK	1987
Ghost	Jerry Zucker	UIP/Paramount	US	1990
Ghostbusters	Ivan Reitman	Columbia–EMI–Warner/ Columbia-Delphi	US	1984
Ghostbusters II	Ivan Reitman	Columbia–TriStar/Columbia	US	1989
Golden Child, The	Michael Ritchie	UIP/Paramount	US	1986
Good Morning, Vietnam	Barry Levinson	Warner Brothers/Touchstone	US	1987
Good Mother, The	Leonard Nimoy	Warner Brothers/Touchstone	US	1988
Good Son, The	Joseph Ruben	20th Century Fox/20th Century Fox	US	1993
Gremlins	Joe Dante	Columbia–EMI–Warner/Warner Brother for Amblin Entertainment	US	1984
Halloween	John Carpenter	Irwin Yablans/Falcon International	US	1978
Heavy Metal	Gerald Potterton	Columbia–EMI–Warner/ Columbia Pictures	US	1981
Home Alone	Chris Columbus	20th Century Fox/20th Century Fox	US	1990
Honey, I Shrunk the Kids	Joe Johnston	Warner Brothers/Walt Disney	US	1989
Indiana Jones and the Temple of Doom	Steven Spielberg	UIP/Lucasfilms for Paramount	US	1984

Film title	Director	Distributor/Production company	Country of origin	Release date
Indiana Jones and the Last Crusade	Steven Spielberg	UIP/Lucasfilms for Paramount	US	1989
Jack and Sarah	Tim Sullivan	Polygram/Polygram	UK	1995
Jazz Singer, The	Richard Fleischer	Columbia–EMI–Warner/ Warner Brothers	US	1980
Jaws	Steven Spielberg	Universal/Zanuck Brown	US	1975
Junior	Ivan Reitman	UIP/Northern Lights Entertainment	US	1994
Jurassic Park	Steven Spielberg	UIP/Amblin Entertainment for Universal	US	1993
Kramer versus Kramer	Robert Benton	Columbia–EMI–Warner/Stanley Jaffe Productions	US	1979
Last Action Hero	John McTiernan	Columbia TriStar/Columbia Pictures	US	1993
Lawnmower Man	Brett Leonard	First Independent/Allied Vision	US/UK	1992
Lethal Weapon 2	Richard Donner	Warner Brothers/Warner Brothers	US	1989
Lion King, The	Roger Allers	Buena Vista/Walt Disney Pictures	US	1994
Look Who's Talking	Amy Heckerling	Columbia Tri-star/Tristar Pictures	US	1989
Look Who's Talking Now	Tom Ropelewski	Columbia TriStar/TriStar Pictures	US	1993
Meatballs	Ivan Reitman	Paramount	Can	1979
Metropolis	Fritz Lang	Pommer/UFA	Ger	1926
Mrs Doubtfire	Chris Columbus	20th Century Fox/Blue Wolf for 20th Century Fox	US	1993
Naked Gun: From the Files of Police Squad!, The	David Zucker	UIP/Paramount	US	1988
Nathalie Granger	Marguerite Duras		Fr.	1972
National Lampoon's Animal House	John Landis	Universal/Universal	US	1978
Nightmare on Elm Street, A	Wes Craven	Palace Pictures/New Line Cinema	US	1984
Nine and a Half Weeks	Adrian Lyne	Palace Pictures/Jonesfilms	US	1985
Octopussy	John Glen	Eon/Danjaq	UK	1983
Out of Africa	Sydney Pollack	UIP/Universal	US	1985
Parents	Bob Balaban	Vestron/Parents Productions for Vestron	US	1988
Parenthood	Ron Howard	UIP/Imagine	US	1989
Platoon	Oliver Stone	Rank/Hemdale Film Corporation	US	1986
Police Academy	Hugh Wilson	Columbia-EMI-Warner/The Ladd Company for Warner Brothers	US	1984

Film title	Director	Distributor/Production company	Country of origin	Release date
Police Academy 2: Their First Assignment	Jerry Paris	Columbia–EMI–Warner/Ladd Brothers for Warner Brothers	US	1985
Police Academy 3: Back in Training	Jerry Paris	Columbia–Cannon–Warner/ Police Academy Productions	US	1986
Police Academy 4: Citizens on Patrol	Jim Drake	Columbia–Cannon–Warner/ Warner Brothers	US	1987
Pretty Woman	Garry Marshall	Warner Brothers/Touchstone Pictures	US	1990
Private Benjamin	Howard Zieff	Columbia–EMI–Warner/Warner Brothers	US	1980
Problem Child 2	Brian Levant	UIP/Universal–Imagine Films	US	1991
Question of Silence, A	Marleen Gorris		Neth.	1982
Quiet Man, The	John Ford	Republic/Argosy	US	1952
Raiders of the Lost Ark	Steven Spielberg	CIC/Lucasfilms for Paramount	US	1981
Rain Man	Barry Levinson	UIP/United Artists	US	1988
Rambo: First Blood Part II	George Pan Cosmatos	Columbia–EMI–Warner/Carloco for Anabasis	US	1985
Return of the Jedi	Richard Marquand	20th Century Fox/Lucasfilm	US	1983
Rocky III	Sylvester Stallone	UIP/United Artists	US	1982
Rocky IV	Sylvester Stallone	UIP/Universal	US	1985
Silence of the Lambs	Jonathan Demme	Rank/Orion Pictures	US	1990
Sleepless in Seattle	Nora Ephron	Columbia TriStar/TriStar Pictures	US	1993
Star Trek–The Motion Picture	Robert Wise	CIC/Paramount	US	1979
Stay Hungry	Bob Rafaelson	United Artists/Outov	US	1976
Staying Alive	Sylvester Stallone	UIP/Paramount	US	1983
Stepfather, The	Joseph Ruben	Virgin/ITC	US	1986
Stripes	Ivan Reitman	Columbia–EMI–Warner/ Columbia Pictures	US	1981
Sudden Impact	Clint Eastwood	Columbia–EMI–Warner/ Warner Brothers	US	1983
Superman IV: The Quest for Peace	Sidney J. Furie	Columbia–Cannon–Warner/ Cannon Films–Warner Brothers	US	1987
Terminator, The	James Cameron	Rank/Pacific Western for Orion	US	1984
Terminator 2	James Cameron	Guild/Carolco Pictures	US	1991
Terms of Endearment	James L. Brooks	UIP/Paramount	US	1983
Three Men and a Baby	Leonard Nimoy	Warner Brothers/Touchstone	US	1987
Tootsie	Sydney Pollack	Columbia–EMI–Warner/ Delphi Productions	US	1982
Top Gun	Tony Scott	UIP/Paramount	US	1986

Film title	Director	Distributor/Production company	Country of origin	Release date
Total Recall	Paul Verhoeven	Guild/Carolco	US	1990
Trading Places	John Landis	UIP/Paramount	US	1983
True Lies	James Cameron	UIP/Lightstorm Entertainment for 20th Century Fox	US	1994
Twins	Ivan Reitman	UIP/Universal	US	1988
Untouchables, The	Brian De Palma	UIP/Paramount	US	1987
When a Man Loves a Woman	Luis Mandoki	Buena Vista/Touchstone Pictures	US	1994
Who Framed Roger Rabbit	Robert Zemeckis	Warner Brothers/Touchstone-Amblin Entertainment	US	1988
Year of Living Dangerously, The	Peter Weir	MGM/McElroy–Peter Weir	Aus	1982

Bibliography

ADAIR, G., *Hollywood's Vietnam* (London: Heinemann, 1989).

ALLEN, R. & GOMERY, D., *Film: History Theory and Practice* (New York: McGraw Hill, 1985).

ALLEN, R. (ed.), *Channels of Discourse, Reassembled: Television and Contemporary Criticism* (London: Routledge, 1992).

ALTHUSSER, L., *Essays on Ideology* (London: Verso, 1984).

ALTMAN, R. (ed.), *Genre: The Musical* – A Reader (London: Routledge, 1981).

ARIES, P., *Centuries of Childhood*, trans. Baldick, R. (London: Peregrine, 1973).

BALIO, T. (ed.), *The American Film Industry* (London: University of Wisconsin Press, 1985).

BARLOW, G. & HILL, A. (eds), *Video Violence and Children* (London: Hodder & Stoughton, 1985).

BARRETT, M. & McINTOSH, M., *The Anti-Social Family* (London: Verso, 1991).

BARTHES, R., *Mythologies* (New York: Hill & Wang, 1972).

BARTHES, R., *Image, Music, Text* (London: Fontana, 1984).

BAUDRILLARD, J., *Selected Writings* (Cambridge: Polity Press, 1992).

BELSEY, C., *Critical Practice* (London: Methuen, 1980). ·

BENNETT, T. *et al.* (eds), *Popular Television and Film* (London, BFI: 1981).

BENTON, T., *Philosophical Foundations of the Three Sociologies* (London: Routledge and Kegan Paul, 1977).

BERGER, B. & BERGER, P., *The War Over the Family: Capturing the Middle Ground* (London: Penguin, 1984).

BERGSTROM, J., 'Sexuality at a Loss: The Films of F.W. Murnau', in *Poetics Today* VI (1985), Nos. 1–2.

BERNARD, J., *The Future of Marriage* (New Haven: Yale University Press, 1982).

BHASKAR, R., *A Realist Theory of Science* (Atlantic Highlands, NJ: Humanities Press, 1978).

BHASKAR, R., *Reclaiming Reality* (London: Verso, 1989).

BORDWELL, D., *Narrative within the Fiction Film* (London: Methuen, 1985).

BORDWELL, D., *Making Meaning: Inference and Rhetoric in the Interpretation of Cinema* (Cambridge, Mass.: Harvard University Press, 1991).

BORDWELL, D., STAIGER, J. & THOMPSON, K., *The Classical Hollywood Cinema: Film Style and Mode of Production to 1960* (London: Routledge, 1988).

BOURDIEU, P., *Structures, Habitus, Power: Basis for a Theory of Symbolic Power* in Dirks *et al.* (eds) (1994).

BROOKS, P., *Reading for the Plot: Design and Intention in Narrative* (New York: Vintage Books, 1984).

BURKE, P., *History and Social Theory* (Cambridge: Polity Press, 1992).

BYARS, J., *All that Hollywood Allows: Re-reading Gender in 1950s Melodrama* (London: Routledge, 1991).

CAMBELL, B., *Unofficial Secrets* – Child Sexual Abuse: The Cleveland Case (London: Virago, 1988).

CARR, E.H., *What is History?* (London: Penguin, 1990).

CARROLL, N., *The Philosophy of Horror* (London: Routledge, 1990).

CHESLER, P., *Sacred Bond: Motherhood under Siege* (London: Virago, 1990).

CHODOROW, N., *Reproduction of Mothering* (Berkeley: University of California Press, 1978).

CIXOUS, H., 'The Laugh of the Medusa', in de Courtivron, I. and Elaine Marks, E. (eds) (1980).

CLEESE, J. & SKINNER, R., *Families and How to Survive Them* (London: Mandarin, 1992).

CLOVER, C., *Men, Women and Chainsaws* (London, BFI: 1992).

COHAN, S. & HARK, I.R., *Screening the Male: Exploring Masculinities in Hollywood Cinema* (London: Routledge, 1993).

CREWE, I., 'Values: The Crusade that Failed', in Kavanagh & Seldon (eds), (1989).

COLLINS, J., RADNER, H. & PREACHER COLLINS, A. (eds), *Film Theory Goes to the Movies* (London: Routledge, 1993).

CONRAN, S., *Superwoman* (Harmondsworth: Penguin, 1977).

CONRAN, S., *Superwoman 2: Superwoman in Action* (Harmondsworth: Penguin, 1979).

CONRAN, S., *Down with Superwoman* (Harmondsworth: Penguin, 1991).

de COURTIVRON, I. & MARKS, E. (eds), *New French Feminisms* (Massachusetts: University of Massachusetts Press, 1980).

DIRKS, N., ELEY, G. & ORTNER, S. (eds), *Culture/ Power/ History: A Reader in Contemporary Social Theory* (Chichester: Princeton University Press, 1994).

DOANE, M., MELLENCAMP, P. & WILLIAMS, L. (eds), *Re-Visions* (American Film Institute, 1984).

DOCHERTY, D. *et. al.*, *The Last Picture Show? Britain's Changing Film Audiences* (London: BFI, 1987).

DONALD, James (ed.), *Fantasy and the Cinema* (London: BFI, 1989).

DONZELOT, J., *The Policing of Families*, trans. Robert Hurley (New York, 1979; London: Hutchinson, 1980).

DYER, R., 'Entertainment and Utopia' in Altman, R. (ed.) (1981).

DYER, R., *Heavenly Bodies: Film Stars and Society* (London: Macmillan, 1987).

EDHOLM, F., 'The Unnatural Family', in Whitelegg *et al.* (eds) (1982).

ELLIS, J., *Visible Fictions* (London: Routledge & Kegan Paul, 1985).

ELSAESSER, T. (ed.), *Early Cinema: Space, Frame, Narrative* (London: BFI, 1990).

FALUDI, Susan, *Backlash: The Undeclared War against Women* (London: Chatto & Windus, 1992).

FELDSTEIN, R. & ROOF, J. (eds), *Feminism and Psychoanalysis* (London: Cornell University Press, 1989).

FINLER, J.W., *The Hollywood Story* (London: Mandarin, 1992).

FLANDRIN, J-L., *Families in Former Times* (Cambridge: Cambridge University Press, 1979).

FOUCAULT, M., *The Archaeology of Knowledge* (London: Tavistock, 1986).

FOUCAULT, M., *The History of Sexuality* (London: Peregrine, 1984).

FOUCAULT, M., *The History of Sexuality, Vol. 3: The Care of the Self* (London: Penguin, 1990).

FRIEDMAN, L. (ed.), *British Cinema and Thatcherism* (London: UCL Press, 1993).

FRIEDMAN, L., 'The Empire Strikes Out: An American Perspective on the British Film Industry', in Friedman, L. (ed.) (1993).

GERAGHTY, C., *Women and Soap Opera* (Oxford: Polity Press/Basil Blackwell, 1991).

GERAGHTY, C., 'British Soaps in the 1980s', in Strinati, D. & Wagg, S. (eds) (1992).

GITTINS, D., *The Family in Question* (London: Macmillan, 1985, second edition 1993).

GLEDHILL, C., *Stardom: Industry of Desire* (London: Routledge, 1991).

GLEDHILL, C., *Home Is Where the Heart Is* (London: BFI, 1987).

GOMERY, D., *Shared Pleasures: A History of Movie Presentation in the United States* (London: BFI, 1992).

GORDON, L., *Heroes of their Own Lives: The Politics & History of Family Violence* (London: Virago, 1989).

GRIFFIN, S., *Woman and Nature: The Roaring Inside Her* (London: Women's Press, 1984).

GUBACK, T.H., *The International Film Industry* (Bloomington: Indiana Press, 1969).

GUBACK, T.H., 'Hollywood's International Market', in Balio, T. (1985: 463–86).

HERMANN, C., *Women in Space and Time*, trans. Marilyn R. Schuster, in de Courtivron, I. and Elaine Marks, E. (eds) (1980).

HILLIER, J., *The New Hollywood* (London: Studio Vista, 1992).

HITE, S., *The Hite Report on the Family: Growing Up under Patriarchy* (London: Hodder and Stoughton, 1995).

HODGE, B. & TRIPP, D., *Children & Television: A Semiotic Approach* (Cambridge: Polity Press, 1986).

HUENG, M., 'Why ET Must Go Home: The New Family in American Cinema', in *Journal of Popular Film & Television*, XI, No. 2: 1983.

HUTTON, W., *The State We're In* (London: Jonathan Cape, 1995).

IRIGARAY, L., 'Woman's Exile' in *Ideology and Consciousness*, No. 1, 1977: 63–76.

JACKSON, R., *Mothers Who Leave* (London: Pandora, 1994).

JAMESON, F., 'Postmodernism and Consumer Society', in Kaplan, E. Ann (ed.) (1988).

JAMESON, F., *Postmodernism or the Cultural Logic of Late Capitalism* (London: Verso, 1992).

JOHNSTON, W.B. & PACKER, A.H., *Workforce 2000: Work and Workers for the 21st Century* (Indianapolis: Hudson Institute, 1987).

KAPLAN, E. Ann (ed.), *Postmodernism and Its Discontents* (London: Verso, 1988).

KAPLAN, E. Ann (ed.), *Women in Film Noir* (London: BFI, 1980, revised edn).

KAPLAN, E. Ann, *Motherhood and Representation: The Mother in Popular Culture and Melodrama* (London: Routledge, 1992).

KAVANAGH, J., 'Feminism, Humanism and Science', in Kuhn, A. (ed.), (1990).

KAVANAGH, D. & SELDON, A. (eds), *The Thatcher Effect: A Decade of Change* (Oxford: OUP, 1989).

KEMPE, R. & KEMPE, C., *Child Abuse* (Suffolk: Fontana/Open Books, 1983).

KENT, N., *Naked Hollywood: Money and Power in the Movies Today* (London: BBC Books, 1991).

KIERNAN, K. & WICKS, M., *Family Change and Future Policy* (Family Policy Studies Centre/Joseph Rowntree Memorial Trust, 1990).

KRISTEVA, J., *Powers of Horror: an Essay on Abjection* (New York: Columbia University Press, 1982).

KRISTEVA, J., 'Oscillation between "Power" and "Denial"', trans. Marilyn A. August, in de Courtivron, I. and Elaine Marks, E. (eds) (1980).

KROKER, A. & KROKER, M., *Body Invaders: Sexuality and the Postmodern Condition* (London: Macmillan, 1988).

KUHN, A., *Alien Zone: Cultural Theory and Contemporary Science Fiction Cinema*. (London: Verso, 1990).

LACAN, J., *Ecrits: A Selection*, trans. A. Sheridan (New York: Norton, 1979).

LAING, R.D., *The Politics of the Family* (Harmondsworth: Penguin, 1976).

LAPLANCHE, J. & PONTALIS, J-B., *The Language of Psychoanalysis* (London: Hogarth Press, 1973).

LEBEAU, V., 'Daddy's Cinema: Femininity and Mass Spectatorship' in *Screen* XXXIII: 3 Autumn 1992.

LEVI-STRAUSS, C., *The Raw and the Cooked: Introduction to a Science of Mythology: 1* (New York: Harper & Row, 1975).

LOVELL, T., *Pictures of Reality: Aesthetics, Politics and Pleasure* (London: BFI, 1983).

MARWICK, A., *British Society since 1945* (Harmondsworth: Penguin, 1990).

McNAY, L., *Foucault and Feminism: Power, Gender and the Self* (Cambridge: Polity Press, 1992).

MEDVED, M., *Hollywood vs. America* (London: HarperCollins, 1993).

METZ, C., *Psychoanalysis and Cinema: The Imaginary Signifier* (London: Macmillan, 1982).

MODLESKI, T., *The Women Who Knew Too Much* (London: Methuen, 1988).

MODLESKI, T., *Feminism Without Women: Culture and Criticism in a 'Post Feminist' Age* (London: Routledge, 1991).

MOI, T. (ed.), *The Kristeva Reader* (Oxford: Blackwell, 1989).

MORGAN, D.H.J., *Social Theory & the Family* (London: 1975).

MURDOCK, G., *Social Structures* (New York: Macmillan).

MURPHY, J.D., *Distribution and Exhibition: An Overview*, in Squire, J.E. (ed.) (1983).

MUSSER, C., 'A History of Screen Practice', in *Quarterly Review of Film Studies* IX, No. 1, Winter 1984.

NEALE, S., *Genre* (London: BFI, 1980).

PARSON, T. *et al.*, *Family, Socialisation and Interaction Process* (Illinois: Free Press, 1955).

PARSONS, A., 'Britain and the World', in Kavanagh, D. & Seldon, A. (eds) (1989).

PARTON, N., *The Politics of Child Abuse* (London: Macmillan, 1985).

PETERS, T., *Thriving on Chaos: Handbook for a Management Revolution* (London: Pan Books, 1989).

PRIBHAM, D. (ed.), *Female Spectators: Looking at Film & Television* (London: Verso, 1988).

RAPP, R., 'Family and Class in Contemporary America: Notes towards an Understanding of Ideology', in *Science and Society*, Vol. 42, 1982.

RAY, R., *A Certain Tendency of the Hollywood Cinema 1930–1980* (New Jersey: Princeton, 1985).

ROBERTSON, A.F., *Beyond the Family: The Social Organisation of Human Reproduction* (Cambridge: Polity Press, 1991).

RODOWICK, D.N., 'The Difficulty of Difference' in *Wide Angle*, No. 1, 1982.

RORTY, R., *Philosophy and the Mirror of Nature* (Oxford: Basil Blackwell, 1980).

RUPPERSBERG, H., 'The Alien Messiah', in Kuhn, A. (ed.) (1990).

SCHAFFER, K.F., *Sex-Role Issues in Mental Health* (Reading, Mass.: Addison-Wesley, 1980).

SCHATZ, T., 'The New Hollywood', in Collins, J. *et al.* (eds), 1993.

SCHILLER, M., *Mass Communications and American Empire* (New York: A.M. Kelley, 1969).

SEGAL, L., *What is to be Done About the Family? Crisis in the Eighties* (Harmondsworth: Penguin, 1983).

SHORTER, E., *The Making of the Modern English Family* (London: Fontana/Collins, 1975).

SIMENAUER, J. & CARROLL, D., *Singles: The New Americans* (New York: Simon & Schuster, 1982).

SILVERMAN, K., *The Acoustic Mirror: The Female Voice in Psychoanalysis and Cinema* (Bloomington: Indiana University Press, 1988).

SMART, Susan (ed.), *Regulating Womanhood: Historical Essays on Marriage, Motherhood and Sexuality* (London: Routlege, 1992).

SQUIRE, J.E. (ed.), *The Movie Business Book* (Englewood Cliffs, NJ: Prentice-Hall, 1983).

STEARNS, P., *European Society in Upheaval* (London: Collier-Macmillan, 1975).

STONE, L., *The Family, Sex and Marriage in England 1500–1800* (London: Weidenfeld & Nicholson, 1977).

STRINATI, D. & WAGG, S. (eds), *Come on Down? Popular Media Culture in Postwar Britain* (London: Routledge, 1992).

STRINATI, D., 'The Taste of America: Americanisation and Popular Culture in Britain', in Strinati, D. & Wagg, S. (eds) (1992).

SULEIMAN, Susan (ed.), *The Female Body in Western Culture* (Massachusetts: Harvard University Press, 1986).

TASKER, Y., *Spectacular Bodies: Gender, Genre and the Action Cinema* (London: Routledge, 1993).

THOMPSON, K., *Exporting Entertainment: America in the World Film Market 1907–1935* (London: BFI, 1985).

THUMIN, J., *Celluloid Sisters: Women and Popular Cinema* (London: Macmillan, 1992).

TODOROV, T., *The Poetics of Prose* (Ithaca NY: Cornell University Press, 1977).

TRAUBE, E.G., *Dreaming Identities: Class, Gender and Generation in 1980s Hollywood Movies* (Oxford: Westview Press, 1992).

UTTING, D., *Family and Parenthood: Support Families, Preventing Breakdown* (York: Joseph Rowntree Foundation, 1995).

WALKER, A., *Hollywood, England: The British Film Industry in the Sixties* (London: Harrap, 1986).

WARD, E., *Father–Daughter Rape* (London: Women's Press, 1984).

WEXMAN, V.W., *Creating the Couple: Love, Marriage and Hollywood Performance* (Chichester: Princeton University Press, 1993).

WHITELEGG *et al.* (eds), *The Changing Experience of Women* (Oxford: Martin Robertson, 1982).

WILLETS, D., 'The Family', in Kavanagh & Seldon (eds) (1989).

WILLIAMS, L., 'Something Else Besides a Mother: Stella Dallas and the Maternal Melodrama', in *Cinema Journal* XXIV, No 1, Fall 1984.

WILLIAMS, L., *Hard Core* (London: Pandora Press, 1990).

WILLIAMS, R., *Problems in Materialism and Culture* (London: New Left Books, 1980).

WILLIAMS, R., *Keywords: A Vocabulary of Culture and Society* (London: Flamingo, 1987).

ZARETSKY, E., *Capitalism, the Family and Personal Life* (New York: Harper & Row, 1973).

Index

259